M000188601

FROM **RESILIENCE**
TO **REVOLUTION**

Columbia Studies in Middle East Politics

COLUMBIA STUDIES IN MIDDLE EAST POLITICS

MARC LYNCH, SERIES EDITOR

Columbia Studies in Middle East Politics presents academically rigorous, well-written, relevant, and accessible books on the rapidly transforming politics of the Middle East for an interested academic and policy audience.

FROM **RESILIENCE**
TO **REVOLUTION**

HOW FOREIGN
INTERVENTIONS
DESTABILIZE
THE MIDDLE EAST

SEAN L. YOM

Columbia University Press
New York

Columbia University Press
Publishers Since 1893
New York   Chichester, West Sussex
cup.columbia.edu
Copyright © 2016 Columbia University Press

Library of Congress Cataloging-in-Publication Data
Yom, Sean L.
   From resilience to revolution : how foreign interventions destabilize
the Middle East / Sean L. Yom.
        pages cm. — (Columbia studies in Middle East politics)
   Includes bibliographical references and index.
   ISBN 978-0-231-17564-7 (cloth : alk. paper) — ISBN 978-0-231-
54027-8 (e-book)
   1. Authoritarianism—Middle East—History—20th century.
2. Political stability—Middle East—History—20th century.
3. Middle East—Politics and government—20th century.
4. Kuwait—Politics and government—20th century.   5. Iran—
Politics and government—20th century.   6. Jordan—Politics and
government—20th century.   7. Middle East—Foreign relations—
Western countries.   8. Western countries—Foreign relations—
Middle East.   I. Title.
DS62.8.Y66 2015
956.05—dc23

                                                         2015013894

Columbia University Press books are printed on
permanent and durable acid-free paper.

This book is printed on paper with recycled content.
Printed in the United States of America

Cover Design: Jordan Wannemacher
Cover Image: © ATTA KENARE/AFP/Getty Images

For Jessica,
my best Reason-for-Coming-Home

CONTENTS

CONTENTS

A NOTE ON TRANSLITERATION AND INTERVIEWS

PROPERLY TRANSLITERATING WORDS from Arabic and Persian into English is a task best left to linguists. To avoid confusion, in this book I have used the most popularized English transliterations for Arabic and Persian terms, including the preferred spelling for people, places, and ideas as they appear in the public record. I refrain from using most diacritics but retain apostrophizing for ʿ*ayn* and *hamzaʾ* (except for the initial hamza).

In addition, personal interviews are cited in notes when relevant. In several cases, those interviewed preferred to keep their identities confidential—a request that every ethical researcher should honor, especially when conducting research in authoritarian states.

ACKNOWLEDGMENTS

AN UNSPARING NETWORK of friends and colleagues supported this project from start to finish. Grzegorz Ekiert, Steve Levitsky, and Melani Cammett were mentors who invested faith in my capacity for comparative research more than a decade ago. In the field, I was steered by special individuals with deep knowledge and warm hearts, among them Mohammad Al-Momany, Marwan Kardoosh, the Sharekh family, Yousif Al-Ebraheem, and Leila Ben Mcharek. I also thank the nearly a hundred individuals interviewed for this project; though only a portion appear in this book, all graciously gave me significant time and shrewd guidance as I navigated new countries. No less generous were the resources and grants offered by Harvard University's Graduate Society and Weatherhead Center for International Affairs, the Foreign Language and Area Studies program, the American Institute for Maghreb Studies, and the American Center for Oriental Research. In this book's early stages, friends and colleagues lent expertise on squaring theory with evidence; among them were superstars Pete Moore, Tom Pepinsky, Wendy Pearlman, Michael Herb, Anne Mariel Zimmerman, and fellow participants at the Comparative Politics Workshop at Harvard.

Over the past few years, another network of gifted colleagues graciously reviewed my work and improved it immeasurably. Among them stand Larry Diamond, Kathryn Stoner, Steve Krasner, and Joel Beinin, all of whom I had the privilege of meeting as a postdoctoral fellow at the Center for Democracy, Development, and the Rule of Law at Stanford University. Since then, numerous scholars intervened to give me further constructive criticism. Among them were Tarek Masoud, Jillian Schwedler, Curtis Ryan, Ellen Lust, Greg Gause, Amaney Jamal, Jason Brownlee, Lina Khatib, David Abernethy, Philippe Schmitter, Saeid Golkar, Quinn Mecham, Mary Ann Tétreault, Lindsay Benstead, Michelle Penner Angrist, Stacey Yadav, Lisa Blaydes, David Patel, Matteo Legrenzi, Larry Rubin, André Bank, Thomas Richter, Oliver Schlumberger, Senem Aslan, Ceren Belge, Kristin Fabbe, Juliane Brach, Debra Shushan, Dafna Rand, Hillel Soifer, Jill Goldenpine, Anya Vodopyanov, and Peter Gran. In seminars, conferences, offices, workshops, hotel lobbies, pubs, airplanes, and coffee shops, they never hesitated to suggest new ideas, encourage my progress, and give professional advice. Finally, since 2010 Temple University has provided me not only a collegial department that welcomed me from the first day but also full sabbatical leave to finish this book just a few years into my appointment. These are the two best gifts any junior faculty member could receive.

Outside the craft of writing stands a special group of supporters. Katelyn Baker-Smith has been a superlative research assistant and sounding board, performing every task with astonishing efficiency and finding humor in the most brutal absurdities. My collaboration with Hicham Ben Abdallah and the unending hospitality of his family in Princeton and Rabat furnished vital perspective and intellectual respite during critical moments. Ana Hagstrand was inspirational and compassionate, generating faith during the roughest storms. I was also blessed to receive the editorial wisdom of Marc Lynch and Anne Routon. The former was patient and encouraging beyond all expectation, and the latter supportive and transparent beyond all belief. They are consummate professionals; the field of Middle East politics is fortunate to have them, and I was lucky to work with them. Michele Callaghan's copy editing skills were a revelation. Last but not least, Whitney Johnson at Columbia University Press ushered these words through the production process, always reassuring me along the way. A first-time author could not have been treated better.

Above all, I finished this book in the arms of Jessica, who never ceased easing my burdens and never stopped reciprocating my love. Her strength has made everything possible.

FROM **RESILIENCE** TO **REVOLUTION**

1

THE ARGUMENT AND THE CASES

T HE ARAB SPRING raised hope that democracy would sweep over the largely authoritarian landscape of the Middle East and North Africa. As national transitions bogged down in violence and strife, however, optimistic forecasts of political freedom quickly gave way to more visceral concerns about stability and order. In many countries, the short-lived triumph of people power did not lead to the creation of resilient democracies that could bridge social divisions and rally popular support behind new leaders. Egypt, Libya, and Yemen have joined postwar Iraq and Afghanistan as examples in which authoritarian regimes were forced to surrender power in the twenty-first century—but whose heirs have not established stable governments of any sort due to unending social resistance and popular unrest. Syria may well join their ranks.

The lesson learned: political order should be democratic, but it should also be *durable*. The type of a regime matters little if that regime does not last very long in the first place or is constantly immersed in opposition and strife. Before liberty, as Samuel Huntington famously remarked, must come "the creation of a legitimate public order."[1] Yet, what determines the durability of any political regime? Here, looking to the past furnishes vital clues to answering this present question. Consider the era when imperialism began to wane—the 1930s to 1950s, when most states in the Middle East began to acquire formal sovereignty from imperial powers. What distinguishes this early era was endemic social conflict in many countries. The kings and presidents representing the first generation of postcolonial leadership lacked mass support. Relying upon traditional elites such as large landowners, tribal sheikhs, and religious authorities, they faced opposition in the form of new urban forces fighting for social justice and democratic reforms, such as labor unions, merchant chambers, and student movements.

These domestic struggles did not unfold in a geopolitical vacuum. After the sunset of colonialism, great powers continued to intervene across the region as they sought resources like oil and gas, coveted strategic assets like the Suez Canal, and amplified proxy clashes like the Arab-Israeli wars. Such hegemons bolstered endangered local regimes deemed focal to their strategic interests through diplomatic, fiscal, and military support. The United States, for instance, rescued Pahlavi rule in Iran and Hashemite dictatorship in Jordan during the 1950s. British troops safeguarded monarchical friends in Iraq during World War II and Bahrain in 1956. By the 1960s, Soviet advisers and arms were flooding Egypt and Syria, backing these states against their pro-Western rivals in the struggle for regional influence. At the same time, other Middle East regimes confronted societal resistance alone, bereft of foreign patronage. The Sabah dynasty of Kuwait and the fledgling Bourguibist presidency of Tunisia garnered little assistance from imperial patrons when they defeated entrenched opposition movements by the late 1950s.

These two catalysts—domestic conflict and geopolitical mediation— combined to form a striking pattern across the Middle East. The *more* that outside hegemons intervened to help local rulers squash domestic opposition, the *less* durable their regimes turned out over time. External support was destructive in the long term, because it deterred national leaders from making inclusive bargains with opposing social forces and encouraged reliance upon repressive and exclusionary institutions. In contrast, autocrats who lacked external patrons were forced to negotiate with domestic rivals, favoring compromise over coercion. Facing the potentiality of defeat, they had to sacrifice much to win more support and through this costly process created more inclusive states that would experience less conflict and instability during future decades. In essence, political order in the postcolonial Middle East was more likely to be durable when founding conflicts between state and society were secluded from geopolitical interference.

STATE-BUILDING AND ITS OUTCOMES

State-building means the creation of new governing institutions to regulate economic markets and impose political rules within a defined territory.[2] This results in new regimes, or the legal structures that control access to power and resources. The *durability* of regimes, in turn, measures two things—longevity plus stability. Too frequently, analysts conflate these terms, resulting in conceptual confusion. For instance, as the Arab Spring showed, it seems all dictatorships are "durable" until the moment they collapse, at which point they are described as having been brittle all long. As a more rigorous conceptualization, I consider any given regime as durable if, over the same time period, it lasts longer than a comparable set of peers *and* faces little to no sustained opposition.[3]

Durability varies in several ways. First, consider an autocratic order that reigns for a quarter century and then collapses in social revolution, such as Iran under the uninterrupted rule of Shah Pahlavi (1953–1979). On the one hand, given that other regimes in the same region have lasted more than twice as long and some still persist today, this case would seem not durable given its short life span and fatal insurrection. On the other hand, long-lived regimes are not identical. Consider Jordan, whose Hashemites have retained power since gaining independence after World War II but only by quelling periodic rebellions from society, and the Sabah dynasty of Kuwait, which has ruled over the same period but far more peacefully, seldom needing to violently suppress a supportive citizenry. Despite their mutual longevity, these cases are qualitatively different: Jordan has persisted under a cloud of regime insecurity necessitating

3

frequent coercion, while Kuwait's rulers have seldom seen their citizens as credible threats. Jordan is a case of tenuous survival, whereas Kuwait comes the closest to embodying long-term stability—that is, durability.

These outcomes of revolutionary collapse, tenuous survival, and regime durability each result from a distinctive confluence of domestic conflict and geopolitical mediation punctuating the early stage of state-building, when rulers have yet to secure full power, social opposition is mobilizing, and few institutions of governance exist. These patterns of historical causation comprise the theoretical framework here, and each deserves careful attention.

GEOPOLITICAL SECLUSION AND DURABLE ORDER: KUWAIT

First, early conditions of geopolitical seclusion contribute to durable regimes. Seclusion, here, does not mean shielding from all external influences; that is nearly impossible. Rather, it means contexts where leaders lack access to great power support, because either their national territories hold little strategic value or they refuse offers of outside intervention due to their complicated colonial past. Without the diplomatic boost, economic aid, and military assistance that come from external support and that could help neutralize domestic opposition, such regimes have a compelling incentive to approach new social forces and make bargains for their loyalty through promises of enrichment via material means or protection from another threat. In essence, autocrats broadened their ruling coalitions.

Kuwait represents this trajectory. In the late 1930s, the stubborn regime of the Sabah family reeled against wealthy merchant opposition, which resisted its despotism and demanded greater political rights. Much to the regime's disappointment, its imperial patron, Britain, refused to deliver the financial and coercive resources necessary to suppress these progressive rivals. Grudgingly recognizing its extreme vulnerability, the leadership was compelled to compromise with the rebels by making liberal concessions and leaving their assets untouched. It also sought to immunize itself from further unrest by deepening ties with its small existing

4

base of pastoral tribes, as well as reaching out to woo new allies in society such as the Shiʿa minority. All of these coalitional overtures to broaden the dynasty's social foundation occurred before the advent of oil wealth transformed the political economy during the 1950s.

Geopolitical seclusion, then, encourages regimes in conflict to broaden their coalitional alliances with society. Such Brumairean pacts are preferable to defeat in conflict but are still costly; they require the surrender of absolutism, alongside new commitments to furnish patronage and protection desired by each group in return for loyalty. Over time, those promises become embedded in the new economic and political institutions that leaders create to govern their territory, from industrialization programs to organs of representation. The goal is to turn citizens into constituents by giving them material and symbolic stakes in the new political order. This also necessitates staying the hand of repression, for repeated coercion against the citizenry breaks down these reciprocal understandings between state and society. Though constraining and expensive, these coalitional investments pay off during severe crises decades later, when events like economic implosion and military conflict again spur everyday people to dissent. Broad ruling coalitions not only reduce the audience for potential resistance but also moderate emergent opposition: critics tend to complain not *if* but *how* their regimes should reign. In turn, because of their proximity to and knowledge of society, leaders carry a repertoire of nonviolent strategies to demobilize confrontations before they spread and radicalize, such as credibly promising democratic reforms, shuffling their coalitions, and reaching out to opposition elites. In essence, broadly based regimes can prevent crises from spiraling out of control by working with, not through, society.

That arc of durability plays out in Kuwait from the 1960s. Regardless of its authoritarian aspirations in the early twentieth century, Sabah leaders recognized that long-term stability required being connected to different sectors of indigenous society from tribes and merchants to Shiʿa and their own sprawling family. Institutionalizing this broad coalition devoured the sheikhdom's oil wealth as the regime initiated costly economic projects and political initiatives from land transfers and trade protections to parliamentary representation and citizenship grants. Yet they paid off starting in the 1980s, which saw a string of successive crises—financial collapse, sectarian tensions from the Iraq-Iran War, then the 1990 Iraqi invasion and subsequent occupation—that uprooted the Sabah dynasty altogether. Throughout this turbulence, the regime defused each crisis in turn: it placated financial losers with material compensation, replaced some Shi'a supporters with newer Sunni Islamists, and negotiated with disgruntled merchants with little desire for revolution. Most of all, it drew upon its deep societal roots in pledging democratic reforms—a compromise accepted by almost all Kuwaitis, who continued advocating the restoration of their autocracy over any other ruling alternative. The result since then has been renewed benevolent authoritarianism, where political blocs fight over the spoils of oil but seldom the irreducible legitimacy of the regime itself.

GEOPOLITICAL SUBSTITUTION AND
REVOLUTIONARY COLLAPSE: IRAN

By contrast, other rulers did reap the assistance of international powers when they stumbled against opposition. In these cases, foreign allies can underwrite the defeat of internal enemies by strengthening incumbent regimes. They may diplomatically boost their confidence to crack down, expand their fiscal resources, and bolster their coercive muscle. Diminishing the cost of repression reshapes the calculus of coalitional strategy: liberated from fear of downfall, previously embattled leaders now have little incentive to bargain with friends and enemies alike—to undertake the costly task of widening their coalitions. Why surrender power and resources to social forces if those demanding actors can be crushed outright? These regimes often restore order believing that coercion, not compromise, represents the winning strategy of governance.

Here, state-building patterns diverge, revealing the second and third causal pathways of the theory. In the second pathway of state-building, conditions of geopolitical substitution—that is, when leaders became so reliant upon great power backing that they failed to raise any real coalitional support—encouraged future revolutions. In such cases, rulers develop their states without having made any commitments to enrich or protect supporters, whether old or new. Economic modernization hoards capital for corrupt cronies; political organizations privilege only an elite few; and brutal repression regulates public life. However, short-term autonomy breeds long-term weakness, because narrowing coalitions distance states from societies. When sudden crises trigger public unrest, autocrats find that decades of detachment from society have produced opposition that spreads quickly due to the many previously marginalized and abused groups. They cannot counter protests by rallying any loyalist factions, lack the credibility to mollify angry crowds with reform promises, and have little knowledge of how to co-opt opposing elites. Left dependent upon repression and great power support, such substitutive dictatorships are highly likely to collapse.

Iran provides a vivid case of geopolitical substitution with revolutionary consequences. In Iran, an Anglo-American intelligence operation restored the Pahlavi Shah to power in 1953 by toppling an elected government backed by popular leftist and nationalist movements. Afterward, the United States provided steady diplomatic, fiscal, and coercive assistance, allowing a regime on the verge of breakdown to assume the offensive and liquidate those in opposition, as well as the sectors supporting them such as students, workers, and intellectuals. The potential victory of such opposition, one aligned against the West and potentially toward the Soviet Union, was unacceptable in Washington. Hence, Pahlavi autocracy reequilibrated without having compromised with opposition or bargained for loyalty. It believed that unconditional U.S. support, and its coercive apparatus, could guarantee future stability.

The governing institutions then in line to transform Iranian society reflected the absence of patronage and protection commitments, as the regime grew more insulated from society. Political parties were talk shops for royal factotums, not forums to rally grassroots support; industrialization and modernization programs alienated old allies like rural landowners, bazaar marketeers, and Shiʿa clergy. When protests erupted in 1978 amid economic crisis, the dictatorship had no tool apart from violence by which

7

to respond. Yet, repression only facilitated the spread of dissent and its radicalization into a revolutionary movement. Against this, the shah had no credibility when promising reforms in return for peace; neither could he organize supporters to neutralize a hostile street or speak directly with resistance leaders. Despite U.S. encouragement and intensifying coercion, the Pahlavi monarchy could not defeat the revolution.

GEOPOLITICAL SUBSIDIZATION AND
TENUOUS SURVIVAL: JORDAN

Not all regimes saturated with foreign support become substitutive. Middle-range outcomes of tenuous survival—longevity *without* stability, due to the periodic threats of uprisings and constant insecurity—can be traced to earlier conditions of geopolitical subsidization, the third causal trajectory of my theory of political regimes. Here, structural factors come into play. Some countries remain uniquely bifurcated by a single ethnic or sectarian division, producing a large communal majority and cohesive minority fearful of majoritarian takeover. That societal landscape makes leaders sponsored by foreign patrons think twice: even after conflict ends, they can capture loyalty from that minority with the promise of protection but still marginalize most other citizens from their coalition to minimize their power-sharing commitment. Subsidized by that international assistance, new economic and political institutions reflect such segregating logic, disproportionately benefiting minority insiders while directing repression and exclusion toward the rest. This promotes a costly strategy of survival. A dispossessed popular audience can give rise to future revolts and strife; but, so long as it retains the negotiated allegiance of the minority base, it stands a good chance of squashing unrest to endure, albeit through violence.

Jordan reveals how such subsidized ethnocracy results in tenuous survival, or longevity without stability. In the late 1950s, the Hashemite monarchy exploited the diplomatic, economic, and military support of Washington to eliminate a leftist-nationalist opposition front that, heavily driven by activists from the Palestinian majority, nearly took power. Such victory, however, did not bring lasting security, as communal tensions escalated between Palestinians and the mostly tribal Transjordanian minority. By the early 1960s, an increasing number of Transjordanian elites feared not government but *lack* of government, of diminishment or even destruction should the demographic majority become political reality. Sensing this opportunity, the regime deepened its protective embrace of this selective base, utilizing more American aid and arms to reconfigure state institutions around Transjordanians—from a powerful royal court linking tribal sheikhs to King Hussein to new public industries that absorbed tribal labor.

Such ethnocratic logic had bloody ramifications in the 1970 Black September Civil War. Then, the regime defeated Palestinian militant groups, drawing upon local resources due to its loyal tribal army and timely Western assistance. Constrained by past commitments, the autocracy recovered by widening the scope of Palestinian exclusion from state institutions even further, more convinced that Transjordanian loyalty could guarantee survival. Economic collapse in the late 1980s exposed the strengths and weaknesses of this assumption. When tribal riots broke out, the regime enjoyed the political credibility, institutional outreach, and social knowledge needed to quickly demobilize unexpected dissent within its base. The primary concession it gave—political liberalization—still reflected communal hostility, as reforms during the 1990s continued to disenfranchise many Palestinians while sheltering Transjordanian interests in renovated institutions like parliament. Communal fear still permeated the coalition between the monarchy and its Transjordanian constituency, creating a deceptive image of longevity: this autocracy persists, but is still haunted by the potential for recurrent opposition within its own society.

Table 1.1 sets out these three cases and patterns in sequential form, demonstrating how a similar coalitional logic accounts for the state-building process and its outcomes.

THE ARGUMENT IN SUM

From these three historical-causal patterns emerges the central thesis, which figure 1.1 unfurls. Geopolitical constraints on state-building

TABLE 1.1

CASES AND PATHWAYS

	SOCIAL OPPOSITION	GEOPOLITICAL MEDIATION	RULING COALITION	REGIME OUTCOME
KUWAIT	Merchant class and dependent maritime labor (1938–1941)	Seclusion: British neutrality, refusal to intervene; regime compromises for survival	Broad: Institutional patronage rehabilitates merchants and labor, rewards tribes, mobilizes Shi'a support	Durability: Mass support during 1980s fiscal crisis and 1990 Gulf War, little threat of domestic uprising
IRAN	Communist and nationalist movements (1946–1953)	Substitution: Profuse U.S. assistance and aid, allowing the shah to destroy opposition and deny grievances	Narrow: Institutions neglect old alliances with clergy, bazaar, and landowners, and repress new popular sectors	Revolution: National insurrection overwhelms regime, despite use of coercion and U.S. support (1979)
JORDAN	Leftist and Arab Nationalist parties (1953–1957)	Subsidization: U.S. support but growing strains divide Palestinian majority and Transjordanian minority	Ethnocratic: Institutions exclude Palestinians and repress urban areas but incorporate Transjordanians into state	Tenuous survival: Endures civil war (1970), popular rioting (1989), and constant communal tensions

in the Middle East posed divergent incentives to early rulers facing domestic conflicts, and consequent coalitional choices produced varying institutional structures that resulted in long-term variations in longevity and stability. If social conflicts compose the initial conditions of state-building and subsequent coalitions and institutional structures represent the domestic variable that influences long-term stability, then geopolitical mediation represents the intervening factor that shapes how early conflict catalyzed different coalitional strategies among autocrats motivated by the same goal of survival.

A few qualifications accompany this proposition. First, initial state-society conflicts represent critical junctures in which the coalitional choices made by political regimes not only break from the past but also inaugurate rapid institutional changes in the state and economy.[4] Second, under conditions of authoritarian rule, the breadth of ruling coalitions is measured by the presence of either patronage or protection—concessions given to secure loyalty from constituencies. *Patronage* means goods and services that enhance the material prosperity of constituencies, such as industrial capital, welfare provisions, and targeted employment. *Protection* entails policies that safeguard the status of targeted supporters from a perceived threat of domination elsewhere, such as political representation, cultural promotion, and other minority privileges.

Third, geopolitics influences this coalitional calculus by lowering the cost of repressive closure. When opposition seems strong, external assistance can make weak regimes stronger. Diplomatic sponsorship, such as public declarations of support, enhances the confidence of leaders to crack down and eliminates the potential for regional backlash from rival neighbors. Fiscal support, such as cash grants, concessional loans,

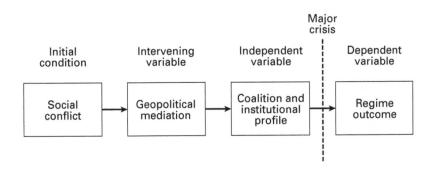

FIGURE 1.1   The argument

and technical aid, staves off bankruptcy and keeps basic organs of government running. Coercive assistance via arms transfers, intelligence operations, and even boots on the ground more directly squashes social resistance. Such bolstering reduces incentives for leaders to bargain with society in order to win more support and stave off defeat, since it provides a shortcut to consolidated power; its absence encourages the forced move of compromising with social actors and listening to their interests.

A COMPARATIVE-HISTORICAL APPROACH

This work aligns with the tradition of comparative-historical analysis, employing the careful study of three historical cases to produce a generalized theoretical finding.[5] Here, the controlled comparison of state-building in Iran, Jordan, and Kuwait since the early twentieth century reveals the argument in full. These cases share key similarities. First, all three countries experienced intense early conflicts involving four broadly constituted actors—the authoritarian regime, its small traditional social base, urban-oriented popular opposition, and a potential foreign patron. Second, these were closed autocracies rather than "hybrid" regimes.[6] Everyday citizens had little means to influence the selection of executive leaders, who ruled until death or deposal. Elections often existed but did not determine the winning coalition, which depended instead upon the preferences of the leadership.

Third, these countries were all late developers where, in Gerschenkronian fashion, the state took the lead in modernizing and transforming predominantly agrarian societies. However, major developmental policies were subordinated to politics. Thus, just like political institutions such as parties, parliaments, and royal courts, economic initiatives like factory projects, land redistribution, and social services reflected coalitional obligations—who to reward, who to protect, who to destroy. Finally, decades after the resolution of early conflicts, these regimes all suffered severe crises involving economic failure that instigated unexpected popular mobilization that disrupted politics, defied authority, and generated uncertainty. These represent valuable windows to observe how antecedent coalitional investments and institutional structures influenced how each regime initially reacted to unrest and in turn how these reactive strategies determined their ultimate fate. This also highlights how early responses to crises play a crucial role in amplifying or neutralizing what begin as small acts of resistance. The Arab Spring demonstrated how crises do not need revolutionary beginnings to have revolutionary endings: the self-immolation of a Tunisian vendor in December 2010 began that regional wave of upheaval, but in almost every subsequent uprising crowds did not swell and revolutionary slogans did not circulate until *after* dictatorships mismanaged the situation by ignoring demands, refusing compromise, and inflicting repression.

Like all small-n approaches in political science, comparative-historical analysis carries the modest disadvantage of having limited scope. The argument here primarily applies to a specific region (Middle East) and time period (postcolonial era). As a qualitative study based on a few cases, I do not create a universal theory of state-building that can perfectly predict outcomes in every other regional and historical context.[7] In methodological perspective, though, the purpose of historical comparison is not to explore as many cases as possible in order to maximize the number of observations. Statistical analyses are far better suited for that task. Rather, analyzing a small number of cases can still produce generalizable insights so long as they are representative of the wider universe of all known cases within a given region and historical period.[8]

In that regard, Kuwait, Iran, and Jordan are not idiosyncratic cases that have no historical peer. Instead, they represent three master categories of geopolitical seclusion, substitution, and subsidization, with each resulting in a different pathway of postcolonial state-building. Under this rubric, other regional countries that historically matched their initial conditions—early conflict, closed autocracy, late development, and major crises—should fall within the theory's purview. Tunisia, Iraq, and Bahrain provide prime examples. The new Tunisian regime of Habib Bourguiba was secluded from French interference in the late 1950s, resulting in the construction of a durable party-state that was derailed by the presidential succession of Zine ʿAbidine Ben ʿAli in 1987—and even then, this republican autocracy persisted for another twenty-four years. Hashemite-era Iraq, like Iran, underwent geopolitical substitution in which heavy-handed British support detached monarchical dictatorship from society and fostered the revolutionary collapse of 1958. Bahrain falls under geopolitical subsidization. British interventions during the mid-1950s enabled the limping Khalifa dynasty to retrench support among its Sunni minority and so tenuously survive but at the cost of incurring regular insurrections from the Shiʿa majority.

A project with unlimited space could explore these and every other relevant case of geopolitical mediation. This book is not that project. The tradeoff of external scope, however, is maximal *internal* validity—ensuring the closest possible fit between theory and evidence. Rather than simply correlate outcomes like revolution or durability with static antecedent variables like oil or culture, my case studies devote empirical detail to tracing out how every theorized causal process plays out over time. By marshaling multilingual evidence from historical monographs, economic surveys, biographical work, diplomatic records, and field-based interviews conducted with government officials, tribal notables, and other authorities, I make visible every step in the causal chain—how social conflicts endangered early rulers, how foreign patrons tipped (or did not tip) the balance of power, how ruling coalitions narrowed or broadened as a result, what economic and political institutions were then created, what levels of repression such emergent states imposed, and finally how these institutional choices influenced authoritarian responses to severe crises decades later. Such meticulous comparative process tracing also allows me to adjudicate rival propositions that purport to explain variations in regime durability in the postcolonial Middle East. The next chapter takes up this challenge and utilizes inductive insights from these three cases to show that culture, economics, rents, coercion, colonialism, and monarchism offer less traction than my argument in explaining long-term outcomes.

A final strength of historical case studies is its encouragement for the oft-ignored tool of counterfactual thinking. The analysis here suggests that, *had* early conflicts been interrupted by different kinds of geopolitical mediation in Iran, Jordan, and Kuwait, then different coalitional and institutional structures could have well resulted and thereby produced regimes and outcomes that would have diverged from history's record. Had geopolitical conditions varied, the Pahlavi dictatorship *could* have outlasted the twentieth century; the Kuwaiti autocracy *could* have brutalized its citizens; the Jordanian monarchy *could* have bridged the gap between Transjordanians and Palestinians. These regimes did not undertake the coalitional decisions and institutional strategies to pursue such alternative futures—not because the gods of history forbid it, but because they simply responded to varying circumstances and pressures with different choices that made sense at the time.

More broadly construed, political actors are seldom consigned to any fate, but the circumstances shaping their choices are seldom equivalent. Admitting that multiple possibilities can spring from any given juncture is necessary to appreciate how long-term processes like state-building and political development play out.

THEORETICAL CONTRIBUTIONS

This study does not explore the prospects for Middle East democracy. A gigantic scholarship has long debated how and why democratization could transform this region by analyzing important topics like civil society, business politics, and state repression.[9] While the Arab Spring showed that questions of democracy and freedom are never far from Middle East politics, it also stressed the equally significant issue of durability, the topic motivating this book. Long-term stability remains the goal of every government, but relatively few achieve it. We must know why.

Neither is this a systemic study about the Middle East as a regional subsystem. International relations specialists see the Middle East as a regional subsystem defined by external forces that swirl across borders, such as ideologies like Arab Nationalism, religion and Islamism, multilateral

15

organizations like the Arab League, globalization and economic pressures, alliances and rivalries, and armed conflicts.[10] These transnational factors come into play at various points in the affairs of every country, and a proper international relations volume would catalogue them all. In contrast, this book has a narrower but more unique purpose that combines two different worlds. It proves how one aspect of the *international* system, great power support, influenced *domestic* outcomes in different states by shaping the coalitional decisions made during the birth of new political order—a powerful interaction that no other work has systematically mapped out.

Given these disclaimers, this work advances theoretical knowledge across three frontiers.

COALITIONS, INSTITUTIONS, AND AUTHORITARIAN REGIMES

First, this book addresses the literature on institutions and authoritarianism. Studies on autocratic politics have reached consensus regarding the importance of institutions: as Jason Brownlee summates, "organizational restraints prolong and expand power."[11] Autocrats who limit their capricious absolutism and rule through institutional arrangements that share power and resources with coalitional supporters, such as dominant political parties and economic patronage networks, last longer and face less opposition. However, while institutions are the antecedent cause of durable authoritarianism, they are not historical givens. They result from prior coalitional choices, which deserve as much attention as institutions themselves. In postcolonial states especially, governing institutions express coalitional politics because the reorganization of the economy and political arena—the transformative processes resulting in new institutions—did not occur until after rulers had resolved their coalitional dilemmas following conflicts with domestic opposition.

In turn, understanding the importance of coalitional politics answers a central question that often stymies institutionalists. If well-crafted institutions can help even the most rapacious dictatorships manage opposition, co-opt dissent, and maintain loyalty, then why do not *all* autocrats create them? This work finds that regimes do not so much choose institutions as they pursue what they believe are optimal coalitional strategies. The intensity of those conflicts *plus* the mediation of outside powers can influence what is perceived as "optimal"—that is, what kinds of social alliances seem to give the best chance of long-term stability from the vantage point of rulers. In essence, my theory complements institutionalism with a corollary emphasis on coalitional logic.

STATE-BUILDING AND GREAT POWERS

The second contribution implicates theories of state-building. The postcolonial Middle Eastern experience shows how the early interventions of hegemonic powers can prefigure the coalitional choices and institutional structures of new states, as well as their regimes. While comparative scholars know well that external forces can influence domestic politics, this study shows that timing matters—that not *if* but *when* outside powers intercede carries great importance. Hegemonic interventions exert profound legacies when they transform social conflicts before leaders have constructed the economic rules and political routines governing their state. For this reason, state formation in the developing world cannot be divorced from the international system constraining it.

This broaches a major headache in discussions of Middle East politics, the tendency to give outside actors too much explanatory weight by blaming them for all regional problems.[12] Dependency theorists, with their searing critique of Western capitalism, and Cold War realists, who saw the Middle East as a strategic chessboard for superpower competition, could not have sat farther apart on the ideological spectrum. However, they both treated regional states as little more than pawns of outside forces, as if every revolution or dictatorship came about entirely from some foreign machination and local actors lacked autonomy and so could not make their own decisions. The antidote to such reflexes is not denying the importance of the international arena but rather replacing blanket statements with specifying *how*, *when*, and *why* geopolitical circumstances can influence the domestic political outcomes.

POLICY IMPLICATIONS AND FOREIGN INTERVENTIONS

Finally, this work relates to ongoing policy debates regarding foreign interventions and international assistance. The historical insights here show that great power support is seldom the answer when new states undergo severe conflict. As postwar Iraq and Afghanistan have both shown, even promising democratic governments can fall into abusive habits when shielded from domestic opposition by hegemonic patrons, whose unconditional support discourages local rulers from mobilizing the mass support necessary to ensure long-term stability. Over the past decade, both countries have suffered repeated bouts of sectarian rivalries, militant insurrections, and separatist flare-ups, showing clearly how these new elected regimes failed to reach into society and secure new sources of loyalty behind the narrow cliques of elites that backed these leaders. By consequence, my theory holds they would have enjoyed far more stability had they been given *less* support from the United States and its allies and instead been encouraged to share power and resources with excluded groups, thereby turning citizens into stakeholders. In an international system still typified by interventions by great powers like the United States, this lesson is invaluable: helping beleaguered rulers in new states overcome the tides of opposition can ironically destroy them in the end.

This also speaks to a recurrent controversy in U.S. foreign policy, namely American support for unsavory allies. Realists often warn that revolutions upend dictatorial client regimes when Washington fails to provide unwavering assistance during crises due to human rights concerns, from the Pahlavi monarchy of Iran in 1979 to the Mubarak regime of Egypt in 2011. With proponents of American hegemony, the policy prescription is unapologetic—when an allied autocracy stumbles into crisis, support all efforts to crush domestic opposition. Yet, as this study suggests, the burden for creating a durable political order rests squarely upon the shoulders of domestic leaders, not foreign patrons. Hegemonic sponsorship does not immunize any state from revolution short of militarily occupying it altogether.[13] Certainly, while well-timed interventions have helped some U.S. client states like Jordan weather periodic revolts provided they also retained a significant local coalition, external allies cannot completely substitute for domestic loyalties. In the Middle East, dictators have lost power not because they lacked outside support but because they lacked support from their own society.

ROAD MAP OF THE BOOK

The remainder of this book develops the argument and validates it through comparative-historical case studies. The next chapter expounds upon the theoretical framework. It addresses rival arguments for regime durability. It also fleshes out concepts of coalitions and institutions, while highlighting the importance of the geopolitical milieu for modern state-building. Chapters 3 and 4 explore Kuwait as the relevant case of geopolitical seclusion and regime durability. Chapters 5 and 6 flip the script and deal with Iran as the representative of a more tumultuous pathway—geopolitical substitution and revolutionary collapse. Chapters 7 and 8 unravel Jordan as a middle-range exemplar of geopolitical subsidization and tenuous survival.

Each chapter pairing constitutes a case study and shares the same internal arrangement. The first in the pair introduces the political regime and the constellation of social forces. Of particular importance are the conservative sectors of each society that supported postcolonial rulers, reflecting preindustrial modes of production and highly mediated structures of power. It explores the social conflicts that threatened these leaders and finally assesses how intervening support by a hegemon—or lack thereof—influenced the resolution of those conflicts. The second chapter of each pair delineates the coalitional strategies and institutional structures resulting from these early conflicts. It pays close attention to whether and how new economic and political institutions conveyed patronage or protection to coalitional allies, and investigates the presence and intensity of repression. Finally, it explores how these coalitional investments influenced the institutional capacity of each regime to maintain power during seminal crises that struck decades later, including how well leaders were able to renew their own bases of support and mollify public unrest because it became costly and violent.

The book's concluding chapter reviews the argument in theoretical perspective. It reiterates the value of addressing issues of authoritarianism and regime durability in the modern Middle East through an approach that links the geopolitical context into domestic explanations. It also connects these insights into contemporary policy issues, in particular how foreign interventions may do more harm than good in conflict-ridden states.

2

COALITIONS, STATE-BUILDING, AND GEOPOLITICAL MEDIATION

BEFORE ELABORATING ON the theoretical framework introduced in chapter 1, it is necessary to review existing explanations that could account for varying pathways of state-building in the postcolonial Middle East. Six arguments rise to the surface: culture, economics, rents, coercion, colonialism, and monarchism. Here, another advantage of systematically comparing historical cases becomes apparent. When tested against the entire range of evidence from Iran, Jordan, and Kuwait, these arguments fail to account for at least one or more of the observed outcomes of revolutionary collapse, tenuous survival, and long-term stability. That disconnect paves the way for a new theoretical perspective, one that emphasizes coalitional politics and great power interventions in order to account for the origins and fates of authoritarian regimes in the region.

EXISTING THEORIES AND PROPOSITIONS

First, consider the still-prevalent culturalist belief that something innate about Middle Eastern societies—Islam, Arab or Persian norms, or some other mysterious essence—dooms these countries toward dictatorship and backwardness.[1] However, such appeals fall short. Adding to scholarship exposing the bankruptcy of using culture to predict politics,[2] the three cases here impart the lesson that cultural *constants* cannot account for *varying* political outcomes. Kuwait, Iran, and Jordan are Muslim-majority countries whose national leaderships experienced very different fates. Whether it overpredicts durability or underpredicts revolution, culture is not a useful explanatory variable.

Second, does economic development bear more explanatory weight? The conventional literature on dictatorships and democracy suggests a straightforward finding: citizens who face sudden hardship due to fiscal downturns are more prone to mass mobilization against the state, the touchstone for authoritarian downfall.[3] More recent analysis frames inequality as responsible for instability and revolution. Acemoglu and Robinson posit a U-shaped curve governing the relationship between economics and politics: middling levels of inequality, rather than widespread absolute poverty or extreme wealth concentrations, bring about conflict due to divergent preferences over asset redistribution held by the middle classes.[4] Intuitively, the Middle East seems conducive to such arguments. Under state-directed development policies, economic output across the Middle East steadily grew until the 1980s. At that point, systemic distortions like the availability of rents, sectoral asymmetries, inadequate revenue extraction, and inefficient administration prevented the economic diversification necessary to ascend any higher on the ladder of globalization.[5]

However, economic underachievement alone in terms of output or inequality does not presage outcomes in Kuwait, Iran, and Jordan. Regarding fiscal downturns, Iran's mild recession in the late 1970s indeed kindled antiregime protests; but, if measured by decline of GDP per capita, then nonrevolutionary Jordan and Kuwait suffered *harsher* slumps over the next decade, yet both autocracies persisted. Levels of inequality likewise inconsistently forecast regime outcomes. Following Benjamin Smith's penetrating critique, the moderate inequality theorized to correlate with authoritarian regime collapse equates to the middle segment of the Gini index—roughly, the 40 to 65 range.[6] However, World Bank data (where available) show equivocal results: Gini scores for Iran and Jordan constantly hovered across this range during the 1970s, but these dictatorships met very different fates by decade's end. Acemoglu and Robinson's argument linking inequality to conflict explains the Iranian Revolution but not Jordanian survival.

A third approach is rentier state theory. It is well known that hydrocarbon windfalls, such as oil reserves and gas fields, generate enormous sources of government revenue separate from the domestic economy. This acutely affects the politics of autocracy. Relieved from taxing the populace, dictators can underwrite large-scale coercion or thwart social discontent through generous welfare provisions.[7] From this large literature emerges an obvious correlation—that the greater the rents, the more durable the regime. However, several problems emerge with this frequently repeated dictum. Hydrocarbon rents are not necessary for longevity or stability; Jordan is hardly the only oil-dry state that has endured to this day, however tenuously. Neither are they sufficient, given the revolutionary uprising that engulfed the Pahlavi regime of Iran and other oil producers throughout regional history such as Iraq in 1958 and Libya in 1969 and 2011.

Why do rentier states experience *both* durability and revolution? As new research has shown, extractive rents theoretically permit a wide range of institutions and policies, but they do not dictate which ones rulers ultimately prefer. Oil and gas revenues constitute a flexible resource that can be harnessed for different goals depending upon preexisting conditions, including ownership structure, leadership preferences, and class relations.[8] Such updated work furnishes an early clue regarding the importance of coalitional politics: the constituent demands and governing strategies in place *before* the advent of rentier wealth will logically shape how that wealth is spent creating new institutions. Sudden riches can either make highly repressive dictatorships even more detached, exclusionary, and brittle, as in the case of Iran during the 1960s and 1970s,[9] or make broad-based autocracies even more inclusionary, populist, and resilient, as in the case with Kuwait during the same oil boom.[10] Hence, while hydrocarbon resources remain an inextricable part of Middle East politics, they must be historicized within the state-building context.

A fourth possibility is coercion. Coercion is integral to not only authoritarian rule but also to the Weberian conception of the state itself as legalized domination.[11] A major assumption among many students of authoritarianism is that coercion represents a robust indicator for long-term stability. Autocracies possessing the moral willingness and physical capacity to inflict violence upon opposition should be durable.[12] Certainly, it is truistic that confident dictators with well-paid armies last longer than quivering incumbents with destitute police. However, longevity is not durability, and coercion does not guarantee stability. The Iranian leadership inflicted relentless cruelties against society through its final years but still fell to revolution when threats of violence failed to stop protesting citizens who simply refused to obey. Moreover, absence of coercion does not necessarily correlate with regime failure. The Sabah dynasty of Kuwait, for instance, has long employed diminutive security agencies designed to maintain rule of law rather than subjugate the citizenry to repressive abuses due to fear of uprising.

The relationship between coercion and durability, the "punishment puzzle," is complex.[13] What the historical cases here underscore is part of this puzzle: why do some regimes desire to inflict more repression than others in the first place? That is, gunmen may guard dictatorships, but not all dictators hire the same number of gunmen. The Middle Eastern experience suggests that coercive routines reflect prior coalitional bargains and political processes. Early on, the Kuwaiti regime did not launch murderous onslaughts against society because it could not *afford* to do so—but, after the 1950s, it never *needed* to do so. Today, the Sabah leadership continues to wield a relatively tame security apparatus, not because it has surrendered its monopoly over coercion but because it still has little reason to believe its citizens wish to overthrow it. As a corollary observation, the Iranian Pahlavi regime constantly assaulted opposition while consolidating power with U.S. aid and arms after 1953. It never felt the need to adopt a more inclusive orientation with opposing groups or learn nonrepressive strategies of dealing with social resistance. Hence, like rents, coercion does weave its way throughout politics but in more sophisticated ways than initially theorized.

Fifth, can colonialism account for variations in regime durability? Before modern state-building were historical periods of imperial governance that could have had powerful legacies. In the realm of economic development, much work has pinned the distal cause of prosperity or poverty in regions like Latin America, Africa, and Asia to colonial governance, particularly in how occupying powers disrupted traditional social relations and configured preindustrial economies.[14] Therefore, regimes inheriting colonial advantages would enjoy more stability after gaining sovereignty. For instance, when colonizers erected centralized bureaucracies, they were able to penetrate and control society more rapaciously—but in cases like South Korea, their successors also benefited by leveraging those institutions to assemble stronger state institutions and more effective economic development strategies.[15]

While colonialism left moral and institutional baggage that still deserves study, whether it adequately accounts for postcolonial regime durability in the Middle East is unclear. The problem is that Kuwait, Iran, and Jordan experienced different kinds of imperial domination. None were colonies, but the regimes that took power following foreign occupation encountered very diverse fates. For instance, the British presence in Kuwait was indirect and light, consisting of little more than a telegraph station and a few diplomats who had neither coercive authority nor administrative responsibility over Kuwaiti subjects. The Anglo-Russian occupation of Iran lasted throughout World War II but not long beyond that. It was brief and did not transform underlying economic and political structures. The Sabah and Pahlavi rulerships, however, pursued very different coalitional strategies following periods of occupation, based upon their perception of what kinds of social alliances could best ensure their future security.

The sixth alternative argument originates from the cases themselves. Iran, Jordan, and Kuwait all present cases of ruling monarchism, a special subtype of authoritarianism. The Arab Spring made this oft-overlooked detail a major factor of analysis. Popular protests during 2011–12 engulfed authoritarian republics like Syria, Libya, Tunisia, Yemen, and Egypt, while most monarchical dictatorships like Saudi Arabia, Morocco, and Oman faced little revolutionary unrest. From this, some analysts argue that Middle Eastern kingships are uniquely durable due to special cultural and religious attributes.[16] Others believe monarchism gives leaders special institutional advantages, such as hereditary succession and familial power-sharing, that allows them to better sidestep enemy elites and better communicate with popular groups within society.[17]

Such assertions about the durability of ruling monarchism ring hollow, however. First, royal exceptionalism is a myth.[18] The Iranian Revolution is hardly the only example of monarchical failure; Egypt (1952), Iraq (1958), North Yemen (1962), and Libya (1969) also suffered uprisings that extinguished their kingships. Neither are Middle Eastern monarchies uniquely powerful and manipulative. Before the twentieth century, the region's monarchies commanded little power, coercive or otherwise; only post-WWII state-building endowed them with ruling institutions and repressive organs that could transmit anything approaching absolutist authority across their territories.[19] Finally, studies distinguishing between monarchies and republics do not account for varying outcomes among monarchies themselves.[20] Such is the puzzle here. Iran's Pahlavi dynasty, the Hashemite monarchy of Jordan, and the House of Sabah in Kuwait experienced very dissimilar fates, and that variation within this subtype of authoritarianism deserves explanation.

Monarchism alone does not explain why Iran, Jordan, and Kuwait vary so much in terms of long-term stability. Neither do culture, economics, rents, coercion, and colonialism, five other potential explanations. Needed instead is a new and more generalized theory, one that engages the fundamental logic at the heart of political order: coalitional strategy.

A COALITIONAL THEORY

All else being equal, autocrats want to retain power. Since leaders in closed dictatorships never need to win competitive elections to do so, the mechanisms keeping them in office include other institutions. For the past decade, this has guided the vast scholarship on authoritarianism—the principle that *institutions* determine authoritarian regime durability.[21] Take, for instance, ruling parties. In historical perspective, autocracies ruled by dominant parties last longer than those headed by militaristic juntas and personalistic strongmen, because the organizational infrastructure of mass-mobilizing parties allow leaders to centralize political resources, resolve elite disputes, and marshal popular support.[22] Parliaments are also useful, even when denuded of legislative authority and driven by sham voting. Legislative councils and representative assemblies help authoritarians monitor society, co-opt opposition figureheads, and distribute patronage to societal elites.[23] In study after study, comparative scholars have shown that regimes with such institutional advantages last longer, and have more stability, than those lacking them.

Why, then, do not *all* dictators create the same institutions to inoculate their tenure? Here, studying institutions alone is less helpful. As Thomas Pepinsky notes, institutionalist theories can be tautological: one cannot argue that institutions cause durable dictatorships, which created those institutions to be durable.[24] The insight given here is that institutions are not exogenous to the power structures of society but instead endogenously result from the choices of political actors struggling over power.[25] They are not just causes but *outcomes* themselves of antecedent processes.[26] Coalitional mobilization is one of those defining processes and so can shed light onto why authoritarian rulers in the postcolonial Middle East embraced such dissimilar institutional strategies when pursuing the same goal of self-preservation.

THE CRUCIBLE OF CONFLICT

In much of the Middle East, ruling coalitions emerged from social conflicts marking the transition from imperial occupation to sovereign state-building. Such rebellions came predominantly from new urban groups, such as students, workers, professionals, merchants, and intellectuals.[27] Such middle-sector groups did not fit into the existing class structure of these preindustrial societies. They were neither peasant nor landlord, tethered to neither title nor debt. They did not represent the protected domain of religious authority, including clerics and seminaries. Neither did they include the holders of petty capital, spanning trade guilds, town retailers, and pastoral tribes. Whereas such traditionally narrow forces tended to support the incumbent leadership, this new urban opposition came from more progressive groups whose identity was shaped by new ideologies emphasizing economic mobility, social justice, and democratic participation. These social actors represented raw materials for new coalition-building.

The keystone to coalitional politics is size. In liberal democracies, the winning coalition necessary to legitimate the governing regime corresponds to the majority of the enfranchised population, calculated by electoral returns. In nondemocratic contexts, however, political inequality is inscribed by law, so power holders have far more leeway in choosing how much popular support to secure. Two concepts from organizational theory shed light on this process.[28] First, coalitional size results from the resolution of two conflicting preferences: the natural inclination to hoard all power and resources, known as the tendency toward "minimum winning" coalitions, versus the perceived need to capture loyalty and support from society, which requires surrendering some power and resources.[29] In historical perspective, one factor repeatedly has nudged leaders toward popular incorporation and away from narrow absolutism: conflicts threatening to destroy them, which forces leaders to win new allies to survive.[30] The crucible of conflict compels coalitional broadening. As Martin Shefter theorized, "political entrepreneurs organize an extensive popular following only if they must overcome *substantial* opposition to gain or retain power."[31] The base objective is survival; if autocrats cannot destroy opposing groups, bargaining is the least bad alternative left. Second, also relevant to coalition formation is the "discount rate," or the propensity of decision makers to discount future consequences in favor of immediate payoffs. Uncertainty raises the discount rate of leaders, impelling them "to concentrate on activities that lead to quick results and immediate reward."[32] Few other events create more uncertainty than costly conflict. Faced, then, with the potential for deposal that comes with protracted struggle, political actors will choose the option that seems to best guarantee their immediate survival. They seldom see, much less predict, the long-run costs and consequences of these immediate and pragmatic decisions.

Across time and space, cases abound in which fierce societal conflicts introduced pervasive uncertainty and convinced rulers to forge new cross-class alliances given their fears of defeat. In postwar Malaysia and Singapore, endemic class warfare convinced dictators and wary elites to band together to avert internecine slaughter, creating the collective impetus for unified parties, militaries, and bureaucracies.[33] In communally fractured polities like Tanzania and Kenya, violent imperial subjugation persuaded nationalist movements to integrate different ethnic factions into their cadres, paving the way for hegemonic ruling parties that neutralized opposition through patronage-driven co-optation after independence.[34] Within the former Soviet sphere of influence, Leninist party regimes became far more willing to compensate dispossessed groups, including ethnic and linguistic minorities, once the unifying ideology of class struggle could no longer mask underlying tensions and rivalries within society.[35] Likewise, after the Berlin Wall fell, the risk of communist recrudescence in those same Central and Eastern European states kept new democratic parties honest, nudging many toward power-sharing agreements with old communist foes that ultimately resulted in less corrupt and more popular governments.[36]

When does conflict truly threaten? Domestic struggles pose an existential danger when leaders lack the ability to suppress opposing groups outright, including the physical resources necessary to contain social opposition and weather any external backlash of crackdown.[37] Regimes are threatened when their coercive units such as armies, security agencies, and police forces are unwilling or unable to disperse challengers and impose political closure; when they lack the financial assets to fulfill public salaries and fight off bankruptcy in order to keep their governing functions intact; and when they fear the diplomatic isolation, potential aggression, and economic sanctions that rival states within the region might levy in response to domestic abuses.

COALITIONAL CURRENCY: PATRONAGE AND PROTECTION

When imperiled by such threats, coalitional broadening becomes a favorable survival strategy. Popular incorporation occurs through bargains between leaders and social forces.[38] Such pacts can result in formalized agreements, as in regimes forged through corporatism, but more frequently they manifest as informal understandings about the patronage and protection to be given by the regime in return for support and allegiance from its societal backers. As outlined in chapter 1, patronage and protection are the currency of coalitional politics. Patronage entails large-scale material inducements. Appealing to the productive interests of constituent groups, such goods not only enhance their prosperity but also link it to the regime's indispensability.[39] For middle-sector classes, examples of collective patronage include public employment, welfare programs, wage protections, price subsidies, business assistance, and other policy concessions.[40] Notably, coalitional patronage given as collective goods differs from the patronage that manifests as individual payoffs for elite cronies, such as appointments, immunities, and kickbacks.[41] Only the former is class oriented, intending to secure the loyalty of an entire group and thus often requiring significant redistribution of resources within the national political economy.

However, not all constituencies desire purely material compensation. As Dan Slater has argued, fear can be an indivisible incentive for coalitional bargaining: in fragmented societies where communal conflicts are endemic, the potentiality of internecine violence motivates some groups to give obeisance to dictators more easily than if the threat of bedlam did not exist.[42] For ethnic and sectarian minorities, for instance, the prospect of majoritarian governance—possibly bringing cultural, economic, or political destruction—often brings about demands for protection. Protection consists of political arrangements and symbolic privileges that enshrine the advantageous status of supportive minorities, such as high-level participation in dominant parties, guaranteed representation in elected parliaments, disproportional employment in the coercive apparatus, and preferential social policies that advance their privileged rank within society. The result is proximity to power; protected supporters under such coalitional promises are able to articulate demands, access leadership, and reap other advantages as they stand far closer to the political center than does the excluded majority.[43]

GEOPOLITICAL VULNERABILITY

If leaders broaden or narrow their coalitions in response to deadly conflicts, it follows that factors that *reduce* the intensity of those conflicts hold immense importance. Here, geopolitical mediation comes into play. It is well-known that states are "Janus-faced" and that the international system can influence domestic politics in various ways.[44] For instance, democratization analysts have shown how hegemonic actors like the European Union can weaken smaller autocratic states through democracy promotion, organizational membership, trade and cultural linkages, and ideational diffusion.[45] Likewise, structural theorists of revolutions have shown in historical perspective that for many teetering dictatorial giants, such as Tsarist Russia, costly military competition with foreign enemies severely drained domestic resources away from state institutions and made them less able to contain mass uprisings.[46]

Theories of state-building also acknowledge the impact of outside forces. Canonical explanations for modern state formation in both East and West heed the dictum that war made states—and warfare was almost always concerned with conquering external rivals. The mere act of waging war against neighbors forced potentates to bargain with new coalitional supporters for resources and create new administrative institutions to control new territories.[47] In England, demands for financial and coercive resources to fuel overseas expansion pushed the Stuart crown into ever-violent confrontations with landed magnates and burghers, precipitating the violent start of parliamentary democracy.[48] In ancient China, warring between provincial fiefdoms sparked the Qin campaign to overpower nearby competitors and forge the first unified imperial administration.[49] Interfeudal war reconfigured provincial rivalries in medieval

Japan, resulting in the Tokugawa oligarchy running a coherent Shogunate state and thus paving the way for the country to become a great power.[50]

All these literatures cast light onto the geopolitical shadows, exposing how great states throughout history have both shaped and been reshaped by the international system. Yet this does not hold much relevance to newer *postcolonial* states that came into existence after World War II, whose leaders focused not so much on warring with neighbors for territorial gain as the more elementary task of maintaining power and controlling their societies.[51] Here, systemic forces critically intervened early on within the state-building process but in ways not described or predicted by past scholars. What distinguished the international system confronting postcolonial states was its organization and structure. The architects of great European and Asian powers competed within an international arena that was neither permeated by norms of self-determination nor asymmetrically lorded over by uncontested hegemons who possessed far more resources and technology. Both conditions had changed by the time state-building began transforming national societies in Latin America, sub-Saharan Africa, Southeast Asia, and the Middle East, not least because *they* had become the hegemonic imperialists.[52] For instance, when much of Latin America gained independence from Spain during the early nineteenth century, local governments frequently warred over territory. Their ambitions, though, were constrained by Anglo-American pressures to maintain existing boundaries, which limited the catalytic effects of warfare.[53] Previewing the post-WWII Middle East, here Westphalian norms and imperial cartography created the outer borders of states while hindering the domestic processes necessary for fleshing out their institutional innards.

Such systemic imbalance between new states and old powers deepened with time. Until the twentieth century, even the most determined imperialists in Paris, London, or Washington lacked the information and technology needed to quickly intervene in distant lands at will. In the era before wireless transmissions and flight, saving a beleaguered ally required considerable time, resources, and manpower. Further, no multilateral organization coordinated global responses to reverse perceived violations of state sovereignty. Both these realities materialized by the mid-twentieth century, when the retreat of Western and Eastern colonialism presaged a new wave of state-building projects in the Middle East, sub-Saharan Africa, and Southeast Asia.[54] Heavily shaped by the global industrialized core, war making and geopolitical competition among newer states became even more constrained given the hierarchical structure of the postcolonial system.[55] Previously, not just the practice but outcomes of wars had been lucrative. Winners could keep what peoples and resources they seized. Inversely, external invasion constituted the primary threat to most leaders, because losing meant surrendering their lands. Now, in newly sovereign regions like the Middle East, when aspiring states attempted to expand in order to become great—or at least greater—powers, as in Iraq's 1990 annexation of Kuwait, external forces halted such adventurism and restored borders to their status quo.[56] When state boundaries did shift or dissolve, it was usually due to civil war, as with the Sudanese division, or else amalgamation with neighbors, as with Yemeni unification.

Three implications flow from such systemic conditions of hierarchy and asymmetry for postcolonial states. First, traditional geopolitical competition lost most of its productive purpose in terms of state formation. Warring did not so much fortify state-builders as drain economic productivity, destroy human communities, impair institutional development, and encourage the rise of nonstate providers of security and services.[57] Second, because they fought frequently but seldom to *survive*, many new states were crippled with fiscal weakness. Most did not inherit from their colonial overlords the institutional capacity to extract revenues from society, and now the hollowness of geopolitical competition had lain even less incentive to develop such mechanisms through societal bargaining.[58] Finally, what neorealists within international relations term the "security dilemma" for many new states came not necessarily from foreign aggression but rather opposition within domestic society.[59] Dictators saw as many enemies capable of ending their reign within their own capitals as in those of regional rivals and neighboring states.

GREAT POWER SUPPORT

Such permeability of postcolonial states to the international system magnifies the effect of hegemonic interventions into the state-building process, such as when great powers United States, Soviet Union, Britain, and France chose to mediate major domestic conflicts. Though the former two enjoyed ascending dominance and the latter two suffered fading paramountcy after World War II, they shared a common set of diplomatic, fiscal, and coercive tools by which they could bolster favored rulers, thereby reshaping the internal dynamics of state-society struggles. Crucially, such interventions were not one-off events. Most hegemons desired long-term alliances with supported regimes, with expectations that relationships would strengthen their strategic interests.

In diplomatic terms, great powers could sponsor a regime through official statements, legislative declarations, and other public affirmations given by executive principals such as presidents, prime ministers, and premiers. Their leaderships could also undertake minatory, or "gunboat," diplomacy—that is, warding off belligerent neighbors and other rival states with veiled threats of retaliation in order to preclude any potential threats of intervention.[60] By giving public support and neutralizing external threats, such moves reduced the cost of repression and augmented the confidence of beleaguered rulers to reject opposition demands.

If diplomatic sponsorship improved the willingness of leaders to quash contentious opposition, then fiscal and coercive strategies of support gave rulers the *means* to do so. Within the broad category of economic aid, which encompasses capital and programmatic transfers intended to improve material well-being, fiscal support refers to unrequited cash grants and concessional loans that immediately enhance the budgetary resources of the recipient regime, thereby nullifying its fiscal weakness. While this is necessary for basic social and infrastructural services to continue, under authoritarian systems the central budget is especially pivotal, because it provides public salaries of civil servants, police, and army—agents of the state who must fulfill their duties in order for the leadership to survive. "When all is said and done, empty treasuries fund no soldiers."[61] In addition, fiscal infusions can enable regimes to better provide goods and services to placate disgruntled groups, beginning the provision of patronage in return for greater support from below.

Finally, coercive backing is a subtype of military aid, which broadly refers to efforts to improve the ability of governments to control and defend their territory using lethal force. However, coercive assistance more explicitly aims at boosting the physical capacity and organizational knowledge needed by the police, intelligence, and military to repress domestic opposition and enforce autocratic directives. This includes the transfer of weaponry—from small arms and ammunition to mechanized vehicles and other equipment—that can be shipped or flown into the country at short notice. Skills and expertise are transferred through trainers, advisers, and other personnel. The donor country can also subvene through the bluntest of all means: utilizing its own forces, ranging from covert operations and intelligence campaigns to direct military operations. The latter was relatively rare during the Cold War, given the shared fear among competing superpowers that recurrent large-scale military interventions could result in cycles of tit-for-tat escalation that might eventually spiral into nuclear war.[62]

Collectively, such mediation helped client regimes by lowering the cost of repression and boosting their capacity to end conflict without making any serious concessions or compromises with society. That is, they made some coalitional strategies appear more attractive and viable than others. To depict this point, take cases of state-building elsewhere. In seventeenth-century England, the House of Stuart could have well crushed its unruly landlords and burghers had it attracted a foreign ally, like the Ottomans, which could have replenished its fiscal reserves and could have landed promonarchist armies on its shores. No such help arrived; the eventual result was parliamentary democracy. Centuries later, another kingship, this one in Iran, utilized American military firepower and economic supplies to squash a democratic opposition front demanding popular voice, botching a vital opportunity to rally a new social foundation, enhance its political accountability, and pave the way for a more pluralistic political order. When the Qin dynasty set out to vanquish other feudal provinces in early China, no outside actor stepped in to impede that campaign of conquest or halt its result—the first administratively unified imperial state in East Asia. Yet in post-WWII Jordan, the United States acted as dutiful umpire by preventing leftist and nationalist opposition parties from overturning the monarchy's autocratic supremacy, preserving its Hashemite ally through substantial conduits of support. As one vision of political order rejuvenated on the East Bank of the Jordan River, another more democratic one disappeared.

INSTITUTIONALIZING COALITIONS

Great power support can transform domestic conflicts by empowering rulers to destroy opposing social groups. However, the lack of such intervention can expose regime weaknesses and hence compel coalitional broadening with contentious opposition through bargains and compromise. Such broadening occurs through patronage and protection, which give recipients new stakes in political order by making the maintenance of the incumbent regime essential to their well-being. Rulers secure not just acquiescence due to threat of punishment but the "enduring and diffuse basis of voluntary obedience."[63] It is here that institutions enter the story. They are the organizational structures that leaders build to enshrine coalitional commitments throughout the state-building process.

Historical examples illustrate how coalitions lead to institutions. First, on the economic level, most Middle Eastern countries after World War II announced impressive plans to modernize their economies through industrialization. Like elsewhere in the developing world, they created bureaucracies to oversee such transformative projects—ministries, councils, and boards held subordinate to the needs of regime survival. When shielded from the input of societal constituencies, as in Iran's 1963 White Revolution, such planning institutions became technocratic wrecking balls, embittering not only traditional producers by destroying the old economy but also alienating new constituencies like urban labor by suppressing unionization. However, when bureaucratic organs consciously took into account coalitional interests, as in Kuwait, the results differed. Development still suffered from inefficiencies, as politics took precedence over competitiveness; but this time, economic institutions targeted specific groups and classes to ensure their prosperity while the state modernized the economy. Similarly, some autocracies assembled militaries with little purpose other than to enhance their international repute and secure weaponry for aspiring generals. This matches many postcolonial dictatorships, among them Iran. Or, as the Jordanian kingship recognized, armies were also forged to economically cement coalitional alliances by providing preferential access to jobs and security to favored minority groups, in this case tribal communities.

The same diversity in function given similar institutional form applies to political entities. Parties, for instance, serve varying coalitional purposes. In durable single-party states, the ruling organization resolves interelite conflicts, circulates patronage, and provides grassroots support to the leadership through national coordinating structures. In Iran, pro-regime parties had all the trappings of such groups from the late 1950s through the revolution. However, in organizational terms, those parties functioned more like social clubs for wealthy elites than mass-oriented associations that poured their energies into recruiting public support. Likewise, when treated like afterthoughts, legislative bodies like elected parliaments played little role in connecting authoritarians to societal trends and public opinion. Again Iran provides a relevant example. By contrast, when autocrats saw parliaments as a useful way to maintain a broad coalition, they invested time and resources to craft them, devising a competitive system of representation, manipulating legislative rules, and embedding patronage networks into its functions. In Kuwait, for instance, the national parliament holds historical importance not because it ever portended democratization, but because it helped the Sabah dynasty monitor society and juggle the loyalties of different constituencies in a highly visible way.

Coalitions seldom freeze. Though they can theoretically broaden or narrow after they become institutionalized, practical considerations limit radical and sudden changes. As decades pass and their reign matures, autocrats find it cheaper to maintain existing economic and political arrangements than to sweep away coalitional alliances and begin afresh. Further, because institutions make regime commitments given to supporters credible by turning promises into actual patronage and protection, they generate long-term expectations that cannot be reversed at whim.[64] A drastic rollback of an institutional investment—inventing a new ruling party, dismantling welfare programs, purging the military of a favored ethnic group—incurs steep material costs, including the prospect of those former supporters becoming opposition and attacking the regime.[65] In short, state-building is a self-reinforcing process: as the practice of politics shifts from the management of conflict to the maintenance of normal routines of law and order, leaders generally seek to keep their boats steady by applying the same coalitional strategies proven successful in preserving power during crises in the past.

Such path-dependent logic implies that radical change becomes less likely as time goes on. Minor coalitional shuffles, however, can occur, given their lower cost. For instance, leaders can respond to minor crises by shuffling their social bases, scapegoating one constituency or incorporating new groups. A prime example rests in Kuwait during the 1980s, when the Sabah regime temporarily stifled the long-protected Shiʿa minority due to security concerns during the Iraq-Iran war, followed by the incorporation of new Sunni Islamist movements into circles of patronage. The autocracy remained a broadly based one, although its peripheries had changed. Coalitions can also decay when unexpected change occurs in the leadership, such as succession that brings to power a new ruler with different views on society. That transpired in Tunisia, when the replacement of Bourguiba with Ben ʿAli in 1987 signaled a change in regime priorities, including the dismantling of a cross-class coalition by hollowing out the mass ruling party and reneging on long-standing commitments of patronage to key sectors like labor—a narrowing strategy that culminated in the 2011 Jasmine Revolution.

FROM INSTITUTIONS TO OUTCOMES

As the institutionalist literature has mapped out, institutional arrangements have enormous consequences for long-term stability because they influence how regimes react to severe economic and political crises. Financial breakdown, defeat in foreign wars, and ethnic rebellions rank among the major shocks that can illicit significant new social unrest, even in countries with extremely popular leaderships. Such periods of tumult, when growing parts of society stop obeying state authority and disrupt political routines, test the coalitional strategies adopted decades earlier.

Broader coalitions provide several advantages to rulers facing such turmoil. Inclusive state-society alliances limit the scope and radicalism of opposition. Rebellious entrepreneurs seldom find it easy to recruit followers among social forces that share deep convictions about the regime's centrality to their well-being.[66] In addition, authoritarians can counter opposition by mobilizing their own loyalists in the public arena who can both combat objectors and broadcast the image that most of society still stands by the existing political order. Moreover, though even supporters may protest their plight, those with vested interests within the system due to long-standing patronage or protection ties are more likely to demand policy change rather than regime change—that is, not *whether* but *how* the leadership governs. The payoffs of a future revolution that could bring an even worse regime to power do not outweigh the costs of reforming the status quo.

These regimes also have viable methods of mollifying opposition without violence. Coalitional ties to popular sectors provide a repertoire of engagement strategies to deescalate tensions. Leaders may offer economic or political reforms to appease public demands, exploiting their record of providing patronage and protection in the past as signals of future credibility. They also have more knowledge about their societies, helping them identify key areas of moderation, the leaders of dissent, and audience appeals.[67] That is, they know *how* to bargain for peace and survival, having learned habits of inclusion and negotiation earlier. Finally, by virtue of all these factors, those standing atop broad-based coalitions and inclusionary institutions generally need to exercise less violent and visible forms of repression. This not only enhances their standing when engaging opposition groups, but it also allows them to absorb protests, criticism, and other attacks without lashing out with indiscriminate violence.

By contrast, narrower coalitions engender institutional detachments between state and society, an environment that encourages concerted opposition. Structural theorists of revolutions long ago noted how small rebellions often blossomed into mass uprisings under conditions of repressive, exclusionary, and personalistic rule.[68] The reason is twofold. First, a small regime coalition engenders a larger audience for opposition leaders who can recruit among excluded groups sharing common grievances. Second, even societal factions without explicit grievances are not heavily invested in protecting the status quo given their prior marginalization from patronage and protection networks. In this environment, what begin as reform campaigns can morph into zero-sum demands for revolutionary turnover: "the lack of routine opportunities to influence state policy tends to push certain groups and individuals toward radical politics."[69] Leaders also have fewer trustworthy allies, which distinguishes Iran from Jordan. Whereas the former could not deactivate social mobilization because it lacked coalitional surrogates, the latter could at least call upon loyal tribal groups who would go to great lengths to ensure the monarchy survived.

Of course, successful opposition mobilization hinges on internal variables, among them coherent organization and unifying ideologies.[70] But also urgent is the institutional capacity of regimes to neutralize dissent before it spreads. Weak linkages with popular forces give leaders a smaller repertoire of nonrepressive strategies. They struggle to understand the perspective of opposition, given their isolation from the underlying social and political trends that produced it. They also lack credibility when offering reforms in return for peace, given their vacuous record and past abuses. Even at the level of street contention, they tend to lack the means to rally committed supporters to counter opposition effectively outside the tired tactic of hiring paid thugs. In essence, they pay for past mistakes. Violence does not always succeed in preserving incumbent rule, either. Repression can radicalize protests and harden moderates, resulting in ever-deepening cycles of mobilization, coercion, and countermobilization.

CLIENCY RELATIONSHIPS

These observations provide a working theoretical model of state-building, one that links early conflicts to coalitional politics and from coalitional strategies plots out appropriate institutional structures and predicted regime outcomes. However, before turning to the chapters that house the case studies, one last dimension of this framework deserves attention: that of cliency. The great power support given to Middle Eastern regimes in the form of diplomatic, fiscal, and coercive assistance were seldom one-off deals. Rather, they inaugurated long-term relationships between the hegemon and the regime. Cliency relations differed from past forms of hierarchical subordination such as colonialism in that they preserved the juridical independence of weaker autocracies in return for concessions of sovereignty to larger states. Great powers intervened within early social conflicts in order to secure client regimes.

Though only lightly conceptualized by scholars, international cliency relationships operationalize the generic logic of patron-client reciprocity at the systemic level.[71] As developed by Mark Gasiorowski, cliency arrangements revolved around the logic of exchange: the larger state enhances the security and stability of the diminutive client state through diplomatic, fiscal, or military assistance, while that client in turn surrenders exclusivity over its sovereignty in order to facilitate its patron's strategic interests.[72] Westphalian sovereignty—the prerogative of each state to determine its governing structures and territorial activity—is seldom holistic and unitary. In the real world, it manifests as a bundle of rights that could be divvied up and traded, like any other good.[73] Thus, in such transactional relationships, client regimes can exchange segments of their sovereignty in return for support from hegemonic patrons.

In the postcolonial era, the most frequent concession given by client states involved control over foreign policy. They often realigned their international stance on regional or global issues to enhance the influence and prestige of supporting powers. During the Cold War, for instance, many American client regimes complied with adopting anti-Soviet positions across diplomatic venues from formal alliances signed through treaties to voting patterns within multilateral organizations like the United Nations. At the economic level, clients also gave many dispensations to their sponsoring patrons. Hydrocarbon exporters could dole out favorable contracts giving external actors preferential access to local oil and gas resources or maintain production and distribution quotas to satiate favored importers. Client regimes could also purchase military goods (e.g., weaponry, equipment, vehicles) from the patron's defense firms. This not only gave financial profit to the patron but also buttressed its regional position as a preferred arms exporter. Other economic concessions include investment protocols and facilitating trade agreements. Finally, client regimes could cede territorial autonomy by giving military basing rights to their patrons, allowing them to situate troops, vehicles, and other assets on their soil in accordance with their regional security goals. They could also assign transit privileges for foreign troops and personnel in the form of safe overland or overflight passage or seafaring rights if they controlled inland canals and oceanic straits.

Table 2.1 illustrates the reciprocity of international cliency. There is no direct correspondence between types of great power support and the concessions of sovereignty given by the client state. For instance, when the United States has given fiscal assistance, it has not always received economic concessions in return. These are neither rank ordered nor linked goods. That said, it is notable that while hegemonic interventions had *domestic* effects by ensuring the internal security of client regimes (left column), reciprocal concessions of sovereignty primarily strengthened the *international* hegemony of great powers by enhancing their broader global interests (right column). For example, Great Britain's domestic

TABLE 2.1

RECIPROCITY AND CLIENCY

GREAT POWER SUPPORT FOR CLIENT REGIME ENHANCES *DOMESTIC* STABILITY	CLIENT REGIME CONCESSIONS OF SOVEREIGNTY TO GREAT POWER ENHANCES *INTERNATIONAL* HEGEMONY
Diplomatic sponsorship (e.g., public declarations)	Foreign policy alignment (e.g., joining alliance)
Fiscal assistance (e.g., budgetary grants)	Economic dispensations (e.g., access to energy resources)
Coercive backing (e.g., arms transfers)	Territorial autonomy (e.g., military basing rights)

economy benefited from the oil wealth of its client states in the Gulf; but other far more important allowances, like foreign policy alignment and military basing rights, enhanced its global capabilities by allowing it to exercise diplomatic and military influence in far-off territories across the world. Evaluating those systemic effects is the conventional task of neorealists and is not covered in great detail throughout the case studies. This conceptual framework of cliency relationships is not exhaustive. Other works have mapped out a fuller range of cliency relationships during and after the Cold War and typologized all the goods and services exchanged.[74] However, it provides the idea necessary to theorize not only how hegemonic interventions (or lack thereof) had such enduring effects on state-building, but also why great powers would want to intercede in the first place.

LOCATING THE EVIDENCE

This chapter has presented a new theoretical framework about state-building and authoritarian regimes in the Middle East. Linking coalitions to institutions, and then institutions to outcomes, I have explained why the coalitional choices made during the critical junctures of national conflicts were so pivotal to the longevity and stability of their regimes. The geopolitical context of this process, which differed from past periods of state formation, clarifies why foreign powers would intervene during those periods of early struggle and in turn how hegemonic support would have powerful long-term effects by shaping early coalitional decisions.

The next chapters present the historical evidence corroborating the argument. To reiterate, the *depth* of external penetration shaped the *breadth* of regime coalitions that in turn helps account for the *durability* of political order. Where countries were most geopolitically secluded, ruling coalitions were broadest, institutions most inclusive in terms of patronage and protection, and prospects for long-term stability the best. When great power support during early conflicts engendered coalitional narrowing, however, different institutions resulted depending on the nature of societal cleavages. Whether subsidized by geopolitical support or substituted by it, though, such regimes relied more upon repression and exclusion. Those that retained the support of entrenched minority groups, as in Jordan, could tenuously survive but at the recurrent cost of suppressing majoritarian dissent, whereas those who repudiated the masses and detached the government from any popular social base altogether were more likely to meet revolutionary downfall.

3

CONFLICT AND COMPROMISE IN KUWAIT

KUWAIT IS THIS book's first case study and introduces the first causal pattern of Middle East state-building—that of geopolitical seclusion resulting in long-term stability. Perched on the Persian Gulf littoral, this maritime principality experienced a social conflict that, relatively secluded from hegemonic interference, induced the Sabah rulership early in its reign to broaden its ruling coalition and share power with social forces. The analysis begins with the seminal figure of Mubarak Al-Sabah, who attempted to assert absolutist authority but met tenacious resistance from merchant-led opposition. The regime lacked the fiscal and coercive resources necessary to suppress them. Foreign intervention here was plausible; after all, the British had already guaranteed Kuwait's external defenses, as the sheikhdom fell under its treaty relations. However, in the end, the British saw little strategic gain in meddling within its internal affairs. Left alone, the Sabah regime was forced to tolerate, and then bargain, with its enemies. Recognizing its susceptibility to domestic dissent, the leadership also sought to widen its bases of popular support by seeking out new allies that had previously sat on the margins of the political economy, such as the Shiʿa minority.

Herein lays the coalition origins of the modern Kuwaiti state that came into being in the 1950s, an autocracy that would soon utilize its newfound oil wealth to distribute patronage and protection to a cross-cutting base of support. That sense of populism and connectedness to society is celebrated by many Kuwaiti historians as stemming entirely from the familial benevolence of the Sabahs. Yet the surrender of absolutist power came not from cultural enlightenment but through reluctant and pragmatic decisions made during dangerous conflicts upon the onset of modern state-building.

SHEIKHS AND MERCHANTS, 1896–1938

The House of Al-Sabah ascended to rulership of a territory very roughly corresponding to modern Kuwait in 1752, when early settlers of the Bani 'Utub tribe, an offshoot of the 'Anizah confederation, selected Sabah Al-Jabir Al-Sabah as their leading sheikh. Theoretically, the Sabah sheikh had considerable power, as he was coterminous with government and his funds equivalent to the public treasury.[1] In practice, though, the affairs of governance operated through frequent consultations with society, because the sheikh had little capacity to enforce any rules. Instead, major policies required the consent of other tribal and communal notables through the custom of *majlis* (council) that allowed societal representatives to voice their grievances. This also gave rise to another function of the Kuwaiti sheikh—to arbitrate major social disputes by serving as an objective third party.[2]

Both consultative conventions and coercive frailty reflected the defining characteristics of preindustrial politics. The economic consequence for the ruling family was constant fiscal scarcity. Kuwait was a city-state whose sheltered harbor lay at the head of the Gulf and predisposed it as a mercantile entrepôt for goods transiting between Ottoman Iraq, Arabian ports, and British India. Until the twentieth century, most of the ruler's revenues came from small customs duties levied on maritime trade, often no more than one percent.[3] The family also owned extensive date garden estates in the nearby Basra Governorate under Ottoman stewardship.

That provided supplementary income, as did profits skimmed from over-land caravan trade, including lucrative arms smuggling.

The Sabah sheikh stood atop a small coalition. The extended clan represented the core political base. The Sabah family maintained its caste-like cohesion through its own majlis, which guided the succession process and mediated disputes between factions.[4] The second part of the ruler's coalition arose from the *badu* (Bedouin, or mostly nomadic residents). In contrast to the *hadhar* (settled) community in the township, Bedouin tribes resided mainly in the desert hinterland and practiced camel pastoralism and some coastal farming.[5] These tribes included offshoots of larger Arabian confederations, such as the respected ʿAjman, Bani Khalid, Dawasir, Shammar, and Mutair, as well as the less powerful ʿAwazim and Rashaydah branches. Though some had customary land claims, the leaders of these tribal formations did not constitute a landowning class. The arid land beyond a narrow coastal strip did not suit anything beyond small-scale cultivation, which precluded tenancy structures of agrarian production.[6] The Sabah family embedded its social ties with this constituency in numerous ways, such as intermarriage, private tributes, and grazing permits. Bedouin tribes also enjoyed regular access to the open-air market of the township, where they could sell supplies and hold meetings.

These tribes, in turn, fulfilled the leader's need for armed manpower. Bedouin tribesmen staffed the royal bodyguard and also served as armed retainers for internal security tasks like protecting land trade caravans. On occasion, the Sabah sheikh could also raise thousands more armed men when mobilizing expeditions to battle rival tribes.[7] Otherwise, he possessed no standing army. Indeed, well into the 1940s, the Sabah ruler never had, at any moment, more than "500 men who could be considered to be responsible for dealing with security issues."[8]

External to this coalition was the hadhar township. Whereas the mostly Bedouin tribes numbered about ten thousand by the eve of World War I, the port community held around sixty-five thousand residents.[9] Three-quarters were Sunni and the other quarter comprised a Shiʿa minority. The maritime economy and its dual sectors of pearling and trading

predominated, such that the majority of these Kuwaitis occupied traditional labor roles such as fishermen, shipbuilders, brokers, and mariners
in the pearling industry. At its pinnacle before World War I, pearling was
the mainstay of Kuwait's productive activity, generating exports exceed-
ing £2 million in value while utilizing seven hundred boats and employing fifteen thousand men.[10] The pearling sector was central to the preoil
economy, and it entailed arduous work for most. Because it was organized
on a profit-sharing rather than wage-earning basis, financial indebtedness
was built into the industry's hierarchical system of labor.[11] Sailors and
divers on pearling vessels labored in dangerous conditions in order to sat-
isfy impossibly large debts to their captains, who in turn often struggled
to pay back their own debts to the merchants and traders who owned the
vessels.[12] This urban labor force lacked internal organization given its dependence upon a powerful business elite. Led by the Asil, a network of the
eight oldest Sunni merchant and trading families,[13] this class occupied the
apex of the preoil economy. They controlled the pearling sector by virtue of owning most of the vessels, providing funds for new ventures, and
selling harvested pearls overseas. Once the summer pearling season had
ended, merchant houses turned to more diversified maritime trading and
smuggling activities. The Sabah family partly controlled the land caravan
routes linking Kuwait to Baghdad and Aleppo, but merchant traders oversaw the oceanic import trade. Routes with British India were most lucrative, with each Asil merchant house accumulating far more revenues per
year than the Sabah sheikh collected through customs and other fees.[14]

Given their wealth, many merchants saw the ruling family as one
among equals. They had the same 'Utub tribal origins as the Sabah and
shared social and economic bonds that enhanced their cohesiveness. Asil
merchants, for instance, often sent their sons to study abroad, a luxury
that few other Kuwaitis could afford.[15] They also dictated the sheikh's
treasury, because import duties and boat fees required a thriving pearling
and trade sector, which their cartel controlled. Many also furnished monies, upon request, to underwrite the Sabah family's own private commercial endeavors. The result was a delicate equipoise: so long as the merchants accepted their titular leadership, the Sabahs would protect their

economic supremacy and leave their enterprises alone.[16] Such an arrangement gave the Sunni mercantile elite a sense of entitlement that distinguished them from the Sabah's purely political domain. Indeed, unlike Sabah-centric histories of Kuwait that saw the royal family as the bedrock of the state, the merchants had their own "noble history, indeed an alternate version of Kuwait's history that celebrated the traders as heroes and reduced rulers to glorified house sitters."[17]

Yet those alternative histories glorifying Sunni commerce exclude the Shiʿa. Compared with their Sunni counterparts in the maritime sector, most Kuwaiti Shiʿa enjoyed some economic security as they dominated petty retail, including the selling of produce, crafts, and imports. By one estimate, the Shiʿa owned more than half of all shops within the city-state.[18] The wealthiest Shiʿa owned merchant trading houses, though they were generally smaller than their Sunni counterparts. However, many Shiʿa differed from the Sunni in originating not from regional tribes but Iran, Bahrain, or the Hasa region of the Arabian peninsula.[19] For that reason, many Kuwaiti Shiʿa, including even affluent merchants and traders, were regarded as newcomers and suffered substantial discrimination. Further, because Kuwait had no established ʿulama, or jurists who interpreted Islamic law and often held leadership positions in Shiʿa communities, the Shiʿa merchants became de facto intermediaries between this minority and Sabah sheikhs, who did not seek out their support so much as work to ensure no violent conflicts exploded into the open.[20]

A REBOOT UNDER BRITISH WATCH

These social forces provided the context to this familial regime's autocratic "reboot," which brought Kuwait under British influence. In 1896, Mubarak Al-Sabah took power by murdering the then-current ruler, his brother Muhammad, as well as another brother. This marked the only violent transfer of power in Kuwaiti history. Kuwait then fell under Ottoman suzerainty, but Sheikh Mubarak moved to establish diplomatic ties with the British.[21] After extended negotiations, in January 1899 Mubarak and the British signed a secret bond that established exclusive treaty relations with London in return for a payment of 15,000 rupees, or £1,500. This Anglo-Kuwaiti accord signified no intention to make Kuwait a colony, nor did it impose legal restrictions on the ruler's domestic authority. It did, however, give Britain prerogative to defend the territory from external threats. That fell in line with London's drive toward dominating the Persian Gulf, which held little intrinsic value. This backwater instead encompassed some of the shipping lanes and supply routes needed by British India, which were vulnerable to pirate attacks and German or Russian intrusions.[22] To foreclose both, the British had crafted similar trucial agreements with other tribal potentates dotting the Gulf littoral, such as Bahrain, thereby turning this strategic area into a British lake.

The Anglo-Kuwaiti treaty appeared to forge a cliency arrangement. It was a geopolitical coup for the British, for it curbed Ottoman territorial ambitions, blocked Russian access to the Gulf's waters, and helped thwart a joint Ottoman-German project to lay a Baghdad-to-Berlin railway. Later auxiliary treaties granted limited territorial concessions. For instance, only British steamships could make port calls. The British later established a Political Agency in Kuwait to house its resident diplomat, who monitored local affairs. Starting in the late 1920s, the Agency claimed its own legal jurisdiction, running a parallel court that applied to Western subjects.[23] The British also constructed local telegraph lines, postal services, and naval refueling facilities and had exclusivity over any local oil deposits.

In external terms, Sheikh Mubarak could now shelter his territory from foreign predation—a major reason why he had inked the treaty. British forces not only deterred Ottoman forays into Kuwait at the turn of the century, but in 1902 also foiled a countercoup by two exiled nephews attempting to reclaim power. During World War I, the British nullified all prior Ottoman claims over Kuwait.[24] British guardianship also blunted threats from the Arabian peninsula. In late 1920, when Wahhabi forces under Ibn Al-Saud invaded Kuwait and besieged the town of Al-Jahra, the British assisted Kuwaiti defenders by buzzing aircraft over Wahhabi encampments and firing warning shots from nearby warships.[25] In 1922 the

British drew up the ʿUqair Protocol, which delimited Kuwait's southern borders and thereby sealed the area off from future Saudi expansionism but at the cost of half its territory.[26] Further imperial cartography in 1923 delineated the northern borders from Iraq, cementing Kuwait's juridical status as a sovereign entity in the post–World War I international system.

In reality, British relations gave the Sabah regime external security but few internal benefits. It did institutionalize Sheikh Mubarak's takeover, as Britain pledged to recognize only him and his male heirs as rightful sovereigns of Kuwait.[27] However, Mubarak desired far more than border controls and diplomatic ties; he desired British resources to strengthen his financial and coercive powers at home. Combative and intolerant, Mubarak's dictatorial leadership broke with past conventions of consultative rule, even if his ambitions outstripped his resources.[28] Critics were threatened and violent punishment became more frequent, shattering the consultative standards that had characterized the mediated relationship between leadership and community. Out of territorial ambition, Sheikh Mubarak also launched numerous desert expeditions into the Arabian peninsula to battle other tribal forces.[29] Such campaigns drew upon the family's modest revenues from sales from date plantations and customs duties, the value of which surpassed the former by almost two to one. What was left underwrote lavish new private expenses for Mubarak, such as a new yacht, motorcars, and a new personal palace.

The British took a passive stance to domestic politics, refusing to intervene on most issues. With little staff, the political agent was no éminence grise; his job was to collect information and advise the ruling sheikh on foreign relations, but neither he nor the supervising British officer for the Persian Gulf, the political resident based in Bushire, Iran, had any authority to supplant domestic rulers.[30] Serving the Indian Political Service of the British Raj, they were to shun involvement in local disputes and focus instead on preserving Britain's imperial exclusivity in the territory over all other powers.[31] The British thus did not allow its troops and arms to be deployed for internal use; so, for policing functions, the Kuwaiti ruler still relied upon tribal retainers. If anything, the treaty undermined the regime by more explicitly setting rules that limited extraterritorial excursions.

For instance, the British limited Sheikh Mubarak's income by banning the arms smuggling trade, from which he skimmed profits, and all but ended his Arabian war-making adventures, which threatened London's détente with the Ottomans.[32] Though not destitute, Mubarak repeatedly asked for financial grants. Yet the British would only entertain requests for loans rather than provide unrequited aid—and even then, they would only give on condition that he seek funds from no other source.[33]

Such difficulties with revenues made the ruler turn inward, which revealed the autocracy's frailties. In 1906–7, Sheikh Mubarak began levying higher customs duties and boat taxes and raised rents on market shops and houses built on common lands.[34] British observers noted that such "heavy taxation was a new feature in the administration" and reported a palpable increase in the complaints against Mubarak discussed in the public.[35] In particular, this elicited angry opposition from the Asil, who felt the ruler had little right to interfere in their commerce. In 1910 a group of merchant elites registered their protest by emigrating to Bahrain—and taking hundreds of pearling boats and their labor crews with them. Their absence proved so disruptive that Mubarak was forced to retract the more onerous taxes and make personal appeals for their return.[36] Following this event, disaffected merchant notables demanded more consultative rule, petitioning to establish a more formal council to counter the regime's autocratic tilt. Mubarak had no counterweight to merchant threats to secede once more, and an uneasy modus vivendi reigned until the ruler's death in November 1915.

Those tensions came to a head during the long tenure of Sheikh Ahmad Al-Jabir (r. 1921–1950). His 1921 succession was controversial; following the family majlis, Sheikh Ahmad won approval from the merchant and trading families on condition that he govern in concert with their proposed twelve-member Majlis Al-Shura, or advisory council. The council had a short and unsuccessful life span, however; it carried only symbolic authority, and internal bickering ended the participatory experiment within months.[37] Sheikh Ahmad had resisted its establishment and had welcomed its dissolution—though with the promise that he would accept a council of advisers later. The old compact between the Sabah clan and the commercial class was crumbling.

The 1930s brought unrest and agitation, mirroring the early rise of Arab Nationalism elsewhere in the region. The Great Depression pummeled the import-export trade sector, while competition from lower-priced Japanese cultured pearls razed the Gulf pearling industry. Overland trade also sagged under the weight of a Saudi land blockade imposed since the 1920s due to border disagreements, intensifying the recession in the city-state.[38] In spite of the crisis, Sheikh Ahmad's attention became fixated on the emergent oil sector. After World War I, British prospectors discovered viable crude deposits in Kuwait. Following negotiations with British diplomats and partners, in December 1934 Sheikh Ahmad signed a seventy-five-year concession treaty with Kuwait Oil Company (KOC), a joint venture between America's Gulf Oil and Britain's Anglo-Persian Oil Company. Although oil would not be exported in commercial quantities until after World War II, the Sabahs received immediate royalties. The KOC concession granted Ahmad 475,000 rupees (about $178,000) upon signing and afterward the greater of either a fixed annuity or a small fee for every ton produced.[39]

At the same time, young merchant scions became more active in politics, hoping to curtail the regime's growing excesses. For instance, Jasim Al-Sagr helped spearhead an underground society called Al-Shabiba, which alongside several other elite clubs helped spread ideas of Arab Nationalism and encourage new forms of dissent. They identified with liberal currents but not with leftism: urban capital did not need communist surrogates. In that capacity as leaders of opposition, the merchants created new organs of governance, such as a Municipality Board and Education Council, which exercised authority over local affairs unclaimed by the ruler. For instance, in 1937, the Education Council began inviting Palestinian teachers to take positions in new Kuwaiti schools. Sheikh Ahmad responded to such initiative by disbanding the council and disrupting the Municipality Board elections and in March 1938 ordered the arrest and flogging of Muhammad Al-Barrak, an opposition activist. By now, the merchant families had organized a united opposition movement. Some appealed for support from King Ghazi in Iraq. Many of the Asil held commercial interests there, and the Iraqi monarchy assumed that any merchant-based regime taking power in Kuwait over the Sabahs would

53

accede to its territorial demands for annexation, which greatly heightened the ruling family's sense of insecurity.[40] The result was an Iraqi propaganda campaign that, over radio and leaflets, called for revolution. Even the British Political Agency pressured the Kuwaiti leadership, suggesting that some political liberalization might be necessary lest open rebellion explode.[41]

In late June 1938, the opposition made its move. Led by Yusuf Al-Marzouq, a faction of merchants organized a secret forum that sent a petition to Sheikh Ahmad, insisting that he honor his earlier promise in 1921 to form a council with consultative powers. Following his refusal, they took the democratic initiative and organized an election among the 150 leading merchant families for a fourteen-seat Majlis Tashriʿi, or Legislative Assembly.[42] Caught off-guard, Ahmad tolerated the new institution for fear of further instability. This Majlis movement enjoyed a groundswell of support. Though participants inflated the scale of their popular following, much of their liberal rhetoric regarding greater participation undoubtedly attracted many townsfolk, including many who stood below the merchants in economic status, such as boat captains and retailers.[43] The Majlis promulgated a Basic Law that formalized its authority over administrative functions like collecting customs duties and allowed it to legislate new social regulations, such as banning Bedouin war dances within the town square and permitting the playing of radios in coffee shops.[44] It soon probed the political limits of Sabah authority. For instance, it dismissed several confidantes and advisers to the sheikh from their administrative positions. It also established civil police units, the first permanent security organs independent of the ruler.[45] And in October 1938, the Majlis attempted to take control over the Sheikh's oil royalties.

This was the red line for Ahmad. The loss of the KOC payments was the last bastion of authoritarian prerogative: surrendering it would mean the family's demise.[46] The move was equally fateful for the opposition, for it represented a "Magna Carta" moment in which the urban center could finally claim political influence commensurate with its economic clout.[47] This was not the future envisaged by Mubarak for his heirs: unable to intimidate and suppress the opposition, the House of Sabah lay in abeyance.

ACCOMMODATION AND COMPROMISE

If left unhindered, the Majlis would have reduced the ruling Sabah sheikh to a constitutional figurehead. Its liberal ideals ran antithetical to the absolutism imposed by Mubarak and sought to restore the old consultative system guarded by new guarantees of elections and participation. There also existed the possibility of greater incorporation with Iraq, which would have reduced the Sabah clan to a decorative dynasty. Here, the geopolitical seclusion of Kuwait to British imperial strategy comes into play. As his position deteriorated in the fall of 1938, Sheikh Ahmad repeatedly stressed the need for British involvement, but the official stance stayed one of neutrality. British Agent Gerald de Gaury and his superiors did sympathize with the sheikh's position and worried about the ideological sympathies of any liberal new regime, but they refused to intervene.[48] In fact, it was de Gaury's initial advice that pressured the sheikh to tolerate the opposition assembly upon its instauration, first by not rejecting the secret petition altogether and second by agreeing to listen to specific merchant demands.

Hence, despite apprehension that the increasingly powerful Majlis would turn anti-Western, the British were unwilling to tilt the balance of power back to the regime. Patronal intromissions would have entailed diplomatic directives to Sheikh Ahmad to crush the opposition or direct threats against the merchants. On the military side, a coercive intervention—from the transfer of weaponry and arms to gunboat diplomacy and troop landings—would have allowed the ruler to attack opposition directly. The resources required would have been miniscule given the small size of Kuwait. Most of all, direct funding would have given the sheikh the resources to counteract the assembly's control of the purse. None of this materialized.

That lack of fiscal assistance was deleterious, because the regime was still tethered to merchant contributions. Kuwait did not begin exporting oil in commercial quantities until 1946, and until then KOC royalties could not substitute for customs revenues and other income. During 1938 and 1939, import duties from maritime trade composed nearly two-thirds of reported revenues of £60,000, or about $290,000.[49] The British simultaneously deprived the ruling family of its supplementary income from its date gardens. From the early 1930s, the Iraqi monarchy claimed ownership over the Sabah plantations, resulting in extended court proceedings. In the end, the Sabahs lost properties valued at £50,000, with only partial compensation by the British.[50]

Such vapidity revealed the weakness of the Anglo-Kuwaiti relationship. For the British, Kuwait had little intrinsic value; its importance lay in keeping the territory away from other great powers. The British cared enough to demarcate its territorial boundaries but had little interest in what occurred *within* those boundaries.[51] In economic terms, the waterway was a mercantilist hinterland: in 1912–13, the value of all British exports to Gulf ports measured under £5 million, whereas worldwide they measured well over £500 million.[52] With a few exceptions, such as ʿAden, Gulf sheikhdoms like Kuwait, Bahrain, and Qatar were considered neither colonies to occupy nor protectorates to administer. In essence, the British could have tipped the scales for the Sabah regime but chose not to do so.

Secluded in geopolitics and limited in options, Sheikh Ahmad faced the possibility of real political demise. He gambled by choosing a mixed strategy of dissolution and compromise. In late 1938, the Majlis blundered by threatening to punish the tribal communities living along the southern coast for allegedly concealing rotten tomatoes in their yields sold to the market. Taking advantage of the outcry, Ahmad called his tribal bodyguard and additional Bedouin to arms.[53] The merchant activists were no match, and the Majlis was dismissed. The sheikh tried to engineer a more docile council over which he would wield veto control, but stormy negotiations with merchant representatives convinced him to dissolve the assembly altogether in March 1939. This sparked public altercations that resulted in the death of one oppositionist and the later execution of another.[54] Other Majlis activists were arrested, while wealthier ones fled to Iraq and India. However, this was only a temporary reprieve, as the source of political resistance—the merchant and trading families and much of their labor—were still the backbone of the economy. It could not be shattered. Within a year, Sheikh Ahmad freed most jailed opposition-ists and within another amnestied the exiled dissidents, allowing them to return.[55] The merchant elite retained their privileges from the possession of their shipping fleets to prevalence over the trading sector. Business continued as usual for a societal faction that had nearly grabbed power.

Reconciling with social opposition and forgiving their transgressions deposited two legacies. For one, it implanted within the Sabah regime a deep suspicion of external meddling. Ahmad never forgave de Gaury for his perceived betrayal and applauded his exit as political agent in May 1939.[56] Though thankful for British protection of Kuwaiti territorial integ-rity, the Sabah rulership became dubious that such a great power could provide any internal advantages to a regime facing societal resistance. Such misgivings would come back to haunt the British during future occa-sions, when they did struggle to carve out more of a domestic role during the 1950s. For another, it enlarged the Sabah leadership's narrow base of support by forcing the sheikh to reach out and secure new domestic al-lies, during and after the confrontation. Mobilizing such a broad-based foundation prefigured the regime's move in a new and less violent direc-tion—an inclusionary pathway of politics, one that preferred compromise and co-optation over coercion and confrontation. The autocracy learned to bargain, extending patronage and protection in order to capture new sources of loyalty.

The Majlis crisis compelled Sheikh Ahmad to reaffirm two pillars of Sabah rule, namely the ruling family and Bedouin tribes. The latter re-mained loyal, not least as the ruler played on their distrust of the wealthy merchants. It was not lost that the "democratic" assembly, which the mer-chants framed as representing the community, had made no attempt to persuade tribal leaders outside the township to participate. The Sabah family, however, required a more creative solution. Several powerful mer-chants had gained the ear of ʿAbdallah Al-Salim, Sheikh Ahmad's cousin who was suspected of harboring resentment for having been passed over during the 1921 succession discussions within the Sabah majlis.[57] Though Ahmad hailed from the Jabir branch, which played rival to the Salim faction for succession, the ruler acknowledged the importance of all descendants of Mubarak within the family.

Most important, Ahmad began a trend of targeted patronage that would ensure that the Sabah clan would continue to close ranks around the incumbent during future crises—the practice of what Michael Herb identified as "dynasticism," or the assignment of key government posts to familial allies so as to give them overwhelming stakes in political order.[58] For instance, the position of chief of the new police force went to another cousin, Sabah Al-Salim, who would later serve as emir, the titular ruler, in the 1970s.[59] In essence, rather than concentrate all power within his personal office, the ruler dispersed elements of political authority across the royal family. Doing so cost absolutist autonomy but also engendered a far deeper and more loyal coalition.

Sheikh Ahmad also mobilized support from Sunni labor and the Shi'a minority. The ruler reminded maritime workers that it was not Sabah maltreatment but sheer indebtedness to merchant overlords that dictated their fates.[60] When the regime did have the financial resources, it would extend unparalleled generosity in giving labor greater assurances. The Shi'a required a more radical approach. Whereas before the regime sought to ensure peaceful sectarian relations, now it took a proactive stance to extend new promises of social, economic, and political protection toward this apprehensive minority. It convinced the Shi'a that only the Sabah family, not any alternative, could guarantee their future prosperity as a valued part of the Kuwaiti community.

Such pledges resonated because many Shi'a feared discrimination and even exile had the Majlis gained more power. For all its liberal ideals, the Arab Nationalism that infused the merchants' discourse too often conflated Sunni with Arab and painted the Shi'a as Persian enemies. The Majlis also won few friends when it dismissed Saleh Al-Mulla, who was a prominent Shi'i and Sheikh Ahmad's personal secretary, in its bid to undercut Sabah power.[61] By late 1938, thousands of Kuwaiti Shi'a— retailers, craftsmen, sailors—had requested British nationality through the Political Agency, convinced that new restrictions were forthcoming. However, the promise of communal protection also struck a chord with wealthier Shiʿa merchants. Many wished to participate in the Majlis, agreeing on principle with the need for more accountability. However, the Sunni merchants denied them entry, reminding them that they as a minority had neither voting rights nor popular representation.[62]

Such alliances did not coalesce overnight. These pacts and promises came about slowly through repeated interactions, especially during World War II, which brought KOC stoppages and general scarcity.[63] They began taking the form of new regime commitments during the 1950s. While the economic and political institutions that would characterize the modern Kuwaiti state would not appear until later on, this decade revealed the first large-scale extensions of patronage and protection to regime supporters. The strategy of inclusive mobilization would have infuriated Sheikh Mubarak, whose authoritarian reboot had been intended to strengthen his family's control over society and immunity from domestic pressures. However, now the creation and sustenance of coalitional alliances became the most logical framework of authoritarian governance— far more attractive than relying upon a distant patron or retreating into a more repressive and exclusionary shell, neither of which had been effective before.

OIL INCOME TRICKLES IN

Oil wealth facilitated this strategy. In 1946, KOC oil production resumed in commercial quantities. At the time, Kuwaiti society was still impoverished, with an annual per capita income standing at approximately $21.[64] The trickle of hydrocarbon revenue became a stream in the early 1950s, when KOC stepped up operations to compensate for the Iranian shutdown. Crude production leapt from sixteen thousand barrels per day in 1946 to over 1.64 million barrels per day by 1961, equivalent to 7 percent of global output.[65] Britain and Kuwait also modified the original KOC royalty agreement with a new fifty-fifty profit sharing agreement, subjecting KOC to an income tax over and above all royalties paid, the latter of which came to be 12.5 percent of posted crude prices.[66] This meant the Sabah regime began reaping a small fortune, with annual oil revenues jumping from $760,000 in 1946 to over $467 million in 1961.[67]

Also characterizing the 1950s was a new incumbent: Sheikh 'Abdallah Al-Salim, who succeeded Ahmad upon his death in 1950 and would rule until 1965. Under his reign, the relationship between the Sabah clan and the merchant class continued to evolve. The old Sunni commercial houses lost much of their political teeth against the regime. To some degree, Sheikh 'Abdallah already had better rapport than Ahmad with the merchants, who remembered his tentative—if unspoken—sympathies to the Majlis movement.[68] However, even if they chose to rebel again, the merchants and traders no longer held the regime's purse strings. Hydrocarbon income allowed the Sabah family to pay off all private debts by the early 1950s. Thereafter, merchant voices found that their access to their old enclaves of influence such as the Municipality Board was dwindling, as the wealthy Sabah clan could now intervene into political affairs more directly. Sheikh 'Abdallah and his cousin, Chief Magistrate 'Abdallah Al-Jabir, further limited the merchants' political reach early on by vetting the memberships of central committees for new administrative domains, such as the legal system and health care.[69] Finally, the regime's repressive capacity grew, albeit slowly. The Kuwaiti army, formed in 1952, sported about two thousand personnel by the mid-1950s, while separate police and public security departments began assuming responsibility for civil affairs.[70] Though initially ill-trained, these represented permanent bodies of salaried, armed men under command of the Sabah family—a luxury it never had before.

More conspicuous was what did *not* happen. Although it could now liberate itself from urban capital and even destroy its merchant rivals once and for all, the Sabah regime did no such thing. The autocracy stayed its hand, even though a crackdown would have cost little. Even the British would have stayed out of the dispute, as their chief concern now lay with the continued production and export of Kuwaiti oil, not the fortunes of an aging elite of trading families. Instead, Sheikh 'Abdallah did the opposite: he neither destroyed nor ignored the regime's old nemesis, but instead he made positive and frequent overtures to ensure their continued success.

Though not yet systematic, state transfers of patronage began to flow into merchant houses. For instance, the ruler required British companies that were bidding for large contracts doled out by the government, such as in transportation, supply, and construction, to take on merchant partners; by the end of the decade, those merchants would squeeze out their British associates altogether. The regime also directed the reinvestment of surplus revenues into new shareholding companies partially or wholly led by merchant and trading elites, giving them entrée in the new economy.[71]

The decade also saw the commencement of the land acquisition program—one of the greatest conduits of patronage the state would give its former rivals over the next few decades. In 1952, the Kuwaiti government began purchasing land from selected owners at highly inflated prices on a massive scale.[72] Initially, Sabah relatives benefited the most. Many appropriated unclaimed lands outside the traditional walls of the city and then funneled public monies into developing those plots into new residential neighborhoods.[73] However, many merchants resold their lands back to the state for enormous profits. Others exploited their financial acumen and personal ties to Sabah princes to shrewdly redevelop these highly valued plots into residential or commercial centers. Nothing regulated these transactions, which one U.S. observer disparaged as a "gimmick" that gave cash to the Asil "on a silver platter."[74] From 1957 through 1963, the state expended $830 million for land purchases, making it the single largest item in the central budget outside of public salaries—more than defense, health care, education, and public utilities combined.[75]

Such initial patronage gives clues to the Sabah dynasty's popular orientation. Another sign was the mediation of internal family disputes, signaling the leader's heightened awareness that authoritarian rule required a minimal degree of familial cohesion. Sheikh ʿAbdallah doled out private goods as personal patronage, continuing to place relatives in lucrative offices and positions within the state apparatus. By the mid-1950s, he had given his relatives hundreds of senior bureaucratic jobs and generous land titles, while also raising the family's financial allowances. Not all dynastic affiliates proved malleable, however. The autocrat exercised caution regarding two especially ambitious relatives: half-brother Fahad Al-Salim,

61

who controlled the public works, health, and municipality departments, and uncle ʿAbdallah Al-Mubarak, who headed the public security force. ʿAbdallah Al-Mubarak was the last living son of Mubarak, and had built up the public security directorate to rival the uniformed civil police under the command of the ruler's brother, Sabah Al-Salim.[76]

In November 1956, Sheikh ʿAbdallah created a new political organ, the ten-member Majlis ʿAlaʾ, or Supreme Council, and stacked it with conservative and loyal relatives.[77] The council not only served as a clearinghouse for advice, but it also helped the sheikh remove Fahad Al-Salim and ʿAbdallah Al-Mubarak from their offices by the decade's end.[78] Such moves against family members were rare but helped foreclose future internal contestation by closing dynastic ranks around the ruler and preventing any relative from gaining too much power. As head of the public security forces, for instance, ʿAbdallah had become antagonistic to other Sabah elders during family meetings, and his dismissal brought widespread applause.[79]

Coalitional broadening ran parallel to another strategic trend. The regime had learned that not the British but its *own* resources could best guarantee its survival. That mistrust of Western meddling influenced the formation of Kuwaiti foreign policy in the 1950s, in which the British Foreign Office in London, having assumed more direct supervision over Gulf affairs since the loss of British India, attempted to assume a more domineering position. In the post–World War II years, the UK still abided by its formal responsibilities that extended from the 1899 Anglo-Kuwaiti Treaty—territorial protection from external threats. However, now it clamored to gain more influence in domestic affairs, recognizing the principality's newfound importance as a major oil producer.

Kuwait produced less than other countries but held more hydrocarbons under its sands; the largest oil field, Burqan Field, was thought to hold 18 percent of world crude.[80] Those reserves held special importance not just for Western supply lines but for the UK itself. During the years from 1956 to 1960, Kuwait supplied more than half of British oil imports.[81] However, KOC no longer held its monopoly, as Sheikh ʿAbdallah had signed concession agreements with American firms in 1948 and 1958 that provided supplementary income.[82] For these reasons, whereas the preoil era was typified by passivity regarding internal affairs, now Britain desired to provide infusions of political and military support in hopes of creating a new cliency relationship.

The regime resisted. In his last years during the late 1940s, Sheikh Ahmad rebuffed suggestions to accept personal "advisers" who, like so many British officials in Iraq, Bahrain, and other client states, could provide a direct link with London.[83] There were some compromises; for instance, in 1951, the Foreign Office persuaded Sheikh 'Abdallah to hire a handful of British financiers and managerial experts. KOC also employed British engineers and technicians.[84] Likewise, in 1953 British officials helped establish the Kuwait Investment Board in London, which reinvested the sheikhdom's surplus oil revenues into the British sterling zone.

Still, the incongruity of London's suddenly offering benefaction to a state it previously treated as a colonial backwater was not lost on 'Abdallah. The ruler rejected numerous requests to implant "political" advisers to streamline the expanding state, instead preferring to keep formal responsibilities within familial circles.[85] He could grant short-term allowances, such as paying for British arms and military training for the fledgling Kuwaiti army, but not any long-term arrangement that would constrain Kuwaiti foreign policy or surrender major territorial concessions.[86] So upset did British officials become regarding this royal defiance that in the late 1950s some in the Foreign Office entertained the idea of simply occupying the sheikhdom and running it as a Crown Colony.[87] Yet the Sabah leadership had little worry. It understood how to survive in a position of geopolitical seclusion and wanted this fading power to surrender its imperial pretensions altogether. It would soon get that wish.

STAYING THE HAND OF REPRESSION

The coalitional strategy of inclusion, combined with the rejection of any reliance upon foreign powers, induced a soft approach for dealing with societal opposition. This became apparent in the mid-1950s, when urban expansion and ideological diffusion led to a brief spate of political unrest. Flush with foreign exchange earnings, the coastal municipality of Kuwait grew faster than its infrastructure allowed; the town became a city.[88] However, holders of traditional occupations—pastoralism, shipbuilding, pearling—could not meet demands for skilled professions like teaching, accounting, and administration. As a result, the state encouraged the immigration of mostly Arab foreigners, such as Egyptians, Palestinians, Lebanese, and Syrians—at a pace so feverish that by the decade's end Kuwaiti nationals had become the demographic minority. Many carried sympathies for Arab Nationalism and leftist ideologies. That wave of expatriate immigration coincided with explosive growth in print media, with daring new newspapers like *Al-Fajr* and *Al-Sha'b* connecting locals to regional events like the Arab Nationalist military coups in Egypt and Iraq.

As a result, an autochthonous movement of Arab Nationalism came into being by the late 1950s. Its members infused Kuwaiti civil society with organizational energies, helping create cultural clubs, educational societies, and professional groups.[89] Such pluralism also resulted in then-resident Yasir 'Arafat's founding of Fatah, a Palestinian national group that would later dominate the ranks of the Palestinian Liberation Organization. Arab Nationalists in Kuwait had much to critique, from the principality's longstanding British connection to the Sabah dynasty's perceived financial excesses with oil revenues; they replaced the merchants as the vanguard of domestic opposition. While they did not support the movement as a cohesive bloc, some merchant and trading families did participate by financing a small but vocal crop of educated Kuwaiti liberals. Ahmad Al-Khatib, for instance, had helped establish the original Arab Nationalist movement during his university years in Beirut in 1952 and helped organize numerous activities after returning home.

This loose urban front first made headlines during the 1956 Suez War, when it launched popular protests in support of Gamal 'Abdel Nasser's regime in Egypt. Sheikh 'Abdallah abstained from deploying the army and instead directed the civil police and public security forces to maintain order with minimal violence.[90] Periodic demonstrations continued for the next several years despite being prohibited, while several underground cells devised a number of bombings against KOC installations. While the police and public security forces utilized different tactics as they fell under different leadership—the public security forces, for instance, favored more physical confrontations—they both fell under orders to exercise considerable restraint when controlling hostile crowds.[91] Though the Sabah leadership perceived Arab Nationalism as a threat, it did not order any campaign of high-intensity coercion. Arrests were targeted rather than indiscriminate, with detainees quickly released or at worst subject to canings. Extrajudicial killings, much less organizational liquidations involving wholesale roundups, were absent. Centers of opposition sentiment, such as the National Cultural Club, operated with only minor interruptions from the authorities. What makes such restraint more remarkable was the legal impunity by which Sheikh ʿAbdallah could have imposed such lethal repression. Indeed, the British pressured the ruler to utilize more constant force against the Arab Nationalists and squash all protest activities after Nasser's moral victory at Suez.[92] Further, many activists were Arab expatriates with few legal rights, which gave the regime considerable latitude in brutalizing them without backlash from any local constituency. Most Bedouin tribes and Shiʿa, for example, did not participate.

In fact, after the Suez unrest, evidence shows the ruler approved just two acts of concerted violence against the citizenry. The first occurred in May 1957, when public security forces assaulted a housing compound holding the Malik family, a distant branch of the Sabah that had returned to commandeer lands. Even that operation instigated considerable disagreement within the regime. Sheikh ʿAbdallah's brother Sabah Al-Salim, the police director, so diverged that upon ascending to the throne in 1965, he paid reparations by absorbing the surviving Malik into the royal family, thus giving them financial security and legal immunities.[93]

The second occurred in February 1959, during a public rally at the Shuwaikh School commemorating the one-year-old merger of Egypt and Syria into the United Arab Republic (UAR) and praising the July 1958 coup in Iraq. The regime provided food for the crowd and allowed the event to continue even when Al-Khatib called for Kuwait's merger into the UAR.[94] Only when Jasim Al-Qatami, a former police officer who had resigned during the Suez War protests, delivered an oratory that attacked Sheikh ʿAbdallah's right to rule and questioned the legitimacy of the Sabah family did the government respond.[95] In the ensuing weeks, public security officers arrested dozens of protesters, shut down several popular social clubs, and suspended several independent newspapers.

Still, most activists received little more punishment than lost jobs and torn passports. Al-Khatib, for instance, would remain active as an opposition figure for the next several decades, attracting government attention but seldom facing the blunt end of any policing tool. Leniency and rehabilitation even applied to Al-Qatami, who had gained favor with the Nasserist regime of Egypt and represented a leading proponent for Arab Nationalism in Kuwait. His brother, Muhammad, had been the Majlis supporter killed in the March 1939 fracas. Within years, however, Al-Qatami was appointed as an adviser to the emir and then undersecretary of the Foreign Ministry—a curious reward for someone who had come as close to any dissenter since the Majlis movement to advocating the deposal of the entire dynasty. These repeated encounters with dissent reinforced two lessons from the 1938 Majlis conflict. First, bereft of foreign patrons, the Sabah regime understood well that it would need to retain a robust social base to immunize itself from any possible unrest in the future. Second, Sheikh ʿAbdallah realized Kuwait's historic ties with Britain had become a major liability, especially with Arab Nationalism ascendant in the region. "The British provided the easy target for opposition, and the Sabahs were guilty by association. It was time to end that association."[96] British policy makers also concluded that, as a result of their declining financial and military resources for pursuits abroad, London needed to scale down the scope of its defensive commitments within former imperial areas.[97] Thus in June 1961, Sheikh ʿAbdallah and Sir William Luce, the political resident in the Gulf, abrogated the 1899 Anglo-Kuwaiti Treaty, although the British maintained an informal pledge to protect Kuwait's territory from external threats.

That promise was summoned weeks later, when the Qasim regime of Iraq revived an old historical claim upon Kuwait. Sheikh ʿAbdallah took no chances that the irredentist threat was a bluff: Iraq's sixty-thousand-strong army outnumbered Kuwait's by more than twenty to one, and its

Soviet-equipped air force dwarfed Kuwait's British-supplied squadrons by nine to one.[98] With Kuwaiti approval, London commenced minatory actions to deter Iraqi action. Coded Operation Vantage, the British positioned thousands of troops near the Iraqi border and prepared for a potential invasion. The Sabah regime then approached the Nasserist regime in Egypt, facilitating entry into the Arab League.[99] Arab League peacekeepers soon replaced the British detachment, and the threat passed. In retrospect, Iraq was likely a paper tiger, given the absence of substantial troop mobilizations near the border. Operation Vantage represented more an opportunity for a fading imperial power to retrench the line and exercise its still-uncontested hegemony over the Gulf.[100]

Regardless, the irony was biting. More than two decades after they were desired by the Sabah leadership, the coercive agents of British power made their presence felt on Kuwaiti soil. Now, however, they were no longer needed—not here and increasingly nowhere else in the Gulf. In November 1967, Britain relinquished the Crown Colony of Aden, its last major installation in the region. British forces assigned to protect its Gulf dominion now consisted of a small task force scattered around its remaining clients: Bahrain, Oman, Qatar, and the Trucial States.[101] Yet continuing budgetary pressures left the British government unable to pay the £12 million annual cost of even this skeletal squadron. In 1971, Pax Britannia in the Middle East ended with the withdrawal of these last naval forces from the Gulf.

With this exit, the Sabah regime would embark upon massive new state-building projects without seeking cliency relationships with other great powers, namely the Soviet Union and the United States, or any other kind of overt dependence on foreign patrons. The economic and political institutions created, and their effects on regime stability, occupy the next chapter.

||||||||||||||||||||||||||||||||||||||||||||||||||||||||||||||||||||||||||||||||||||||||||||||||||||||||||||||

This chapter advanced this book's theory about regime durability. At a critical juncture, a lack of British support forced the Sabah leadership into a position it did not desire: one where survival required compromising with powerful opposition, as well as sacrificing additional resources and power to woo new supporters like the Shi'a minority. Power was consolidated through bargains rather than brutality. The timing of this conflict, and the absence of hegemonic support, left powerful legacies on future economic and political institutions. They would materialize as early as the 1950s, when the regime collected its first sustained oil revenues and decided to not suppress its societal foes that had nearly toppled it decades earlier but instead to protect and enrich them. This came alongside maintaining its newly broadened coalition of other societal allies. In the coming decades, access to more oil wealth would not make this regime more repressive and narrow despite having the resources to be so but instead would deepen its cross-cutting social base and enrich almost every constituency across society with carefully targeted transfers of patronage and protection.

If the British intervened to allow the Sabah rulership to defeat its merchant opposition *without* bargaining in the late 1930s, would the regime have embarked upon a different path? The evidence suggests so. A dynastic leadership with access to British financing and troops would have had little need to tolerate any bold experiments in democratic power sharing, much less pardon and reintegrate those involved in such seditious efforts. Neither would it have felt such urgent pressures to reach out and secure new supporters to allay its domestic insecurities and reinforce its grasp upon authoritarian power. In historical reality, though, the British did not intervene—and though it stung the House of Sabah greatly, over the long-term it would prove to be advantageous for its future stability.

4

INCLUSION AND STABILITY
IN A POPULIST AUTOCRACY

K UWAIT'S REGIME LARGELY stayed its hand of repression when dealing with pluralism, dissent, and opposition in the latter half of the twentieth century. This chapter shows why. Constrained by the connected interests and expectations of its constituents, Sabah leaders seldom felt comfortable enacting wide-ranging violence to keep domestic order during crises, instead preferring to negotiate their way out of trouble. As the last chapter showed, such an inclusionary style of governance stemmed from the hard compromises made in the late 1930s, when the regime was forced to broaden its coalition in response to geopolitical seclusion from British support.

This chapter traces the institutional consequences of that coalitional strategy upon national development, revealing how new economic and political institutions after the 1950s kept the Sabah family in close contact with Kuwaiti society through the provision of patronage and protection to different coalitional allies. This made the autocracy well prepared to deal with two disastrous crises, the 1980s financial collapse and the 1990 Gulf War, which nearly ended its rule altogether. During these hurricanes, the Sabah regime could draw upon nonviolent strategies to deal with opposition, a repertoire of engagement that reflected its past investments in keeping the national leadership connected to different societal trends. It shuffled its coalition in response to heightened sectarian tensions fueled by regional conflict in the early 1980s, temporarily demoting one group, the Shiʿa, while promoting a new constituency, the Sunni Islamists. It also made credible promises to consider new political reforms to placate resurgent democratic opposition. Above all, it was able to convince almost all Kuwaitis in exile during the Iraqi occupation that, for all its flaws and mismanagement, the Sabah dynasty was still the most viable choice of leadership for the country. Its success in convincing the citizenry to restore authoritarian rule despite nearly a decade's ravages of economic and military chaos exposed how much its historical coalitional strategy allowed for durable political order, one characterized by constant state-society dialogues and minimal coercion.

THE OIL ERA BECKONS

From the 1960s onward, Kuwait accrued enormous capital surplus from its hydrocarbon exports, which in most years contributed at least 90 percent of all revenues. It featured all the classic fiscal and social indicators of a heavily oil-rentier state, among them nonexistent taxation and universal social services. By the late 1970s, the state had assumed control over the hydrocarbon industry, with its own Kuwait National Corporation Company buying out KOC and most other Western interests.[1] Such nationalization meant that the Sabah autocracy alone lorded over the oil sector and its financial proceeds during a period of rising global demand. Like other Gulf oil producers, the 1973 OPEC embargo that tripled the market price of crude yielded an incredible bounty for Kuwait, while the 1979 doubling of crude prices generated still more profits.[2] By the mid-1970s, spectacular rates of growth had pushed per capita incomes, consumption rates, and living standards to median Western levels.[3] Figure 4.1 charts economic growth during these two decades, with revenues outstripping expenditures almost every year. Much like Iran, hydrocarbon revenues spiked after the early 1970s, providing Kuwait with the majority of its rents long after the Sabah regime had settled upon its coalitional

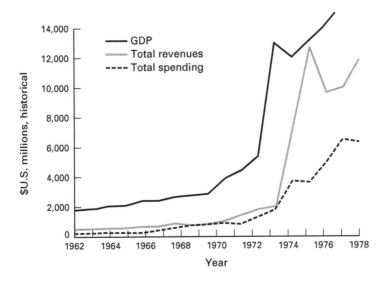

FIGURE 4.1   Kuwait's economic growth, 1962–1979

Sources: World Bank (serial); Kuwait Central Statistical Office (1990).

strategy. However, also like Iran, that Kuwait *had* such oil wealth tells little about *how* it would redistribute those rents across society. The 1960s and 1970s reveal the institutionalization of the inclusive coalitional logic crafted earlier, as indicated by the large-scale and targeted transfers of patronage and protection to different social groups in order to maintain their support for Sabah rule.

Before reviewing evidence for these inclusionary institutional commitments, the way that the Sabah autocracy began linking citizenship to oil-fueled social and economic entitlements merits attention. Like other oil-rich Gulf states, the regime addressed those formerly dependent upon the maritime economy in a straightforward way: it employed them, turning echelons of seafaring laborers into a new state-dependent bourgeoisie. The central administration rapidly expanded in size after the 1950s, soon becoming engorged with ministries and agencies whose size far exceeded their modest functions, with thousands of new bureaucrats often lacking

71

the skills needed for new office-based roles involving technical and managerial tasks.[4] The welfarist use of public employment as one form of collective entitlement to citizens became obvious to outside observers. One World Bank team lamented the "low productivity" of government offices where "the amount of work done by each person or section is often small because there sometimes simply is not enough work to fill the day."[5] By 1976, half of the national labor force worked in the civil service, despite a quarter being illiterate and nearly a third not having completed primary education.[6] Such rentierism predictably required considerable budgetary expenditures. For instance, recurrent outlays on public salaries, which often increased to keep pace with living costs, typically consumed up to one-half of all government spending.[7]

As a corollary, while the vast majority of all Kuwaitis could obtain public employment of some sort, the rest of the economy began requiring a large expatriate workforce. Most Kuwaitis stayed sequestered under state employment, while other Arabs, and increasingly Asian workers, dominated the private sector.[8] The division between citizens and everyone else sharpened in December 1959, when the government issued a naturalization decree stipulating that only those who could provide proof of familial habitation in Kuwait before 1920 qualified as citizens. Naturalization was rare and required minimum residency of ten years for Arab and fifteen for non-Arab nationals. As a result, foreign workers had few economic protections and almost no political rights. Falling through the cracks as well were some outlying tribes that could not prove their historical residency with legal documentation often due to their nomadic nature, despite some having social and economic roots in the area long before 1920. These tribespersons became the *bidun*, short for *bidun jinsiyyah*—those "without nationality."[9]

Kuwait was not alone in creating this stratified model of citizenship, one dependent upon the repurposing of oil rents into domestic entitlements. More relevant is how the regime promulgated such policies *without* feeling the need to create a large coercive apparatus to maintain domestic order at the same time. As figure 4.2 illustrates, combined military and police spending shrunk as a percentage of total spending, from about

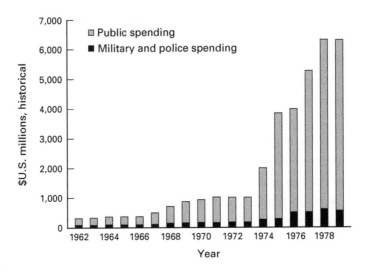

FIGURE 4.2   Kuwait's spending on repression, 1962–1979

Sources: ACDA (serial); Kuwait Central Statistical Office (1990).

25 percent in 1962 to less than 10 percent by 1980, or from about $60 million to over $600 million. Much of that increase stemmed from expensive one-off purchases of advanced weaponry—planes, missiles, radar, and so forth—designed for external deterrence, not internal use. The regular army and public security directorate within the Interior Ministry never increased dramatically in size, with both payrolls hovering around ten thousand personnel until the 1980s.[10]

Of course, Kuwait's small population, which grew from 300,000 to 1.4 million during the same period, could account for such slim figures. However, qualitative evidence suggests instead that the Sabah leadership did not believe repressive controls were either necessary or appropriate for Kuwait. Sheikh ʿAbdallah and his advisers agreed in the early 1960s that the army's sole purpose should be to deter external aggressors like Iraq, not any internal stabilizing function.[11] The military was invented *because* of Kuwaiti statehood, not to achieve it: "[Kuwait] could not be the only Gulf entity without an army. . . . It was expected by the world but not necessarily desired by Kuwaitis."[12] Indeed, few Kuwaitis saw the military as a viable career path, given the availability of better paying civil positions elsewhere within the state. Thus most personnel, including junior officers, were bidun or non-Kuwaiti Arabs, an uncomfortable fact that resulted in conscription being imposed in 1978.[13] Still, evasion rates were high, and the majority of career personnel remained non-Kuwaiti.

Likewise, the Interior Ministry's public security and small intelligence department were neither trained nor equipped to engage in high-intensity coercion. Upon its establishment in 1962, the Interior Ministry's primary concern was containing Arab Nationalism, policing expatriates, and deporting troublemakers.[14] As a result, extrajudicial acts of violence were rare, much as collective opposition action seldom occurred. The entire 1960s, for instance, registered just one strike, a twenty-four-hour work stoppage among oil workers, and one instance of anti-regime violence, a 1969 bombing in protest of the rigged elections two years earlier.[15]

Yet social and political life was not inchoate. After the 1950s, the Kuwaiti press had become among the liveliest in the region. The merchant-backed *Al-Qabas*, Arab Nationalist *Al-Tali'a*, and other daily papers, alongside nearly a hundred weeklies and monthlies, provided an expansive space for public debate, with only the affairs of the Sabah family remaining off limits.[16] Several newspapers with merchant backing, such as *Akhbar Al-Kuwayt*, even positioned themselves as proregime outlets, embodying their new alliance with the ruling family.[17] The government also enforced few associational restrictions, which enabled a plethora of professional organizations, social clubs, and student groups to operate with loose regulatory oversight.[18] Civil society was vibrant and growing.

This should not connote that the Sabah regime desired democracy. On the contrary, the royal leadership sought to weaken its critics from the 1960s onward in various ways, but this was to be achieved through softer forms of manipulation and constriction, not through battering repression. For instance, vote rigging in the 1967 elections for the Majlis Al-Umma, the unicameral parliament created in 1962, engineered numerous opposition deputies with Arab Nationalist sympathies or merchant backing out of office.[19] In 1976, the regime suspended the Assembly for several years in response to uncomfortably open invectives, dismissed the elected boards of several professional associations, and closed the Independence Club, popular with former Arab Nationalists.[20] Such moves were accompanied by temporary press restrictions and sporadic arrests of dissenters who lashed out at the Sabah ruler or his family openly. Hence in comparative perspective, the exercise of state violence against the citizenry was light. The worst years of coercive "excess" in Kuwait prior to the crises of the 1980s, all told, were still more lax than the "best" years of repression under most other dictatorships.

As leniency characterized the domestic arena, disengagement from superpower rivalry typified Kuwaiti foreign policy. After the abrogation of British treaty relations in 1961, Kuwait presented itself as an independent emirate, with the ruling Sabah sheikh now assuming the title of emir, or prince. Its external vulnerability, however, remained the same, with Iraqi incursions from the north a constant worry. Yet neither Sheikh 'Abdallah nor his successor, Emir Sabah al-Salim, desired a close-knit relationship with another Western patron, believing instead that a more independent course of "generous" neutrality could secure international goodwill. One plank of this strategy entailed foreign aid. After the 1961 Iraq crisis, Sheikh 'Abdallah established the Kuwait Fund for Arab Economic Development, or KFAED.[21] From 1962 through 1989, KFAED distributed 361 development loans equaling $5.73 billion among sixty-five Third World countries, with half going to other Arab states for political purposes. Among pan-Arab causes, Kuwait helped finance the Palestinian Liberation Organization, which already derived considerable private funding from Palestinian expatriates in Kuwait, and delivered funds to Jordan and Syria to support their resistance to the 1978 Camp David peace accords between Egypt and Israel.[22]

Further evidence for this independent foreign policy lies in the regime's studious avoidance of superpower alignments during the Cold War. For instance, Emir Sabah al-Salim was cautious about his dealings with the Johnson and Nixon administrations in the United States, as he did not wish Kuwait to be regarded in the Arab world as a Western client.[23] After the 1982 Israeli invasion of Lebanon, some parliamentarians even threatened to cut diplomatic ties with Washington and to suspend oil shipments to the West.[24] In 1983, the emir also refused to receive the new American ambassador, Brandon Grove, because he had once served as consul in East Jerusalem.[25] Meanwhile, Kuwait ranked among the first Gulf states to open diplomatic ties with the Soviet Union in the 1960s and frequently extended its oil surplus to Soviet bloc states. For instance, in 1974 it gave a $40 million loan to Hungary and in 1976 financed a new petroleum refinery in Romania, agreeing to supply it with 160,000 barrels of oil daily.[26] While such cordiality might be defensible as pragmatism, equally striking was the tactic of purchasing arms from most major suppliers without prejudice. During the 1970s, Kuwaiti spent $650 million on U.S. weaponry, but they also spent billions more acquiring French aircraft, British tanks, and Soviet missiles and ground systems.

PATRONAGE: THE MERCHANTS AND *RAISON DE FAMILLE*

The mostly noncoercive approach taken by the Sabah regime reinforced its primary strategy of institutionalizing and preserving its coalitional commitments. Sabah Al-Salim, the former head of the civil police, succeeded his brother, Sheikh ʿAbdallah, in 1965 and would rule until 1977. Emir Sabah reigned over a period of not only renewed unity within the royal family but also large-scale patronage transfers to the regime's former foes: the merchant and trading elites.

Despite that national control over the oil industry gave it unparalleled wealth, the Sabah autocracy continued to enrich the merchant class with new economic policies and programs. The land acquisition program continued to funnel money to this group. In total, from 1952 to the mid-1980s the state expended more than $10 billion on this program, of which an estimated $6.5 billion went to the wealthiest eighty merchant families.[27] Moreover, Emir Sabah protected the merchants' newfound commercial monopolies in real estate, insurance, finance, construction, and other nonoil sectors. First, he discouraged royal relatives from entering into economic ventures that could compete against them. This raised complaints, though side payments in the form of greater financial allowances, participation in the land program, and political appointments appeased them. In fact, the state often fortified merchant firms and conglomerates with its own capital, such as by purchasing various assets in national shareholding companies led by merchant elites at above-market rates—but never a majority stake. Thus by the end of 1979, the state owned 35 percent of all outstanding shares listed by these firms.[28]

Second, the regime also did not interfere with the rise of the Kuwait Chamber of Commerce and Industry (KCCI), which fostered greater cohesion between the merchants and facilitated political lobbying efforts.[29] Noninterference manifested as a significant policy because Emir Sabah now had the independent wealth necessary to penetrate and dismantle such civic organizations; the choice to not do so, much like the withholding of royal interference in merchant businesses, was deliberative. Third, various protectionist measures facilitated merchant profits. The Central Bank's hedged monetary policy and extremely generous credit terms shielded the Asil's semiprivate enterprises from almost all competition. In addition, the 1964 Imports Law and 1965 Industries Law limited the rights to establish businesses to only Kuwaiti nationals, which required all non-Kuwaiti companies to adopt a local partner to operate. Petty traders exploited the sponsorship system by taking huge cuts of profit from foreign firms, often for little more than giving their legal signatures to sponsorship documents. The wealthier families took special advantage of the luxury import sector, where they partnered with Western multinationals to grab licensing and franchising rights to sell cars, appliances, and other expensive goods to the prospering urban populace. By the late 1970s, one of the Asil clans, the Ghanim, was running the biggest General Motors dealership outside the United States.[30]

These economic payoffs had political analogues. As the merchants became more dependent upon state resources, their status within the ruling coalition evolved as well. Though they would lack formal independent venues of political influence beyond the KCCI, merchant elites were never frozen out of policy making. In December 1961, Sheikh ʿAbdallah had convened the Majlis Ta'sisi, or Constituent Assembly, which was charged with writing the constitution. The assembly's composition mirrored the social changes of the late 1950s. Of the twenty elected seats, ten went to merchants and five to Arab Nationalists. Eleven unelected spots went to Sabah relatives to balance out the composition, including the next three emirs: Sabah Al-Salim, Jabir Al-Ahmad, and Sa'd Al-'Abdallah.[31] The assembly's more than thirty meetings featured heated debates between the regime and its critics. The fact that so many societal activists received such a central place at the bargaining table underscores the preference of the ruling family to keep its primary opposition as close as possible, rather than insulate itself from their interests.[32] These discussions resulted in a compromise-driven constitution that embodied some of the democratic reforms envisioned by the 1938 Majlis. It replaced the Supreme Council with a cabinet-based government that, though appointed by the emir and headed by a Sabah prince, was theoretically accountable to the fifty-seat parliament. This outcome pleased many of the older Asil merchants, for it provided at least the veneer of contestation in the manner desired by the Majlis movement. It would furnish some minimal degree of accountability, against the wishes of many Sabahs.

This would mark the last time the merchant class would carry such political influence. The new system also fell short of its democratic affectations in various ways. Parties were prohibited, which undercut electoral mobilization. Voting rights were also limited to male citizens; the inaugural January 1963 parliamentary elections featured just 16,900 registered voters. The assembly wielded limited powers of legislative review, acting primarily to authorize laws handed down by the government. The requirement that all ministers also serve as ex officio deputies also diluted any potential opposition bloc, since cabinet members were chosen by the Sabah prince serving as prime minister. It did have some check against executive power; though the emir wielded the uncontested right to suspend parliament at any time, while in session elected deputies could not only hold public debates but also question cabinet ministers through their right of interpellation, followed by a vote of confidence. More important than these semidemocratic functions, however, was parliament's role as a bellwether of the regime's coalitional trends. Due to its political visibility and proximity to royal power, legislative politicking—which deputies sided with ministers, which ones criticized official policies, which ones voted for certain laws—allowed Kuwaitis to see which groups had become ascendant and which forces were waning in relation to the regime.[33]

The first parliament that convened in 1963 featured just five merchant deputies, representation that would not vary much over the next several decades. This fit into the institution's deeper purpose of securing the loyalties of the older Bedouin tribes and Shiʿa minority. Still, major merchant and trading houses could reach policy makers through the KCCI, which held numerous contacts with princes of the Sabah family. The well-educated scions of the Asil clans also received invitations to high-ranking offices in government due to their managerial expertise.[34] Tellingly, the only three commoners in Sheikh ʿAbdallah's first cabinet in January 1962 hailed from merchant families. Until the 1980s, they would never occupy less than a third of any cabinet's ministerial portfolios.[35] This engendered a continuous, if gradually declining, channel by which they could transmit their business interests to royal ears.

Meanwhile, the regime also continued practicing dynasticism to ensure the continued unity of the ruling family, in particular its many dozens of princes with varying aspirations. The prohibition against political parties aimed to not only discourage mobilization among merchants, Arab Nationalists, and other liberal trends but also to ensure that the prime minister, as the emir's appointee, would always remain a royal—more specifically, the crown prince. At the same time, Sabah princes were discouraged from running for legislative seats, which were earmarked for other constituencies.[36] Instead, royal ambitions gained fulfillment through political appointments. The inaugural cabinet government in 1962 featured eleven royals out of fourteen serving ministers. Although future governments would display more diversity, the *wizarat al-siyada*—the "sovereignty" portfolios, which encompassed the premiership, Interior, Defense, Finance, and Foreign Affairs ministries—would almost always go to trusted Sabah relatives. Familial aspirants also staffed the senior echelons of the military and bureaucracy, as well as the emir's royal court, which provided information and advice to the ruler separately from his appointed cabinet. Such political goods, alongside hefty financial allowances and other privileges, also extended toward branches of the extended Sabah clan no longer in the succession line due to the rupture created by Mubarak. They still had a place at the familial majlis, and their support was considered valuable.

PROMOTING TRIBES AND PROTECTING SHI'A

The merchants and extended Sabah clan received economic and political patronage that not only enhanced their status but also tied it to the regime's prosperity. The tribal Bedouin and settled Shi'a community likewise received various enrichments, with the latter gaining significant protections as well. These groups resided on the margins of the preindustrial political economy, but they now garnered attention as important coalitional allies.

In practice the preoil social division between *badu* and *hadhar*, rural and urban, was often porous. Nomadic tribesmen and settled townspeople shared constant social and economic interactions.[37] The regime, however, sought to both exploit and exacerbate this dichotomy in order to reify the Bedouin tribes as a powerful independent force within society, one that would be extremely supportive of its rule. Such "desertization," shifting the tribes from the economic periphery to the political heartland, occurred in several steps.[38] First came geographic acculturation, as the government pressured nomadic and seminomadic tribes to adopt sedentary lifestyles in fixed residential neighborhoods. By the late 1960s, thousands of tribal families were fleshing out new urban areas like Jahra and Fahaheel. Many of these new housing projects were modest in accommodation and kept distant from older and more settled neighborhoods in the city.[39] Paradoxically, by removing the nomadic aspect of Bedouin tribalism—the one trait that actually did distinguish badu from hadhar in terms of social practices—these strategies helped sustain the new fiction that tribal Kuwaitis were culturally distinctive from their more settled counterparts.

This went hand-in-hand with the granting of citizenship to Bedouins, which not only enabled political integration but also distinguished these Kuwaitis from the growing population of foreign workers. The regime went about naturalizing as many Bedouin as possible, sometimes by accepting very tenuous family claims as "proof" of pre-1920 residency. Most of the 220,000 residents that gained Kuwaiti citizenship from 1965 to 1981 at the discretion of the Interior Ministry, for instance, had tribal backgrounds.[40] Then came economic protection. With traditional modes of pastoralism and migratory production fading, the tribes benefited from not only social services made universal by oil rents but also means-tested allowances that targeted their lower-income status, such as housing benefits. They also received access to new jobs in the state, although early on they gravitated to policing work and military employment—fields where widespread illiteracy would not raise problems.[41]

Desertization did not so much make the Bedouin tribes wealthy as it introduced them to middle-class patterns of sedentary consumption. Politically, they would also move closer to the authoritarian center through institutional means. Informally, both Emir Sabah Al-Salim and his successor who assumed power in 1977, Emir Jabir Al-Ahmad, made clear to numerous sheikhs through dialogues that, despite the country's dizzying pace of urbanization, the "traditional" values of desert tribal life would remain the backbone of Kuwaiti culture (as defined, of course, by the ruling family).[42] Such assurances often came through outreach efforts by royal liaisons, or private visitations via *diwaniyyah*—the weekly gathering of all men from an extended family to share news and discussion. Social policies also reflected deference to tribal conservativism. One example was the emir's continual reluctance to enfranchise Kuwaiti women despite constant pressures from merchants and their liberal colleagues; universal suffrage, in fact, would not come until 2005. Finally, Sabah affinity with Bedouin tribal constituencies endured through familial links. By the summer of 1979, Emir Jabir (then aged fifty-three) had married over 130 times, almost all with women from the noblest tribes, which signified the cultural primacy many older tribes had in the "new" Kuwait.[43]

The promotion of tribal interests also involved facilitating strong Bedouin representation in the National Assembly, with the assumption that such nominally conservative tribal figures would back royal initiatives and counter legislative criticism by opposition-minded deputies. Uniquely, this strategy did not require the creation of political parties, which remained prohibited. Rather, the Sabah leadership encouraged distinctive blocs in parliament to informally coalesce on basis of shared tribal affiliations. For the Bedouin, this represented a major elevation of status. Whereas most tribes had never held any formal representative platform before, now prevalence in parliament enshrined a newfound proximity to the royal center—one mediated not by raids and arms but law and bureaucracy. With access to state resources, they could also obtain economic benefits for their tribal communities directly, such as new development projects and preferred employment in choice ministries.

Electoral gerrymandering made this tribal ascendancy possible. Within the 1962 Constituent Assembly, one of the loudest debates centered upon the number of electoral districts for the new parliament. Merchant and Arab Nationalist voices desired a single national district with proportional representation, while most Sabah royals desired twenty separate electoral constituencies.[44] The compromise was ten districts with five seats each; but half of those districts were deliberately drawn to encompass a preponderance of Bedouin voters.[45] Every elected parliament hence had an identifiable tribal bloc. Many tribal deputies indeed fulfilled Sabah expectations in endorsing government policies while countering opposition pressures. For instance, whereas many merchants and liberals assailed the 1976–1981 parliamentary suspension as unconstitutional, tribal elites supported the move.

In return, the regime continued delivering tribal patronage through the institutional channel of elections. Before the February 1981 elections, the regime raised the number of districts from ten, with five deputies each, to twenty-five, with two deputies each. This adulterated the few areas where the merchants and old Arab Nationalists had thrived. It also sealed the predominance of certain tribes by encasing these communities in new smaller districts, which encouraged greater *intra*tribal politicking rather than competition with outside groups.[46] In many of these new districts, vote buying and other informal practices skirting electoral law thrived. Some sheikhs began regularly holding *intikhabat far'iyyah*, primary elections that were technically illegal but allowed by state authorities.[47] The Rashaydah, 'Ajman, and 'Awazim tribes often held such primaries in various neighborhoods, with the effect of predetermining the ballot well before the election.

As a result of all these institutional manipulations, the Bedouin dominated the parliament. In total, tribal deputies outstripped every other bloc in parliament, ranging from nineteen seats after the 1963 elections to twenty-seven following the 1985 contest. Out of 300 total seats in these six assemblies, tribal deputies claimed 136 (45.3 percent), compared with the merchants' twenty-three and seventy-one by Arab Nationalists and their successors, leftists and liberal independents.[48]

Parallel to the assimilation of tribal interests, the regime also cultivated the loyalties of the Shi'a minority through various protection schemes. The Shi'a benefited from the overall pace of economic growth. Many entered state employment, and a few families—including that of Saleh Al-Mulla, Sheikh Ahmad's secretary infamously dismissed by the 1938 Majlis—exploited new state contracts to create commercial conglomerates that rivaled the Sunni Asil.[49] This extended into the retail market, in particular luxury goods and consumer durables. The Ghanims, one of the wealthiest Sunni merchant houses, might have held the General Motors license, but the Shi'a Mulla family received representation rights to Chrysler vehicles, while the Buick brand under GM was given to another Shi'a family, the Behbehani. Shi'a organizations, including religious associations, also flourished within civil society. For instance, the Jama'iyyat Al-Thaqafa Al-Ijtima'iyyah, or Sociocultural Society, became a clearinghouse for Shi'a political sentiment, and operated with little state oversight.

The primary mechanism of incorporation, though, was political protection. Given its historical fears of marginalization, convincing the Shi'a minority that Sabah rule best served their interests required embedding the community into new institutional vessels of representation.[50]

The National Assembly served this purpose. Electoral architects drew two of the original ten districts to heavily overlap with Shiʿa enclaves, and parliamentary campaigning in those areas brought out powerful expressions of Shiʿa politics. Until the 1980s, every parliament featured between six to ten Shiʿa deputies, while customarily at least one cabinet post was reserved for a Shiʿi. Shiʿa business luminaries continued to serve as intermediaries with the regime. However, now parliamentary deputies and ministers enjoyed access to royal officials, increasing the density of communal contact. Electoral campaigning also provided a protected space for the expression of Shiʿa Islam in ritualistic terms, such as celebrating a shared identity that departed from the Sunni-oriented Bedouin cultural discourse fueling Kuwaiti nationalism. Like the Bedouin, Shiʿa neighborhoods abutting Sunni areas within the same electoral constituency also held informal primary elections with royal complicity so as to not split votes with competing Sunni candidates.[51]

Proportionately, these steps barely conveyed the demographic punch of the Shiʿa, who constituted more than a quarter of the populace. Neither did this strategy eliminate the everyday prejudices still held by some Sunni Kuwaitis.[52] However, they delivered an emotive pledge to many Shiʿa that resonated: while there were still reasons for some to fear bigotry from fellow citizens, the emir made clear they "should not fear *the state*."[53]

The institutionalization of an inclusionary coalition linking all these societal groups put the Sabah autocracy on sturdy footing. It would reap the advantages of these investments during the mid-1980s through early 1990s, when it faced two extraordinary shocks under Emir Jabir—economic crisis followed by the Iraqi occupation.

COALITIONAL SHUFFLING AND CREDIBLE REFORMS, 1980–1990S

The Sabah regime of Kuwait successfully demobilized popular challenges during major crises by leveraging its long-standing ties of trust and reciprocity with society. The coalitional investments made earlier paid off in several ways. Broad-based mobilization had shrunk the domestic audience for opposition activists. Even when Iraqi forces deposed the Sabah regime during the Gulf War, most social groups remained wedded to the autocracy's restoration and proposed no other ruling alternative. It also gave the emir a repertoire of nonrepressive strategies to deal with dissent, in particular effective bargaining spaces and the credibility to propose popular reforms. This prevented tensions from escalating into violence and enabled dialogues with moderate opponents.

Kuwait's defining crisis began with fiscal calamity that originated from two sources. The first was the Suq Al-Manakh stock market crash. In the 1970s, the expanding economy had benefited not only the old merchant elites but also a new generation of businessmen taking advantage of easy credit and state support to amass small fortunes. Both groups began trading in a small stock exchange. A brief hiccup in 1977 convinced the government to introduce new regulations, such as banning any trade in offshore firms. While the traditional merchant group clung to this older bourse, new investors flocked to an unregulated stock exchange, the Suq Al-Manakh. The Suq operated on the fringes of the financial world. The targets of its trading were offshore Gulf companies that often existed only on paper and whose shares were traded through forward transactions bankrolled by postdated checks with high premiums. The bubble burst when a single postdated check bounced in August 1982, precipitating a massive run. About six thousand investors found themselves with nearly thirty thousand worthless checks totaling $90 billion of debt, more than four times the GDP.[54] The collapse soon spread to the older bourse, spreading liability to existing firms. Atop this, the state absorbed the cost of intervention as it provided new loans to protect the most exposed banks, bailed out small traders through credit extensions and buyouts, and disciplined the most indebted dealers.[55]

The second source of economic difficulty came not long after the global oil bust buffeted Kuwait. The record profits of the post-1973 oil bonanza disappeared when crude prices began tumbling in the early 1980s. In 1980 the oil-exporting Gulf kingdoms recorded $248 billion in oil exports, but this figure plunged to just $42.67 billion in 1986.[56] To some degree, Kuwait was better prepared than its neighbors were, as the national oil industry had a diversified portfolio of not just upstream crude extraction but also downstream petrochemical operations. The state also possessed significant financial reserves thanks to overseas investments made by the Kuwait Investment Office and its parent agency, the Kuwait Investment Authority, in preceding decades.[57] However, even a modest diminishment in oil revenues created severe budgetary arrears, once the overhead of the Suq crash added to the existing cost of public employment, social transfers, and capital investments. Figure 4.3 shows the swift reversal of financial fortune, with expenditures outstripping revenues annually starting in 1983. Clearing the massive liabilities left by the Suq crash alone had consumed $6.6 billion by 1984.[58]

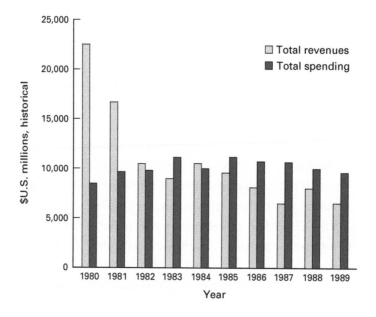

FIGURE 4.3   Kuwait's fiscal crisis, 1980–1990s

Sources: World Bank (serial); Kuwait Central Statistical Office (1990)

The drop in investor confidence accompanying unexpected fiscal emergency resulted in a wider recession, as the GDP contracted 37 percent from 1980 to 1986. Stagnant salaries and rising living costs resulted in diminishing household incomes for the first time in decades. The regime was forced to enact selective austerity measures, with budgetary planners recognizing it could no longer "spend its way out of trouble."[59] Among other cuts, hiring freezes took hold across the public sector. The government also reduced larger transfers like the land acquisition program, which diminished by nearly 70 percent during 1982–1985.[60] Some in the Finance Ministry even suggested putting fees on previously free services like health care and raising the price of subsidized goods like utilities.[61] The financial crunch also affected foreign policy, in particular Kuwait's longstanding stance of "generous" neutrality. Overall foreign aid payments dropped 91 percent from 1980 to 1988.[62] The 1980–88 Iran-Iraq War also exacerbated the crisis. Given its forward position to the conflict, the Kuwaiti regime nearly tripled its military and security spending over the decade. Emir Jabir also permitted Iraqi aircraft to fly through Kuwaiti airspace and Iraqi military supplies to transit through its port and provided over $13.3 billion in financial loans and grants.[63]

What further aggravated this economic decline was external instability. After the Iranian Revolution, the new Islamic Republic called for Shiʿa coreligionists across the Gulf to overthrow their Sunni regimes. As some Kuwaiti Shiʿa celebrated the downfall of the shah, some royal insiders wondered whether this sectarian minority would indeed revolt against its Sunni regime.[64] Many feared revolutionary copycats, so much so that in October 1979 the government took preemptive action by prohibiting all public meetings of more than twenty participants.[65] In reality, the Shiʿa community was hardly rebellious, but social change had made it less cohesive than before. Many wealthy Shiʿa merchants bemoaned the revolution, not least because they had many commercial interests in Pahlavi-era Iran. However, the 1970s had seen the ascent of newer entrepreneurs and successful businessmen from more modest backgrounds, including the new leadership of the Sociocultural Society, which had become less dependent upon Shiʿa merchant backing. Some of this new generation welcomed the rise of the Islamic Republic and supported the new activist Shiʿa ideologies brought to Kuwait by ʿulama previously expelled from Iraq and Iran.[66] Among the most prominent of these Shiʿa movements provoking religions and political tensions against Sunni regimes was the Daʿwa, which became active in Kuwait.

Within the heightened climate of sectarian tension and regional instability caused by the Iran-Iraq War, this politicization of religious identity left the door open for public violence. The country suffered a string of terrorist incidents by Daʿwa and other pro-Iranian militant networks. Through the mid-1980s, these groups orchestrated attacks on Kuwaiti diplomats abroad, multiple hijackings of Kuwaiti airliners, and numerous bombings within the kingdom itself. Three of the more noteworthy events were the December 1983 suicide bombings against the U.S. and French embassies by Islamic Jihad and Daʿwa; a failed assassination attempt against the emir in May 1985, for which Islamic Jihad took credit; and botched bombings of oil facilities in 1986 and 1987.

During these fiscal and sectarian troubles, the regime exploited the advantage of its broad-based coalitional strategy to keep an even keel. Though more outspoken about their parochial identity than before, few Kuwaiti Shiʿa cheered on these terrorist attacks or desired the toppling of the Sabah dynasty. The bombings had mostly involved expatriates rather than citizens, and Emir Jabir and his advisers did not believe the entire minority was categorically disloyal. However, they also understood the need for a strategic response in order to allay their many other Sunni allies. Their decision was to ride the sectarian wave by rotating the Shiʿa out from the ruling coalition, thereby reassuring major Sunni constituencies while keeping plans to rehabilitate this minority once the crisis had passed. Such a risky strategy of coalitional shuffling rested upon the ruler's close contacts with Shiʿa notables, in particular merchant liaisons and parliamentary deputies, who could be trusted to not mobilize loud resistance to these moves given the promise that such demotion was temporary. In the eyes of many communal representatives, the regime's assurances that the Shiʿa still held a central spot in politics were credible.

Temporary suppression by a preferred familial dynasty still appeared more desirable to suffering no protection at all under a less tolerant Sunni regime.

With that understanding, the regime went about drawing temporary lines of exclusion. Many Kuwaiti Shi'a, already targets of social discrimination, found themselves under increased harassment. After the 1983 bombings, the regime pursued prosecutions through state security trials, deported thousands of Shi'a (though mostly Iranian and Iraqi expatriates), and fired Shi'a officers in the Interior Ministry and military.[67] Further, the raising of parliamentary districts from ten to twenty-five prior to the 1981 elections had the effect of dividing mostly Shi'a areas. Partly for this reason, Shi'a representation in the National Assembly dropped from ten seats to just four after the 1985 contest.

As the Shi'a faced coalitional relegation, the regime appealed to a new social current—Sunni Islamists. Trends in Kuwait emulated the rise of Islamist movements elsewhere in the Middle East following the 1967 Arab-Israeli War and the retreat of Arab Nationalism. In Kuwait, the major two Islamist groups were the Jami'at Al-Islah Al-Ijtima'i (Society for Social Reform) and Jami'at Ihya' Al-Turath (Heritage Revival Society). Taking advantage of the electoral district changes that weakened Shi'a representation, Sunni Islamist candidates announced their arrival in national politics by winning four assembly seats in 1981 and five in 1985. Under royal patronage, their cultural influence grew. For instance, they helped stymie efforts to extend women's suffrage, an issue long backed by liberal merchants, captured board roles in civil society groups, and endorsed conservative public policies like the complete prohibition of alcohol.[68] Some also pressured the emir to extend new rules inspired by their conservative interpretation of shari'a, the canon of Islamic law, to all spheres of life, although here the ruler pushed back, knowing well that this could estrange the family's other coalitional partners as well as less conservative Sabah princes who had little wish to see Kuwait become a "replica of Saudi Arabia."[69]

If the Shi'a could be massaged into quiescence, then liberal proponents—the ideological successors to the Arab Nationalists, whose influence had faded by the 1980s—proved to be a tougher challenge. The jump to twenty-five constituencies prior to the February 1985 elections unexpectedly allowed many oppositionists to return to parliament, including longtime critics like Ahmad Al-Khatib and Jasim Al-Qatami. They joined Islamist deputies in pursuing an independent course, criticizing the government for its alleged mishandling of the Suq crash and the recent spate of terrorist violence. In May 1985, Minister of Justice Salman Al-Dua'ij resigned due to corruption accusations, marking the first time that parliamentary pressures had booted a member of the Sabah family from a cabinet position. Two other royals, Minister of Interior Nawwaf Al-Ahmad and Minister of Oil 'Ali Al-Khalifah, also found themselves threatened by parliamentarians with interpellation. Such legislative resistance in the context of the Iran-Iraq War proved too much, and in July 1986 Emir Jabir suspended the assembly altogether, justifying that its bickering threatened national unity at a time of regional war. Jabir thereafter ruled by decree, and mildly repressive statutes followed, including the continued prohibition against public meetings and new censorship laws that limited press freedoms.

After the Iran-Iraq War ended in 1988, a new opposition bloc drawing upon merchants and liberals coalesced to demand the restoration of the constitution, including the National Assembly's reinstatement. In late 1989, a forty-five-member committee representing this constitutional movement presented Emir Jabir with a petition signed by more than thirty thousand Kuwaitis to recall parliament. Public security forces cracked down on several of this constitutional movement's weekly diwaniyyah meetings and even arrested dozens of participants. However, the crisis did not tumble into further popular mobilization and violent retaliation for several reasons. First, opposition leaders in the late 1980s found it difficult to recruit a truly national audience beyond their staunch core of liberals and merchants. While Sunni Islamists lent some encouragement, most tribal communities and Shi'a constituencies did not; they still believed that the emir would backtrack in due time.[70] For them, public resistance against the regime did not hold overwhelming appeal.

Second, the constitutional movement held very limited goals. From its initial creation through diwaniyyah meetings and business networks to the more organized petitioning seen during 1989, this liberal bloc did not embrace any revolutionary discourse. Its leaders desired to restore certain constitutional elements as well as parliament but at repeated junctures made clear that they were neither against the Sabah family nor calling for any radical transformation in the state's economic institutions and social representation, including the legalization of political parties.[71] Desired instead was the *restoration* of past regime tolerance of societal pluralism not the creation of an entirely new political order. Thus, though many merchant elites today lionize the 1989 constitutional group as the logical successor of the 1938 Majlis movement, in historical perspective they demanded far less change and systemic reforms than with its predecessor.

Third, the Sabah leadership never committed to high-intensity coercion and instead sought negotiated solutions rather than zero-sum ultimatums. The insecurity created by the Iran-Iraq War and local terrorism spurred the regime to increase the size of the military and public security forces by several thousand personnel. Yet, despite that augmented capacity, Emir Jabir's first response was to bargain. He offered concessions on several issues, such as loosening some press laws and associational restrictions, and assigned Prime Minister and Crown Prince Saʿd Al-ʿAbdallah, among other royals, to hold dialogues with opposition elites to this effect. The brief detention of protesters became the bluntest physicality shown, and even that elicited discomfort within the ruling family.[72] That the regime's initial reaction was so lenient implies an embedded preference for compromise rather than coercion. It suggests that the exercise of repressive violence was constrained by the weight of expectations wrought by previous decades of state-society relations. "[Emir Jabir and his advisers] believed that if critics began getting killed, there would be real outrage because those things seldom happened before . . . most did not think they could get away with it. So the regime had to find other ways to cope."[73]

Ultimately, the emir did furnish a compromise settlement, although it fell short of opposition hopes. Instead of reinstating the parliament, Emir

Jabir instead ordained a new legislative body, Al-Majlis Al-Watani (National Council), which had far more limited consultative authority than the old parliament. Such an orchestration did not go over well with the liberal and merchant voices of the opposition, but they were not the target audience. The royal leadership instead hoped that closer groups, in particular the Bedouin, would rally behind the council on the basis of their old historical alliance. The assumption was only half right: while formal groups, including most Islamists, boycotted the council elections, many Bedouin participated in the exercise rather than side with the opposition. Still, the significance of the National Council lies not in its distance from opposition demands but rather the fact that such an arrangement made sense to the regime in the first place. Even when it could not entertain the stipulation of restoring parliament in accordance with the constitution, it chose to induce a new institutional option with the expectation that *other* supporters within its coalition would back it—thereby providing a nonviolent counterpunch to the opposition in ways that physical repression could never deliver.

RESTORING AUTOCRACY AFTER OCCUPATION

The council had operated for hardly a month when Iraq invaded in August 1990. This brought home the final and most traumatic segment of Kuwait's crisis. Already economically reeling and politically churning, the principality now suffered regime overthrow and military occupation. While many merchants and other wealthier citizens fled, as did most of the Sabah family, the Bedouin and Shiʿa communities that stayed behind rejected the "provisional" government imposed by Iraq, which garnered little support from the citizenry given its pledge to wipe away the remnants of Sabah rulership. Likewise, Emir Jabir's unity conference held with exiled Kuwaiti representatives in Jeddah, Saudi Arabia, in October 1990 promised its participants that the regime would restore parliament and the constitution upon its reinstallation to power. Among those party to this pact were merchant elites, liberal activists, Shiʿa factions, Sunni

Islamists, and a larger group of independents, with tribal luminaries notably linked to the latter two.

The unpopularity of the provisional regime and the ability of the deposed Sabah leadership to rally these forces cannot be attributed to some function of nationalistic pride. The Iraqi invasion presented Kuwaitis with a rare opportunity to impugn Sabah legitimacy and call for a fully democratic, or even revolutionary, alternative. It came after years of financial crisis, political unrest, and new opposition. As the Arab Spring showed, further, citizens in authoritarian countries invaded by foreign actors have no instinct to champion their regime out of instinctive patriotism if they genuinely desire a new political order. Rather, in Kuwait support for the restoration of a deposed autocracy stemmed from the stickiness of coalitional links laid forth during the state-building process.

As expected, during the decade following the Gulf War, the Sabah regime ceded ground to an ever-evolving coalition of popular support but was affixed as always in the logic of the old order—reciprocal understandings of allegiance in exchange for patronage and protection. In accordance with promises made during the occupation, upon his 1991 return Emir Jabir recalled parliament and removed most of the legal curbs on the press and civil society imposed during the 1980s.[74] The Sabah regime retained its authoritarian prerogatives, and the restored National Assembly did not gain any new powers over the royal executive. Still, the October 1992 parliamentary elections marked the return of the constitutional system. Those contests saw a renaissance of lively campaigning from candidates representing the entire spectrum of society. Many were first-time candidates who pushed the boundaries of normal criticism outward with daring critiques of the Sabah regime (though not Emir Jabir himself), bringing up past events like the 1986 suspension of parliament, the 1990 failure to anticipate the Iraqi invasion, and the lack of long-term reconstruction and development planning after the occupation.[75]

In addition, U.S. diplomats pressured the regime to hold those contests on time.[76] Many in the first Bush administration had encouraged Emir Jabir's plan for electoral restoration, not least because they needed to justify the costly Gulf War to an American public suffering from its own economic recession.[77] For the Sabah regime, the economic situation was far worse, though, as the state faced an outright fiscal emergency. Kuwait had bankrolled much of the U.S.-led coalition's military efforts, which drained its coffers (and in particular, its overseas investments) by over $66 billion. The low price of oil, the cost of wartime repairs, expectations to maintain prewar social provisions, and new initiatives designed to assuage public opinion, such as the blanket forgiveness of all private debts, resulted in record budgetary shortfalls by the mid-1990s.[78]

Politically, however, pluralism returned. Though the ban against parties remained firm, both old blocs and new political factions emerged with vigor, including Shi'a activists drawn into the open by the promise of toleration by the restored regime. During the 1992 elections, turnout approximated 85 percent, matching the 1985 rate despite the government having registered more than eighty-one thousand total voters, an increase of over 50 percent from the 1985 registration pool.[79] Thereafter, Emir Jabir fortified ties with the old merchant elite, a renewed alliance culminating in the ascent of Asil merchant Jasim Al-Khurafi as speaker of parliament in 1999. Younger merchant activists, however, backed new movements that desired even more political reforms, with some envisioning constitutional monarchism under the Sabahs as a long-term goal, a system where the emir's executive power would be considerably curbed by a more authoritative parliament. Organizers from the constitutional movement helped create the Democratic Forum, which became a standard bearer for many liberals. Twice in the postwar decade these liberal actors secured a third of the assembly's seats, thanks to the newfound support of many Shi'a as well as through aggressive appeals to young voters.[80] While wealthier Shi'a merchants retained close relationships with the royal family, middle-class households—those employed in the bureaucracy and public enterprises, mainly—gravitated to liberal blocs. Others still created new Shi'a associations advocating closer relations with Iran and more religious recognition.

The Bedouin demographic, too, had evolved. Some younger tribesmen did not hold their elders' hostility to progressive urban politics, while many others showed sympathy to the Sunni Islamists. By the early 2000s, the Islamists had ascended to become the largest bloc in parliament, with public polls regularly showing them as the most popular of all ideological proclivities, including the leftist and liberal currents.[81] Still other tribal deputies decried the growing disparity of wealth between Bedouin communities and nouveau riche urbanites, whose ever-expanding neighborhoods helped turn outlying parts of Kuwait City into urban sprawl that abutted, and sometimes encompassed, older tribal areas.[82] The removal of lingering media controls in 2006, meanwhile, allowed for a new surge of print outlets that complemented an already vibrant blogosphere, bringing into the public domain controversial new debates about Shiʿa identity, Sunni Islamism, and tribal sentiments.[83]

Such liberalization resulted in frequent struggles between the Sabah leadership and a more vocal parliament, the latter eager to impose more restraints upon the autocratic executive. By the mid-2000s, deputies in the National Assembly were regularly exercising their right of interpellation to question cabinet ministers about alleged corruption and wrongdoings.[84] Further, in 2005, Emir Jabir bowed to liberal pressures by promulgating women's suffrage, more than doubling the size of the electorate and satisfying a core reform demand. The brief reign of Emir Saʿd in 2006, who succeeded Jabir but struggled with physical and mental frailties, hit parliamentary resistance from the start, triggering his abdication after just ten days. His successor, Emir Sabah Al-Ahmad, gave further ground with the 2007 reduction of electoral districts from twenty-five to five— a move backed not just by a grassroots campaign of liberal youths and merchant backers but also by many Islamists and tribal Kuwaitis.[85] The former believed their rising popularity would translate into greater success in larger multiseat districts, while the latter complained that population growth in Bedouin areas had resulted in malapportionment within the old system. Thereafter, legislative relations with the House of Sabah settled into a tempestuous but predictable pattern, with the emir ritualistically dismissing parliament and calling for new elections every time political disputes on the legislative floor threatened to spill over into the public.[86] Demonstrations during the Arab Spring further brought tens of thousands of Kuwaitis onto the street for various ends, with the common refrain calling for an end to government corruption and greater transparency in royal affairs.

While louder than it had been for decades, such contestation masked the silent bulwarks keeping the Sabah regime in place. Discord in contemporary Kuwait, symbolized by the oft-rambunctious nature of parliamentary politics, has denoted not the *failure* of democratization, which was never ordained by historical trends and never inevitable, so much as the *success* of the regime's inclusionary strategy of authoritarian rule, one highlighted by far less repression and more accountability than most other dictatorships. Since the late 2000s, the most divisive issues that have resulted in parliamentary suspensions or national scandals, such as the payoffs of economic privatization, Islamization of educational curricula, and corruption investigations into state officials, have incited frustration about *how* the Sabah autocracy rules but not *that* it should still rule, both for the present and for the indefinite future.[87] The major opposition blocs that level accusations of misconduct against officials and sometimes threaten electoral boycotts—merchant-backed liberals, Sunni Islamists, and Bedouin deputies—have questioned the wisdom of state policies and criticized appointed royals, such as the prime minister. Yet, for all of the shifts and dramas, such politics have never resulted in any concerted opposition demanding a ruling alternative, much less threatened enough to merit the use of violent clampdowns by the small coercive apparatus. Though their ideas and positions have changed, major social forces stayed attached to the regime in ways that have discouraged the very acts of rebellion that not only became the regional norm during the Arab Spring but had also defined Kuwait's preoil history.

||||||||||||||||||||||||||||||||||||||||||||||||||||||||||||||||||||||||||||||||||||||||||||||||||||||||||||||||||||||||||||||||||||||||

This chapter demonstrated how the theoretical effects of geopolitical seclusion in the early twentieth century resulted in a coalitional and institutional chain of events that ultimately produced a durable nondemocratic regime in Kuwait. Coalitional strategies of inclusion crafted by the Sabah autocracy required that the state-building process institutionalize the large-scale transfer of patronage and protection to different sectors of society. Such an approach to governance also meant a foreign policy of neutrality throughout the Cold War, as this was no client regime. The timing of oil rents is crucial here: had the regime struck immense geological wealth decades earlier, when opposition nearly dethroned it, the ruling institutions created would have been far more repressive and exclusionary following the 1950s. Instead, from the 1960s onward, the Sabah dynasty strengthened its ties to Kuwaiti society, maintaining close proximity to major groups even though it now possessed the power and resources to turn away from such coalitional commitments. Such investments generated tremendous returns during the economic and military crises of the late twentieth century, when the regime could mobilize its cross-cutting alliances to defuse dissent and maintain steady power.

In essence, Sabah autocracy is *durable* because it is *constrained*: durable, because it does not face any realistic threat from domestic society seeking to unseat it, and constrained, because the very ties of patronage and protection that link it to a broad-based social foundation also foreclose reacting to pluralism in openly violent ways. Such durability seldom makes headlines, but should not be taken for granted. In the Kuwaiti case, astute coalitional choices facilitating long-term stability sprang from a practical confluence of geopolitical seclusion and domestic conflicts—not from any inherent cultural element and not from the vision of the regime's modern patriarch, Mubarak the Great.

The opposite occurred in Iran, the case study that occupies the next two chapters.

5

CLIENCY AND COERCION IN IRAN

IRAN REPRESENTS THE opposite of Kuwait, embodying the causal pattern of geopolitical substitution resulting in revolutionary collapse for the governing regime. This chapter analyzes the Iranian case beginning with the seminal state-society conflict in which the ruling Pahlavi monarchy was nearly overthrown by urban opposition. Popular mobilization starting in the late 1940s made clear the regime's domestic vulnerabilities from its small base of elite support to the regime's severe fiscal and coercive shortages. Mohammad Mossadegh, the main leader of the national opposition, seemed poised to unseat the Pahlavi kingship when the United States intervened. Many scholars are drawn to this period for Operation Ajax—the Anglo-American coup in 1953 that deposed the elected government of Mossadegh and restored the shah to power, becoming one of the most controversial events in modern Iranian history. The analysis here finds the years *following* Ajax to be equally important.

After the coup, Washington delivered vast flows of diplomatic, fiscal, and military assistance, which allowed a Pahlavi regime starved of oil revenues to ruthlessly liquidate urban dissent and so scuttle any potential bargaining. The result was coalitional narrowing. By 1960 the renewed Pahlavi autocracy exhibited not just extreme intolerance against any dissent but also the concentration of sweeping powers into the hands of the shah, which began to alienate the traditional religious, landowning, and commercial groups that identified with Pahlavi rule. At the time, the shah and his advisers believed that, with contentious social forces under control, they could create new economic and political institutions necessary not only to modernize Iranian society but also to preserve their rule indefinitely. They had every reason to be confident. Saturated with American support, this autocracy intent on remaking its national political economy had little desire to hold itself accountable to societal constraints, including even the interests of its oldest allies.

A COALITION AND A CONFLICT, 1925–1953

The Pahlavi monarchy was born during the 1921–1925 period of political disorder, when army officer Reza Khan seized power in Tehran from Soltan Ahmad, the last shah (king) of the long-ruling Qajar dynasty. Adopting the Pahlavi surname, the new Shah Reza sought to unify the fragmented country and resolve the administrative chaos that characterized Qajar rule.[1] Peripheral regions that had enjoyed some autonomy, such as Khuzestan, were occupied. Though safer from internal toppling than its Qajari predecessor, the regime lacked the means to govern large areas beyond Tehran. It could quash revolts and uprisings, as it did with many nomadic and seminomadic tribes, which had long threatened the dynastic center.[2] However, it lacked the means to do much else, such as provide social services, upgrade the rural economy, or impose rule of law.

Instead, the regime left major arenas of public life under the sway of traditional actors representing the pillars of preindustrial society. The first comprised landowning elites from the rural sector. Iran was still a heavily agrarian country well into the 1950s; out of a total population reaching 16 million, two-thirds lived in rural areas. Landowning inequality was extreme, with a privileged class of notables subordinating a large peasantry and sharecropping class through a labor-intensive feudal system. Though small-scale cultivators existed, most tenants were haunted

99

by indebtedness and poverty, which rendered them dependent upon these oft-absentee landlords.[3] Primitive technology and lack of credit compounded the problem by depressing yields, keeping the indebted further enchained to their masters. One study in 1950 estimated that out of 50 million hectares of arable land, just 4.6 million produced viable crops.[4] Landowners also enjoyed the customary right to obtain more revenues by raising rents and confiscating the properties of insolvent families. Their fiscal contributions to the government enabled them to control local officials, including the electoral boards that regulated the ballot box, which all but guaranteed their dominance in parliament.[5] The wealthiest stratum wore the informal moniker of the "Thousand Families."

Next was the bazaar. Bazaars were central marketplaces and thus hubs of social interaction in towns and cities. Among those embedded in this commercial sector were petty proprietors including shopkeepers, retailers, and workshop owners; guildsmen and artisans of various crafts; and traders and merchants, many of whom scraped local profits, although a few dipped into transnational commerce. Though not homogenous, most bazaar districts revolved around a common set of financial structures, social norms, and legal understandings, which helped diffuse similar political preferences among its constituents.[6] What often drove bazaar interests was presumed noninterference from above—or abroad. Its mobilizational potential had earlier manifested during the 1905 Constitutional Revolution. Then, anger over British trading concessions helped spearhead a contingent alliance with many ʿulama, enfeebling Qajar rule and helping create the national parliament, the Majles.[7] However, few opposed the Pahlavi kingship, partly because efforts to spread commercialized manufacturing against bazaar interests were so inconsistent and partly because Reza himself did not see the bazaar as a threat, and so seldom intervened in its affairs.

The final group was the ʿulama, the large Shiʿa clerical sector led by jurists and scholars but that also encompassed an armada of students, clerks, and cultivators reliant upon various religious assets accumulated over time.[8] Under the authority of the jurists, those assets included shrines, seminaries, mosques, institutions of vaqf (charitable and religious endowments), and religious taxation. Since Shiʿa Islam had become the state religion several centuries earlier, the ʿulama brandished many social duties, such as leading Friday prayers, administering education, and pronouncing matters of law. By the 1930s, the city of Qum, less than a hundred miles from Tehran, had come to host the most important centers of Shiʿa religious instruction, and its ayatollahs held considerable influence over the ʿulama in other towns and seminaries. They shared close ties with the bazaar, as the latter not only paid religious taxes but also tended to value piety.[9] Their imprint came through reciprocal ties with political power: the clergy's hierocratic identity had compelled past Qajar rulers to seek their explicit approval, which was given in return for their social and economic autonomy over vast swathes of public life.[10] The first Pahlavi sovereign was no different in seeking that religious legitimation. By the late 1930s, relations slightly soured as Reza Shah began questioning the clergy's educational and religious monopolies and chafed at the idea of subjecting his policies to their moral approval.[11] However, the regime lacked the means for any comprehensive resistance, and on the eve of World War II the state-clergy alliance held strong.

The predominance of these old classes showed in parliament. Theoretically, the Majles had substantial clout, as it could vote against the government. However, two-thirds of all deputies from the 1920s through 1950s came from large landowning families, including not only rural aristocrats but also ʿulama and wealthy merchants.[12] As a result, its main role was not so much to check executive power but to run parallel to it. Landowners also dominated cabinet positions. During the period from 1941 to 1953, for instance, all twelve prime ministers either came from the titled landowning class or else were army generals with blood ties to those Thousand Families. They, alongside trusted senior bureaucrats and officers, operated most ministries on behalf of the monarch. The royal court handled protocol but also cast its own aura of influence and likewise was packed with trusted advisers and dependents who lived off the throne's purse. Such a closed system was not devoid of intrigue, as grudges and vendettas made for unpredictable elite drama. However, political order as a whole did not involve any kind of mass participation.

NEW URBAN OPPOSITION

World War II spurred urban mobilization against this dictatorial structure, commencing over a decade of monarchical marginalization at the hands of efflorescent opposition. In August 1941, Allied forces invaded Iran, with the Russians occupying the north and the British moving into the oil-rich south from reoccupied Iraq. Under pressure, Reza Shah abdicated in favor of his son, Mohammad Reza.[13] The new shah inherited an increasingly fractious society whose growing urban centers were giving rise to new forms of political activism.

The most prominent of these new urban actors was the communist Tudeh Party. It drew upon workers in industries like transportation, oil, and light manufacturing, which had grown considerably during Reza Shah's reign thanks to new state investments. By 1940, non-bazaar enterprises employed 170,000 workers, but both employers and the government discouraged wage-bargaining and union organizational efforts.[14] Tudeh filled this gap and advanced new demands for political participation and economic justice through protests, strikes, writings, and even Majles sessions where a handful of vociferous deputies attacked the crown's landed allies.[15] Other new groups emerged too, from Azeri and Kurdish separatist movements to radical Islamic organizations critical of the established ʿulama of Qum and other religious centers, who were seen as too subservient to Pahlavi interests. Still, the Tudeh had the most popular appeal and beyond labor attracted numerous students and youth activists. At its apex, it claimed forty thousand active members operating over a thousand national cells, with 355,000 affiliates belonging to labor unions alone.[16] Its newspaper, *Rahbar*, boasted the biggest circulation of any print media. Tudeh also had several clandestine militant wings, including one that recruited hundreds of army officers.

The postwar period saw the end of foreign occupation, but it also saw economic recession and political clashes. The government was unable to ameliorate food shortages, heightening inflation, increasing unemployment, and diminishing commerce. Urban conditions were not much better than the impoverishment characterizing the countryside, as nearly two-thirds of city and town dwellers lived in slum conditions. However, the new shah continued governing through a small phalanx of loyalists. Almost all of the over three hundred vacancies in the twenty-four cabinets formed between August 1941 and November 1948 were filled with the same seventy or eighty propertied notables and royalist officials.[17] As Tudeh grew in size and influence, this regime reacted with repression. It attempted to stamp out party meetings, arrest outspoken activists, and in 1949 banned the party outright through martial law. By then, another urban opposition bloc had captured headlines: the National Front. If the Tudeh represented wage earners and students, then the National Front embodied the smaller but more affluent salaried professional class.[18] Led by Mohammad Mossadegh, the Front grew out of a *dowreh*, or small political circle, that had drawn affluent patricians and liberal intellectuals. Upon its broadening into a popular grouping, it attracted teachers, lawyers, civil servants, and other educated graduates, with the cities of Tehran and Esfahan becoming active bases of mobilization. Its nationalist platform sought constitutional monarchism, land reforms, social democracy, and above all the expulsion of British interests.[19]

This anti-imperialist position made the Front contingent allies with the Tudeh, creating enough opposition momentum to seriously challenge the Pahlavi regime. At the turn of the 1950s, nationalizing the British-run oil industry became the flashpoint of public controversy. The British had discovered Iranian crude deposits in 1908 and thereafter established the Anglo-Persian Oil Company (APOC) to capitalize and operate the new industry. Yet, like other states bound to royalty agreements with Western firms, Iran garnered a paltry concession as its share of oil revenues. From 1932 to 1950, Iran received just over £100 million as its royalty fee from its entire hydrocarbon sector, whereas the British government reaped twice as much by taxing the company's massive profits.[20] Though Mohammad Reza attempted to renegotiate the treaty on favorable terms, such as a fifty-fifty profit-sharing agreement that mirrored what Venezuela had just obtained in similar negotiations, the shah's meetings with British diplomats, executives from the now renamed Anglo-Iranian Oil Company, and

U.S. mediators throughout 1950 failed to reach such a conclusion.[21] For the National Front and Tudeh, exiting any sharing agreement and simply expropriating the AIOC became a point of nationalist pride. For the regime, resisting increasingly strident calls for outright nationalization and instead revising the royalty agreement on its own terms was a test of authority. For the British, it was a strategic Rubicon, as losing control over the AIOC's oil assets would hurt the West at a time of heightened fears regarding the growth of Soviet influence in the Middle East. Nationalization also would deprive London of foreign exchange, given the sizable tax revenues garnered from the AIOC every year. That loss could not be taken lightly given the general state of fiscal scarcity in postwar Britain. Even with cheap fuel imports, the British government could not afford to deration petrol until 1950.

The Qum ʿulama, the conservative backbone of the Shiʿa clergy, had earlier rejected the communist aspirations of the Tudeh, as did much of the bazaar and landowners. Most established ʿulama also did not warm to the National Front, believing the shah and the monarchy to best guarantee their religious and landed interests.[22] On the other side, though not always in harmony, the Front, Tudeh, and smaller opposition groups authored a steady campaign of demonstrations, rallies, and meetings that surged ahead in early 1951. Relentless mobilization enabled the Front to begin winning adherents from more traditional groups, including clerics like the Ayatollah Seyyed Abol-Ghasem Kashani, as well as some bazaar retailers.[23] In April 1951, following the assassination of the shah's premier, General Haj Ali Razmara, the Majles nominated Mossadegh as new prime minister, which the shah refused to recognize. After the Tudeh coordinated further disruptive strikes, including some in oil facilities, the shah capitulated and ratified Mossadegh's appointment. Now led by the leftist-nationalist opposition, the new government pushed the shah aside and nationalized AIOC, triggering a Western embargo against Iranian oil exports that, combined with British sabotage, ground the oil industry to a halt.[24] Still, by 1952 Mossadegh was more popular than ever, and in January the National Front and its allies procured a parliamentary majority. Tudeh candidates alone secured about one-fifth of the vote. As Mossadegh was anointed *Time* magazine's Man of the Year, the shah and his allies began worrying about the future of Pahlavi rule itself given the spectacular ascendancy of the National Front.

Yet monarchical resistance was futile. In July 1952, when Mossadegh attempted to assume greater control over the military, the shah exercised his royal sanction to dismiss the premier and cabinet. Soon after, the Front and its allies responded with mass protests and crippling strikes across the country, with the cities of Tehran, Esfahan, Ahvaz, Kermanshah, and Hamadan witnessing the largest uprisings. The police and army could not contain five days of bloody rioting, which claimed several hundred casualties.[25] The shah then relented, first ordering the military to stand down and then returning Mossadegh to office. As he began implanting his own bureaucrats within official agencies and cabinet ministries, the triumphant premier landed another blow by securing emergency powers from the Majles. Among the empowered government's initiatives was further sidelining the shah by cutting the royal budget and restoring lands expropriated by his father Reza Shah.[26]

By 1953, the Pahlavi monarchy's banishment to the hinterland was now in full swing. Not just anti-Western but antiroyalist views had spread throughout the urban public. In July, the Tudeh staged a huge rally that boldly called for an end to monarchy. What aggravated these tensions and partly fueled many of these protests was the worsening economic situation, manifest in stubbornly high living costs and unemployment. Nationalization had ironically crippled the oil industry and so starved the government of much-needed export revenues.[27] Still, the opposition continued capturing the levers of state power. In August, Mossadegh held a successful plebiscite to dissolve the Majles and rule by decree, with the final vote tallying 1,441,156 in favor against just 694.[28]

Whether Mohammad Mossadegh would have created a new democracy if left unattended is a worthy counterfactual question. The opposition was not without its own fault lines; for instance, many Tudeh activists and liberal allies refused to endorse the Majles dissolution, worrying that they had just replaced one dictatorship for another. More certain, however, is the historical reality that the Pahlavi crown had reached the nadir of its power by the summer of 1953, with the possibility of regime termination looming large. Personal accounts of this crisis portray the shah as isolated and fatalistic, only realizing too late the mistakes made with the AIOC negotiations and Mossadegh's meteoric rise.[29] He and various advisers even considered exiting the country on several occasions, knowing well that any temporary "leave" of absence was euphemism for exile. They remembered this was how the Qajar dynasty ignominiously ended—during a European trip that became, for its last shah, a permanent vacation.

The old regime was unable to resist the popular campaign of the National Front and its allies for several reasons. None were external, as Iran faced little threat of belligerency from neighboring states, including the Soviet Union. Rather, the shah could not match the opposition's mobilizational capacity to incite collective action on the street. Thanks to its unifying principles and organizational infrastructure, Mossadegh and other leaders could assemble public protests in order to counter political setbacks. Moreover, because it still languished under its stingy AIOC royalty agreement, the shah's regime lacked the financial resources to palliate popular anger through material largesse, for example through announcing new development programs, reform packages, or public wage and salary increases. This was problematic because the economic slowdown worsened during the oil crisis: from 1946 to 1953, not only did living costs rise consistently but the overall balance-of-payments hit record negative deficits.[30]

Likewise, the regime's coercive agencies were inadequate to control urban spaces. The civilian police had proven incapable of dispersing large-scale demonstrations, due to poor training and lack of manpower. Within the army, Mossadegh had replaced many officers with his own allies, making the shah and his aides wary of their loyalty.[31] Even before that, however, wartime occupation had atrophied much of the military force that the shah's father had built. While some units remained cohesive and willing under royal command, problems with low morale, outdated equipment, and inexperience meant that the army as a whole was unreliable. This was partly why Tudeh could recruit a clandestine network of at least six hundred officers and paramilitaries in its militant wings.[32] For good reason, the royal decision to return the army to the barracks after the July 1952 rioting sprouted from the fear that prolonged exposure to opposition sentiments would result in defections.

Finally, the British could not bail out the shah. Neither the embargo nor international legal prosecution had reversed AIOC nationalization. The British government also struggled with its own postwar social and financial shortages, resulting in its gradual surrender of other imperial obligations across the region.[33] If any foreign capital could rescue the shah from his pending doom, it would not be London alone.

A CLIENT CREATED, DEMOCRACY SMASHED

Observers of Iran in August 1953 could be forgiven for presuming the imminent downfall of the Pahlavi crown. Within weeks, however, the situation had reversed. How a triumphant Mossadegh found himself in jail and a demoralized shah found himself back in power is the stuff of diplomatic intrigue and Iranian collective memory. However, it is also just one part of the wider story. A royalist coup d'état, planned months earlier through the American and British intelligence agencies, removed Mossadegh at his zenith. This audacious project, code-named Operation Ajax by the Central Intelligence Agency, has received exhaustive treatment elsewhere.[34] More relevant here are the strategic reasons behind the act, which restored Pahlavi rule, oriented Iran toward a cliency relationship with Washington, and made the regime see American support as more important than its own popular standing.

Upon World War II's conclusion, it was difficult to forecast Iran's future importance for Washington. The United States had a small diplomatic mission in Tehran; it considered the Pahlavi regime a potential ally but doubted the shah's leadership. Indeed, many in the Truman administration blamed him for the breakdown of the 1950 AIOC talks, especially his ardent desire for a Venezuela-style fifty-fifty revenue split, which had emboldened the opposition to gather support for complete nationalization.[35] Thus, until 1953, Iran received little bilateral support. The entire

U.S.-Iranian military relationship consisted of an unarmed American advisory mission that provided occasional instruction to Iranian army officers.[36] Economic aid was almost nonexistent, with a few million annually given for humanitarian issues like public health and education.

In the early 1950s, however, two geopolitical factors conjured enough momentum for American decision makers to embrace the Pahlavi dictatorship. First, policy principals in the new Eisenhower administration evoked concern for Iran's vast oil reserves, which until the AIOC's nationalization had provided much of NATO's energy needs. Solidarity with Britain did not play into this. Indeed, many wished to break London's monopoly on Iran's oil industry and claim their own profits—a desire satisfied after Mossadegh's successful toppling, when the British begrudgingly gave a large stake to American firms. Others evinced worry about the economic and energy security of European allies. American dollars might have financed the Marshall Plan, but Saudi and Iranian oil were the fuel. After the cessation of Iranian oil production in 1951, NATO countries in Europe lost $700 million when they were forced to import oil from more expensive sources, like Kuwait.[37]

Second, American policy makers feared that Iran would slide into the Soviet Union's sphere of influence. By 1952, with the new doctrine of Soviet containment in full effect, key voices in the Eisenhower White House believed that Moscow would intervene in Iranian affairs.[38] The leftist-nationalist opposition was particularly seen with suspicion. Early on, American officials recognized that the antiroyalist Tudeh had become the only independent political organization with "any real degree of support among the people" and believed that the National Front's "revolutionary" agenda backed by its "fanatical" leaders would bring unceasing instability that could facilitate a communist takeover.[39] And if Iran fell under Soviet influence, so too would the rest of the Middle East—including the oilfields of the Persian Gulf, the crucial transit zone of the Suez Canal, and even the North African states abutting Southern Europe. This would be catastrophic to the United States, in terms of both strategic capabilities and superpower prestige around the world. As one period study observed regarding the loss of even a single pro-Western oil producer:

The whole uncommitted world would see the writing on the wall. NATO would be outflanked. Once in control of Middle Eastern oil, Moscow would have its grip on Europe's jugular vein. It could hardly be long before our European allies would be forced into accommodation on Soviet terms, leaving the United States isolated. In the words of the President, Soviet control of the Middle East "would have the most adverse, if not disastrous, effect upon our own nation's economic life and political prospects." He might have added, without exaggeration, upon our national security and our survival as a free nation.[40]

Such domino-effect thinking saturated U.S. policy making toward the Middle East for the next three decades. However, the United States overestimated Soviet intentions in Iran based upon misleading clues. By the late 1940s, Soviet propaganda was broadcasting anti-Western tropes across the region, encouraging new opposition movements like Arab Nationalism to look to Moscow for revolutionary inspiration, not least because of its recent role in preventing Nazi domination in the Middle East.[41] Outwardly, the Soviet government thus encouraged the National Front and Tudeh's advances. However, it hardly considered intervening more overtly within Iranian politics. For one, while the two countries shared a 1,200 mile border, Western military forces had entirely departed after World War II, so Moscow's southern flank was under no danger. In addition, the cost of invading and occupying such a large country was prohibitive.

Finally, the Soviet leadership did not see the popular opposition as strategic partners. Mossadegh's insistence that historical Azerbaijan lay under Iranian sovereignty rather than Soviet jurisdiction soured relations, leading Moscow to dismiss him as an agent for "big bourgeoisie."[42] Moreover, Soviet liaisons were wary of Tudeh's internal factionalism and ideological varieties. Stalin's death in March 1953 also began a period of turmoil within the Soviet political establishment, distancing it even further from Iranian affairs.[43] Still, perceptions mattered more than reality. Anglo-American fears, combined with discomfit at AIOC's nationalization, transformed initial U.S. caution toward Mossadegh into outright hostility and antagonism throughout 1952. In June 1953, when the Mossadegh-led government quietly asked for emergency economic aid given its nearly bankrupt treasury, the Eisenhower administration refused and instead suggested that Mossadegh resolve the British and AIOC dispute first—a position it knew Mossadegh would never take, as he had cut off relations with London.[44]

Iran thus became the second major commitment by Washington to protect a Middle Eastern regime from overthrow, the first being the Truman administration's support for Turkey. Operation Ajax exemplified this strategic turn, and it cut down Mossadegh at his apex. It succeeded despite several missteps and involved a lively cast of characters—CIA officers, British MI6 personnel, Western diplomats, military liaisons, the shah himself, pro-Pahlavi generals, conservative politicians, and numerous street contacts and opposition informants. The operation culminated on 19 August 1953, when Iranian partisans and army officers arrested Mossadegh and most of his cabinet, after which General Fazlollah Zahedi, one of the shah's most loyal retainers, became the new prime minister. Not long after, the shah returned to Tehran having fled a week earlier, at the height of the coup's disorder.

Operation Ajax is popularly portrayed as having singlehandedly restored Pahlavi rule.[45] However, while the coup dispatched anti-Pahlavi figureheads, it did not destroy the infrastructure of resistance. Thousands of activists and cadres from the Tudeh, National Front, and other groups were still willing and able to mobilize as they had months earlier. Moreover, the shah struggled with familiar weaknesses—budgetary shortfalls, an uneven coercive apparatus, and wavering confidence. The difference maker—indeed, the *kingmaker*—was American support. The United States enabled the Pahlavi regime to decimate its urban enemies, sanitize the political arena of all opposition, and enact restrictive martial law by furnishing diplomatic, fiscal, and coercive assistance that turned the momentous conflict between state and society into a one-sided rout.

Before exploring the content of American support, it is necessary to explore its destructive effects. After the coup, the Zahedi-led cabinet launched coercive sweeps that targeted the workers, students, activists, and intelligentsia backing the opposition.[46] Mossadegh and other National Front leaders languished in jail. Across the country, the regime ordered the military and policing units it trusted to suppress all public dissent, including shuttering the media and civic associations. They further cracked down on peripheral areas with tribal communities and ethnic minorities like the Kurds, many of whom had become increasingly vocal during the Mossadegh years.

The Tudeh, too, bore the brunt of this repressive wrath. The regime purged several thousand functionaries from various bureaucratic departments and agencies on suspected charges of Tudeh membership and eliminated over five hundred officers who had not supported the royalist coup through show trials, imprisonments, and executions.[47] Loyal military officers then combined covert infiltrations with vicious assaults to destroy Tudeh party cells. The leadership committee was identified and dismantled. Thousands of activists faced mass arrest; some were executed, while others fled the country. By 1955 the Tudeh "was almost completely crushed" as an organized group.[48] Some pockets of National Front activism continued underground, however, sustained by the intellectual and financial resources of its members. Finally, the regime pacified the Majles by rigging the 1954 elections to return a familiar crowd of landlords and magnates. This robbed the legislature of some of its hard-earned political authority acquired during Mossadegh's time in office.

By the late 1950s, these campaigns had razed the terrain of societal pluralism. Press censorship returned while many potentially political groupings, such as unions and syndicates, were dissolved or folded into state-run organizations. Ethnic minorities and tribal communities also faced new restrictions. When the dust settled, the Pahlavi dictatorship stood alone, having conquered its enemies and regained control of the state.

THE ENORMITY OF AMERICAN SUPPORT

Such reequilibration could not have occurred without copious American support, which bolstered the willingness and capacity of the regime to dominate society. The diplomatic bolstering came quickly.

Following the coup, U.S. decision makers made explicit that the shah had become an essential ally of Washington. Shortly after his return, the shah received a congratulatory message from Eisenhower, while later in December Vice-President Richard Nixon visited the country to evoke further confidence in his rule.[49] In late 1954, the shah spent two months in America, while Tehran began hosting frequent delegations of U.S. policy makers from congressional leaders to various cabinet secretaries.[50] By the late Eisenhower administration, sustaining a pro-Western (and thus anti-Soviet) Iran had become the cornerstone of U.S. grand strategy in the region. Maintaining the longevity and stability of the Pahlavi dictatorship intersected with a host of other regional goals, such as opposing the Nasserist regime of Egypt, ensuring other Western client states like Iraq and Jordan remained stable against the tide of Arab Nationalism, and not only renewing but ramping up Iranian oil production for Western consumption. In March 1959, the governments inked a mutual defense agreement, liberating the shah from worrying about the integrity of his sovereign borders with the Soviet Union and Iraq, whose monarchy had just fallen to its own nationalist revolution.

Securing Iran's external sovereignty was one thing; safeguarding its internal order was another. Iran could not draw upon its oil wealth when the shah returned to power, given the oil industry's stoppage. Indeed, after Operation Ajax, it would take several years to fully reactivate the oil sector, a process that Anglo-American interests dominated. AIOC, now renamed British Petroleum, collaborated with five American oil firms to create a new consortium that gave each side a 40 percent stake, with the remainder granted to Iran. The consortium reassumed control over all aspects of the hydrocarbon sector from production and pricing to marketing and transport.[51] However, this restoration would take several years, so in late 1953 the fiscal outlook looked dark. At this moment, U.S. economic aid saved the regime by essentially plugging in all budgetary gaps. Figure 5.1 shows how until 1957 Iran was more of an aid-dependent state than an oil-rentier one. Hydrocarbon revenues did not match U.S. foreign aid receipts until 1957, when each measured $140 million. In 1954, for instance, the government received over $110 million in U.S. assistance but only $37 million from oil.

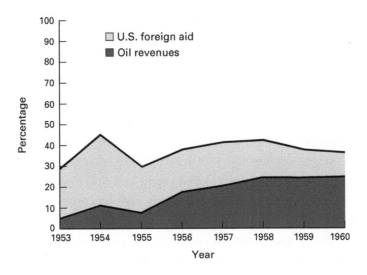

FIGURE 5.1 Aid and oil as percentage of Iranian budget, 1953–1960

Note: Iranian data for 1953–1954 normalized to account for official exchange rate change in 1955. U.S. foreign aid includes grants and loans.

Sources: Katouzian (1981); Gasiorowski (1991); USAID (serial); Central Bank of Iran (serial)

In total, Iran would receive nearly $1 billion in American foreign aid from 1953 to 1960, half for economic purposes. After assuming the premiership in August 1953, the Zahedi government received a $5 million payment from the CIA to help pay public salaries by month's end.[52] That was a huge boost, as government payrolls had been only irregularly given during Mossadegh's last year. More subsidies followed. Weeks after the coup, the Eisenhower administration transferred an urgent $43 million emergency cash grant to relieve the regime's fiscal crisis. In the four years between 1953 and 1957, Iran would harvest over $250 million in economic grants, with another $116 million in low-interest loans given through the Export-Import Bank and other agencies. Such funds, euphemistically called "special assistance" by the State Department, essentially allowed the otherwise-bankrupt regime to have a viable budget until the oil industry returned online. Martial law was not cheap, and U.S. officials recognized this. In 1954, $27 million in cash transfers was directly earmarked for the Finance Ministry so that it could either maintain or raise the salaries of civil servants, oil workers, and police and military personnel.[53] Another use of funds entailed the creation of numerous temporary public works programs whose products included low-cost housing and new roads. By the late 1950s, a hundred thousand new laborers had contributed two million days of work through such initiatives.[54] Though most of these projects would not extend into the 1960s, the goal was more immediate in absorbing unemployed young men into a paid labor force, thereby keeping them off the streets at least for a few years.

A lesser known but equally important use of American tax dollars was to defray living costs. From 1953 onward, U.S. grants and loans helped finance large-scale imports of consumer goods that had become scarce during the recession, such as sugar, automobile parts, and hospital drugs.[55] Such currency inflows also allowed the Central Bank to stabilize the Iranian rial's exchange rate and halt rampant inflation. Food prices also benefited from U.S. agricultural aid programs, which through 1959 had donated over 116,000 tons of surplus wheat, rice, beans, and other foods. They did not ship straight to Iranian families: instead, government officials would allocate and sell them to domestic mills at cost, thereby turning donated food into state revenues. At the household level, food costs indeed rose more slowly than other cost-of-living factors, such as rent, for the remainder of the decade.[56]

By 1957, Iran had become one of the largest U.S. foreign aid recipients outside NATO. However, when its oil wealth began to eclipse American contributions, Washington changed strategies. Fungible cash grants for general budgetary use were no longer urgent. Instead, using the rhetoric of development and growth, the United States transferred project-based technical assistance in fields like agriculture, education, forestry, public health, and mining. American technocrats entered the country in volume, with over nine hundred civilian advisers residing in Iran by 1960.[57] Some sought the tiny private sector, restructuring the banking and regulatory environments to invite Western investment. Many others worked in various administrative positions, with the Agriculture, Finance, and Interior

Ministries attracting the most attention. Such involvement went far beyond administrative reform and managerial suggestions; for much of the decade, American advisers helped formulate internal budgets, forecast expenditures, and account for all fiscal grants.[58] They also helped inaugurate the $1.1 billion Seven-Year Development Plan in 1955, which intended to expand social services, upgrade infrastructure, and capitalize new industries in a bid to help stabilize the economy and reduce social discontent. Though it became bogged down under corruption and wastage, the plan provided the state with new experience in central planning and economic transformation.[59]

Officially, the Eisenhower administration sought to enhance the development and prosperity of Iranian society. One report from the US Agency for International Development (USAID) saw the Iranian people as locked in a "life-and-death struggle," for they were "pre-occupied with providing for the necessities of life—food, clothing, and shelter" but without "experience in the science and the art of government."[60] The reality was that technical assistance was designed to enhance authoritarian stability by keeping the economy afloat and relieving the burden for greater social spending. As a result, many of these grants and loans were "administered in a loose, slipshod, and unbusinesslike manner," with earmarked monies often disappearing due to outright incompetence or corruption on the Iranian side.[61]

Washington also worked to reorganize and boost the Pahlavi monarchy's weak coercive apparatus, ensuring that it could retake political control and defeat opposition forces. During the seven years from 1953 to 1960, the United States transferred nearly $450 million in security assistance. The objective was twofold: create a military to ward off potential Soviet intrusions and improve internal policing and intelligence capabilities to prevent future uprisings.[62] For the regime, however, both objectives bled into a blunter quest—to permanently monitor, and if necessary destroy, any popular threat from Iranian society that could endanger its rule. Notably, whereas American military financing to other countries up to that point usually consisted of loans, Iran received mostly credits and grants. This allowed the regime to rapidly beef up its repressive agencies,

TABLE 5.1

SUPPORTING IRANIAN COERCION, 1953–1960 (IN $U.S. MILLIONS, HISTORICAL)

	U.S. MILITARY AID*	IRANIAN MILITARY SPENDING**	MILITARY AS PERCENTAGE OF TOTAL PUBLIC SPENDING	MILITARY MANPOWER
1953	20.6	33	20.7	
1954	25.6	52.8	28.8	
1955	15.5	66	22.5	135,000
1956	23	81.8	26.5	
1957	82.5	110.9	27.3	
1958	104.9	149.2	28.5	143,000
1959	84.6	184.8	29.2	
1960	85.3	187.5	27.1	205,000

Iranian data for 1953–1954 normalized to account for official exchange rate change in 1955.
*Includes grants and loans.
**Includes expenditures on armed forces as well as internal security but not the Organization of Intelligence and National Security, known under the Iranian acronym SAVAK.

Sources: Hurewitz (1982); Gasiorowski (1991); USAID (serial); Central Bank of Iran (serial)

since it could spend far beyond its means to purchase technology, skills, and weaponry from its preferred supplier, America.[63]

Table 5.1 reveals a predictable trend of securitization in step with American involvement. Between 1953 and 1957, Iran more than tripled military and police spending from $33 million to $111 million; from there to 1960, and a decade beyond, the military and police would consume between one quarter and one third of an ever-rising national budget.

More telling is the qualitative evidence. One U.S. military delegation, the Military Assistance Advisory Group, or MAAG, helped modernize and professionalize the Iranian armed forces. MAAG supervised the shah's purchase of armored vehicles, combat jets, and other lethal weaponry. It also encouraged the expansion of manpower, as the United States wished the Pahlavi ruler to have a large standing army. Thus from 1953 to 1960 the armed forces nearly doubled in size to 205,000, with the army being the largest component. Though conscription (instituted by Reza Shah in 1926) still existed, this jump came from new efforts to recruit and retain career personnel.

MAAG also oversaw the transfer of skills and expertise in repression. This required extensive contact with American muscle, which came in kind: during this period at least ten thousand U.S. military personnel passed through Iran, training their counterparts on weaponry, mobility, communications, and operations.[64] MAAG's senior officers provided direct advice to the shah. Likewise, Iranian officers began traveling to study at American service institutions, with some two thousand having done so by the mid-1960s.[65] The only major concession that the United States did not demand was permanent basing facilities in the country.

Despite its size, the army could not govern Iranian society directly. In 1957, with the economy somewhat recovered and the opposition defeated, martial law ended. By then, the regime had a powerful new tool of repression. The U.S. intelligence community helped found Sazman-i Amniyat Va Ittila'at-i Kishvar—SAVAK, the Organization for Information and State Security. What began in September 1953 as an army intelligence unit organized by a CIA officer and trained to disembowel the Tudeh movement through infiltration became, in 1957, the state's domestic intelligence agency.[66] The CIA trained thousands of SAVAK officers through the 1960s and provided strategies of surveillance, interrogation, and propaganda strategies that its Iranian counterpart would later unleash against the citizenry.

By the early 1960s, SAVAK would establish its presence in most areas of Iranian society—the bureaucracy, university classrooms, unions and syndicates, private workplaces, and various civil associations; among its duties was to monitor society, vet government employees, and eliminate perceived threats. The CIA maintained a large mission in Tehran, as well as listening stations throughout the country attuned to Soviet military operations and missile movements.[67] Hundreds of American officers also came for the less glamorous mission of improving the national police and rural gendarmerie. American trainers sought to upgrade civilian policing with better equipment and skills so that, once martial law ended, they could instill enough of a sense of legal order that would deter not only normal crimes but also subversive activities within civil society, especially any sign of leftist or nationalist politics.[68]

Enveloped with diplomatic, fiscal, and coercive assistance, Iran began its cliency relationship with the United States. By 1960, with Pahlavi authoritarian rule reestablished, "the U.S. embassy in Tehran was as important a power centre as the Shah's palace."[69] The regime fulfilled its part of the deal by ramping up its pro-Western foreign policy, which Washington saw as a major moral victory. Just months after Operation Ajax, the shah restored diplomatic relations with Britain. In 1955, Iran helped organize the Baghdad Pact, a collective defense treaty linking the UK with monarchist Iraq, Pakistan, Turkey, and Iran. The resulting multilateral entity, the Central Treaty Organization (CENTO) was modeled after NATO, though it was seldom convened. The shah also emitted a more consistent anti-Soviet discourse within Iranian diplomacy. He recognized the need to hold at least affable ties with the bordering Soviet Union, but he refused to entertain any sustained alliance. He and other officials understood well that "the British were no longer a match for the Soviets" in this era of imperial retreat and that only the Americans could hypothetically protect Iran during war.[70] As one example, the shah rebuffed Soviet efforts to sign a nonaggression treaty in January 1959 in a curious way. He invited a Russian delegation that included the deputy foreign minister to Tehran for discussion—only to ignore them until their departure.[71] Such personal attachment to U.S. protection grew tighter after the July 1958 revolution in neighboring Iraq exposed the wave of Arab Nationalism spreading across the region. He knew the toppled Hashemite kingship well: the deposed ruler, King Faisal II, had once asked for the hand of his daughter, Shahnaz, in marriage.

AN IRON FIST AND A PEACOCK THRONE

At the domestic level, the shah saw U.S. backing as the best guarantor of authoritarian survival. This depressed any incentives to approach social opposition through bargained compromises and inclusion-ary gestures. After Operation Ajax, had the United States left the emas-culated regime to its own devices, the shah would not have been able to extirpate the Tudeh and National Front despite Mossadegh's fall.[72] While unrealistic to imagine a Pahlavi-opposition alliance, the regime could have been forced to consider negotiated, and thus nonviolent, options to broaden its coalition and gain more popular support. For instance, since trade unions were the heartland of Tudeh activism, it could have adopted the issue of labor rights, allowing for greater unionization and wage-bargaining among urban workers. The shah could have also championed greater equality and more aggressively allotted the monarchy's Crown Lands to impoverished villages—a process with which he had dabbled in 1950 but then had halted under Mossadegh.

Regarding foreign policy, the shah could have dismissed the coup-installed Zahedi government as a Western stooge and then called for a fairer oil treaty with British and American firms, burnishing the fictive image of a nationalist king putting popular interests first. The regime could have also maintained an anti-British position rather than so eagerly restoring relations with London after the conflict, a move that angered much of the urban public. Likewise, the shah could have presided over more inclusive cabinets by appointing oppositionists to bureaucratic and administrative positions, key opportunities for elite co-optation. How-ever, as Richard Cottam noted, while "such an act would have had real promise of producing stability and legitimacy," it would have required an illusion of tolerating pluralism "and it was quickly apparent the Shah had no interest in doing that."[73]

None of these possibilities materialized because the shah and his ad-visers felt no pressure to sacrifice anything while under the auspices of American protection. The substitutive effects of such geopolitical inter-vention left three legacies, all of which encouraged coalitional narrow-ing. First, the regime became accustomed to utilizing coercion as the preferred means of political regulation. This created habitual distance between the leadership and any group, class, or organization with con-travening interests: rather than speak to dissenters to assess the depth of any grievances, the autocracy instead would eliminate the loudest voices and cow the rest into obedience. The army, police, and SAVAK developed institutional identities not as vehicles of patronage or protection for any single group within society but rather as fiercely loyal organizations that buffered the Pahlavi ruler *from* society. Their fiscal needs overrode the concerns of all other ministers and technocrats, constituting a major reason why the 1955 Seven-Year Development Plan failed.[74]

Second, the leadership became subsequently personalistic. By 1960, the shah had made decision making increasingly reliant upon his will and only delegated authority to a small inner sanctum—acolytes like Manuchihr Ighbal, Asadollah Alam, and Jafar Sharif-Emami, who comprised what one observer called a personal "state within a state."[75] As a result, government officials began suffering very erratic careers throughout the 1950s, with the shah realizing that he needed to frequently shuffle his deck of elites to prevent any individual from advancing too quickly. Such abrupt discharges ended the premierships of Fazlollah Zahedi in April 1955 and Hossein Ala' in April 1957, despite their fidelity. This capriciousness even extended toward SAVAK, whose head Teimur Bakhtiar was dismissed in 1961 and later assassinated. Such unpredictability continued for the next two decades. It indicated not so much the paranoia of an insecure despot so much as the concomitant refusal to concede any degree of power to those he did not personally trust.

Finally, the relatively costless consolidation of authoritarian rule in the post-1953 years weakened the regime's ties to traditional social bases— the 'ulama, bazaar, and landlords. Until the mid-1950s, it seemed these alliances would last, as each group had a vested interest in Pahlavi rule. For instance, most 'ulama welcomed the Tudeh's destruction, as they saw secular communism as anathema. The regime found partners in conservative figures like the Grand Ayatollah Seyyed Hossein Borujerdi and Ayatollah Muhammad Mosavi Behbehani, and collaborated with the clerical establishment in the persecution of the Baha'i religious minority. The bazaar was likewise treated well, even though some proprietors had backed the opposition. The regime only imprisoned two merchants for their support of Mossadegh, avoided price controls, kept the army out of marketplaces, and allowed trade guilds to continue electing their elders.[76] Finally, rural landlords also continued orbiting the royal nucleus. Most of the Thousand Families found Mossadegh's socialist rhetoric appalling and welcomed his fall. In return, electoral rigging enabled them to recapture two-thirds of the 1954 and 1956 Majles elections.[77]

However, in the late 1950s, signs of coalitional narrowing emerged, as the regime began putting forth policies that clashed with these constituencies. The shah felt less constrained to heed them: after all, it was not they but a combination of internal suppression and external support that had saved his throne. For instance, as part of the Seven-Year Development Plan, the regime flouted an agrarian reform law in 1959 as necessary modernization, only to elicit angry—and successful—resistance from landowners and Shiʿa clerics fearing the consequences of land redistribution.[78] The regime repelled clerical resistance to expanding women's rights, an idea championed by a new generation of technocratic advisers. In addition, planned urbanization schemes made public boasted of future factories and business parks but made little mention of the bazaar and its traditional workshops and districts.

This creeping detachment also manifested in the political sphere. After martial law ended in 1957, the regime masked its oppression by declaring a new period of electoral contestation. It created two parties—Melliyun (National) and Mardom (People)—each headed by a trusted political subordinate—that would supposedly encapsulate all societal interests and allow for mass participation. The Melliyun was designed as the loyalist party, whereas Mardom was to be the opposition. They were even designed from the top down as identical organizations, with a biennial congress, provincial and national committees, and party newspapers.[79] However, foreshadowing future party-building efforts, the shah was satisfied more with the façade of party-based politics than its actual operation. The Melliyun and Mardom were weak vehicles driven by individualistic interests rather than by grassroots activism. They lacked a dedicated membership cadre who, in sharing an ideological platform, could recruit new members by engaging new local audiences across the country.

As a result, their hand-picked deputies—vetted by SAVAK and often the shah himself—shared such overlapping interests that they became known as the "yes" and the "yes, sir" parties.[80] Representatives of the "opposition" Mardom, for instance, seldom spent time on the legislative floor discussing government policies: "it is, in fact, hard to discern any party influence in the functioning of the majlis."[81] Equally important, these two parties irked many rural magnates, whose success came from dominating their districts as independents. When independent candidates could run, as in the 1960 Majles contest in which some former National Front activists participated, the regime rigged the elections anyway.

This trend of reorganizing politics and the economy in accordance to the shah's increasingly disconnected views would bloom in the 1960s. Starting then, the bazaar, ʿulama, and landowning elite would come under attack by various new reforms launched in the name of transforming Iran into an industrial powerhouse. What would remain was the slenderest of bases for authoritarian power—the royal coterie, the coercive apparatus, and American support.

||||||||||||||||||||||||||||||||||||||||||||||||||||||||||||||||||||||||||||||||||||||||||||||||||||||||

In Iran, geopolitical substitution occurred after the United States rescued Pahlavi autocracy in 1953. The social conflict wracking urban politics at the time was no passing skirmish; it represented the division between the old guard and a new middle-sector demanding economic justice and democratic reforms. Only a U.S. government unwilling to accept regime change in a pro-Western oil producer bordering the Soviet Union saved the day. As its capacity to impose political control expanded under Washington's tutelage, the Pahlavi leadership believed that a combination of unrelenting repression and unending U.S. support could deliver future stability. Indeed, with the threat of popular deposal becoming more distant by the late 1950s, the shah had little reason to listen to the restive public. This growing gap between state and society would have enormous consequences on the economic and political institutions soon created to modernize the country.

Without the American intervention, the Pahlavi regime could have persisted but only in a weakened form. Indeed, without Operation Ajax, the shah might have never returned to Iran. Even after his return, he would not have been able to destroy opposition movements like Tudeh and the National Front so thoroughly or reoccupy urban areas that had seen constant protests so violently, given the autocracy's lack of resources and skills. The shah could have retained a diminished leadership but only through bargains with opposition, including allowing the elected Majles to continue exercising considerable powers of governance as it did under Mossadegh. The regime would have also felt far more pressure to widen its coalition of support, such as by reaching into newly mobilized groups like labor and students in order to both placate existing hostilities while preventing any more uprisings. In historical reality, Washington *did* step in to fill the breach. In doing so, it helped plant the seeds for the monarchy's future demise.

6

EXCLUSIONARY POLITICS AND
THE REVOLUTIONARY END

I N MOST NARRATIVES of Iranian history, the last shah is often described as a tragic figure—a despot so riddled with megalomania and obsessed with Western modernity that a mass revolution was fait accompli. The evidence shown in the previous chapter revealed an interesting twist in this popular characterization: the Pahlavi regime did not become extremely personalistic and exclusionary until after outlasting the domestic conflict of the early 1950s. The ease by which the shah could not only endure those troubles but also destroy opposition with American backing helped spawn the coalitional tendency toward narrowing that, as historians know well, detached the Pahlavi leadership from societal interests and paved the way for the revolutionary end. Only recently have newer biographies of the shah acknowledged that only after being restored to power did he and other officials begin justifying repressive absolutism as the "natural order" of things.[1]

The institutions created after such coalitional narrowing manifest in the White Revolution, an ambitious plan to modernize Iran. Such policies did great economic and political damage to traditional sectors of support that still stood with the Pahlavi regime, such as landowners and ʿulama. Worse, they failed to mobilize the beneficiaries of economic development, such as newly landed farmers, to replace those lost sources of traditional loyalty. Provisions of patronage and protection on a collective scale were nonexistent, as the regime relied upon few classes or groups within society beyond a small stratum of dependent elites. It also lacked constructive methods of dealing with social resistance apart from violence. This spelled trouble in 1978, when small antiregime demonstrations began in the context of a mild recession. These protests were neither revolutionary nor armed, but the state lacked the institutional ability to neutralize such dissent through peaceful means. Not only could opposition leaders, from ideologues and students to bazaar merchants and the ʿulama, recruit from an enormous audience of discontent citizens, but the regime also could not negotiate with these opponents for peace, for it lacked the credibility necessary to offer assuaging reforms. Revolutionary crowds paralyzed the country despite the monarchy deploying repressive violence. In the end, not even American support could prevent the shah from fleeing the country for the last time.

THE WHITE REVOLUTION OF 1963

By 1960, another economic downturn had hit Iran. Serious balance-of-payments deficits arose, as rising import costs and other expenditures outpaced oil revenues. Austerity measures checked inflation but depressed employment and wage levels, giving rise to new protests. Unexpectedly loud demonstrations broke out in response to the orchestrated 1960 Majles elections, which landed elites dominated.[2] In May 1961, thousands of teachers launched a strike to demand higher salaries, to which the police responded sternly. A subsequent rally over the economic situation attracted seventy thousand people, including many old National Front activists.[3] In January 1962, student riots at Tehran University elicited army intervention.

The specter of urban unrest returning compelled the shah to consider unprecedented economic and political reforms. The clearest signal was promoting ʿAli Amini to the premiership after the May 1961 teachers' strike. Unlike others in the shah's covey, Amini had ascended the ministerial ranks as a more independent operator. His appointment coincided with the recognition that the state, after a decade of recovery, could now engineer policies on a national scale without relying upon societal intermediaries. Its swelling bureaucracy had become one of the leading sources of employment for educated Iranians. By the late 1950s, over two hundred thousand worked for the public sector, with the majority having been hired in the previous decade.[4] However, Amini barely lasted a year. His anticorruption investigations came close to touching the shah himself, while efforts to trim military spending, which in 1961 consumed more than a quarter of the budget, met terminal resistance. Still, Amini's stewardship paved the way for new policies, in particular land reform, which would become the basis of the modernization program dubbed the "White Revolution." In January 1963, the shah announced this eponymous national program, ratifying it in a hasty referendum that returned nearly six million votes in favor and just 4,115 negating.[5] The White Revolution encompassed a comprehensive package of land reforms, industrialization, and enfranchisement, supplemented by new social and educational provisions.

From the start, the White Revolution was created not in collaboration but in *opposition* to Iranian society, in particular the regime's old coalitional trifecta—the landlords, bazaar, and clergy. For the shah and his mandarins, the regime was on a manichean mission to enlighten a backward nation, and any who opposed it were antediluvian reactionaries. This was an ambitious leap toward a "Great Civilization," one that would make Iran not only a progressive example for the rest of the Middle East but also the industrial envy of the West.[6] Such a campaign was influenced by the shah's American exposure. During his many visits to the United States, he had marveled at the mechanized plants, bourgeois consumption, and sprawling cities that seemed like desiderata of modernization. That prosperity came before democracy was never questioned. Despite the waning number of absolutist monarchies left in the world, the shah argued Iran was a cultural exception whose people would always accord him "both the right and the obligation" to rule.[7] The long tenure of Prime

Minister Amir ʿAbbas Hoveyda, whose premiership spanned 1965–77, provided the continuity to implement these ideals.

Propelling such exclusionary state-building were the intertwined impetuses of oil wealth and U.S. support. During the period from 1961 to 1972, Iran weaned itself off American economic assistance. Figure 6.1 depicts this transition, with U.S. foreign aid dropping from $147 million in 1961 to virtually zero by 1972, whereas oil revenues increased from $283 million to nearly $1.6 billion. By the early 1970s, income from gas and petrochemical production plus older royalties from the controlling Anglo-American consortium constituted over half of national revenues.[8] Other kinds of aid were scaled down as well. With fiscal grants gone, economic assistance

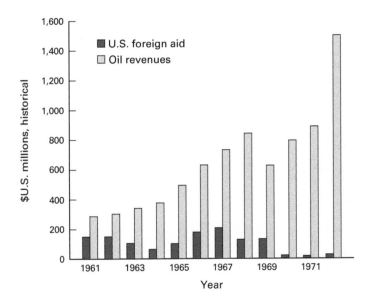

FIGURE 6.1   U.S. foreign aid and oil revenues in Iran, 1961–1972

Note: U.S. foreign aid includes economic and military components. Most economic assistance ended in 1967.

Sources: Bharier (1971); USAID (serial); Central Bank of Iran (serial)

through technical support and targeted loans stopped altogether in 1967. Military support continued through training and advisory functions, but by the mid-1960s the shah was expected to purchase arms outright.[9] At the same time, the availability of oil rents reduced incentives to improve domestic revenues through tax collection. A 1967 survey found that 25 percent of all tax income returns were missing due to evasion and noncompliance, a trend that worsened over the next decade.[10]

Critically, the vast majority of Iran's rentier wealth accumulated a decade *after* the White Revolution began reconfiguring society. Hydrocarbon wealth amplified coalitional narrowing into institutional form but did not create it. The 1973 oil embargo by the Organization of Petroleum Exporting Countries (OPEC), which Iran helped establish in 1960, brought hydrocarbon windfalls to a new high. Figure 6.2 plots out the resulting wave of new expenditures. Gross fixed capital formation, a use-

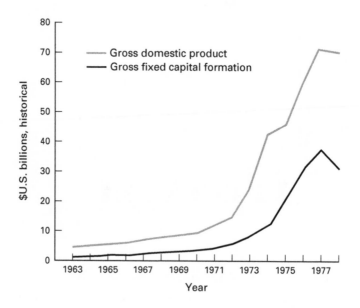

FIGURE 6.2   Iranian state investment and economic growth, 1963–1978

Sources: Bharier (1971); World Bank (serial); Central Bank of Iran (serial).

ful indicator for state investment into the domestic economy, slowly rose from $1 billion to $3 billion annually throughout the 1960s before reaching $8 billion in 1973 and peaking at $37 billion in 1977. The GDP registered a similar breakneck pace, jumping from $4.7 billion in 1963 to over $70 billion in 1977. However, such mammoth spending resulted in excess liquidity and hyperinflation. Inflation averaged over 12 percent from 1973 to 1976 and crested at 27 percent in 1977.[11]

The other catalyst for Iranian state-building was the United States, as Iran remained a client even as it gained fiscal independence. The 1958 destruction of the Iraqi monarchy had shocked American diplomats and exposed Britain's retreating imperial shadow. The loss of that British client regime helped patch up what Anglo-American tensions remained from the 1956 Suez Crisis and hastened discussions on how to contain the dual threats of Soviet communism and Arab Nationalism.[12] Those perceived threats underlay the Kennedy White House's insistence for the shah to implement land reforms, even to the point of recommending the appointment of Amini.[13] Modernization theory was at work, as some U.S. analysts were convinced that *rural* uprisings represented the greatest menace to Iran's stability—a strange conclusion given that leftist and nationalist movements drew upon the urban middle sector.[14] However, such pressures upon the shah for reform emphasized economic change, not democratization. Iran's geopolitical value as a barrier against Soviet advancement and pro-Western energy supplier required an authoritarian client regime at its helm. Thus the United States remonstrated little when the government stamped out public protests throughout the early 1960s, reinstated martial law, and rigged the 1963 Majles elections.[15]

The Johnson administration more steadily backed Pahlavi rule, and in return the shah was among the staunchest non-Western leaders in backing the Vietnam War. The regime continued to give concessions to the United States on its home soil. A seminal example was the Status-of-Forces Agreement (SOFA) signed in October 1964, which granted U.S. military personnel in Iran immunity for all crimes.[16] It was the most generous SOFA inked with any U.S. ally and incendiary for Iranians who remembered past Western occupations. Another concession was allowing the

CIA to operate intelligence stations monitoring Soviet missile activities, as well as granting overflight and landing rights for its spy planes. The regime was also careful to maintain controlled but consistent ties with Moscow, characterized by occasional arms purchases and energy deals. It exchanged crude oil with Soviet bloc states in Europe, such as Czechoslovakia, in return for assistance in creating industrial plants.[17] Still, no other single country save the United States preoccupied the Iranian ruling elite. The prevailing belief was that much like in 1953, America would rescue the monarchy if another crisis exploded—such was Iran's importance. Between the U.S. Embassy, MAAG officers, visiting delegates, private contacts, and policy principals in Washington, the shah and his advisers constantly interacted with agents of American power.

LAND REFORM: DISSOLVING RURAL ARISTOCRACY

Large-scale land reforms under the White Revolution began with laudable intentions. By the late 1950s, Iran was over two-thirds rural and counted some fifty thousand permanent villages. Of these, nearly ten thousand belonged to just 2,250 absentee notables, 6,885 were held by the ʿulama as part of their *vaqf* endowments, and 2,167 had belonged to the Pahlavi monarchy itself as Crown Lands.[18] Premier ʿAli Amini and his Minister of Agriculture, Hasan Arsanjani, advocated the redistribution of these lands to downtrodden tenants. Neither the communists nor the National Front had garnered much support outside cities, and empowered peasants could appreciate the shah for emancipating them from feudal obligations. In January 1963, Arsanjani convened a peasant congress in Tehran to discuss these plans, drawing over 4,200 rural delegates.[19]

Reforms began with a curt mandate: no landlord could own more than one village. Through rentals and exchanges, the state reallocated thousands of deeds and properties to landless tenants. Smaller landowners owning less than a village were targeted later on. By March 1963, the state had redistributed two thousand villages in part or whole to the rural underclass, creating over 120,000 new peasant landowners.[20] After a decade, the government trumpeted the program as complete. In total, 787,000 new farming households had been created due to the receipt of new estates.[21] In addition to land grants, the government created agricultural cooperatives to provide financial credit and logistical support to small cultivators and families. Other productive investments included mechanization, irrigation, and additional capital inputs.[22] Finally, it conceived new programs to enhance education, improve health care, and manage water resources in peripheral regions. The Literacy Corps was one such initiative, bringing educational access to villages that had seldom, if ever, received services from the government.[23]

However, while these schemes indeed reconfigured property relations, they also began dismantling the regime's constituency of large landowners. Many rural notables were shocked at the indiscriminate nature of the program, but the shah brooked no resistance. Martial law under Amini's premiership allowed land reform proposals to come into effect, since the landlord-dominated Majles had been suspended. The shah vilified complaints from provincial magnates, calling many absentee landlords "black reactionaries" to his White Revolution.[24] Further hardline tactics included the removal of local bailiffs in some areas to encourage peasant mutinies, while ignoring landowner complaints of lawlessness. That was worthy of note since the United States had helped create the rural gendarmerie, which numbered thirty-five thousand in 1966 and was supposed to keep order in the countryside.[25] This heavy-handed approach differed from the way the monarchy released its own Crown Lands. It gave some villages to friends and supporters, while the rest was sold at market rates to cultivators, entrepreneurs, and investors, resulting in massive profits.[26]

Most large landlords were not reduced to penury, although they did suffer significant losses. For instance, the government purchased many estates at a price between 100 to 180 times their annual tax contributions; however, so many landowners had grown accustomed to underpaying their taxes with state complicity that this meant substantial loss of wealth.[27] Still, many were able to leverage their social capital to partner with new industrialization ventures, giving their land not to tenants but public enterprises and thus enriching themselves further as agents of the state. Many re-created their aristocratic lifestyles in cities, sinking much of their savings into property speculation and other fields of profit. Through various connections, many elites still held onto some rural properties well into the 1970s. The overall effect was the *political* destruction of this dominant stratum. The loss of feudal tenure laws meant the extermination of collective status. Another indicator was that their representation in the Majles dropped to less than a quarter by the late 1960s and continued diminishing afterward.[28] What further sped this demotion was the regime's increasing reliance upon official parties to convey the spirit of popular participation in parliament, whereas in the past most landlords had run as independents.

Land reallocation, however, did not replace the old class of barons with a new political surrogate. The formulation of rural initiatives had been technocratic, with one of the few opportunities of popular input being the one-sided referendum for the White Revolution. As a result, while the regime imagined it had created a generation of patriotic yeomen with unfettered mobility, in reality it failed to mobilize new cultivators into any unified organization that could provide information and support to the monarchy. The incoherent results of rural reforms speak to this. First, land programs reinforced old patterns of insecurity.[29] Redistribution reproduced inequality at the local level by awarding differently sized plots to tenants based upon preexisting cultivation rights. Thus sharecropper families, nearly one-third of the rural populace, stayed landless. "It makes no difference to the peasant whether his landlord owns one village or 600 villages; he will still have to pay rent and be at the landlord's mercy."[30] Another third received parcels less than two hectares, far less than the eight to ten needed for household subsistence. Moreover, of the 1.3 million landowners expropriated, the majority were petty landlords rather than titled notables; for them, the loss of even small estates was impoverishing.[31]

Second, the regime showed little commitment to its initial dream of cultivating a nation of patriotic yeoman. The credit-based agricultural cooperatives languished out of neglect; they shrank from 8,400 to 2,800 by the late 1960s due to inadequate managerial expertise and technical resources. Instead, planning agencies began commercialization in hopes of maximizing the agrarian sector's export potential.[32] The state collaborated with private partners to establish eight quasi-public agribusinesses, ninety-three farming corporations, and thirty-nine new production co-operatives. They garnered epic infusions of government subsidies, long-term credit, and low-interest loans; per hectare, they received fourteen times the financial assistance than what agricultural cooperatives gave to farmers.[33] Most of all, collectivized agriculture required the reallocation of plots already earmarked to peasants and sacrificed food production in favor of cash crops. That, plus rising consumption, turned Iran into a net food importer in 1974. Further, by reducing demand for tenant labor, industrial farming spurred the migration of over two million rural poor to cities, where they often faced greater hardships in shantytowns.[34]

All this underscores the Pahlavi leadership's failure to mobilize reform beneficiaries into political bulwarks. Even excepting rural migrants and peasant families displaced by agribusinesses, there were still hundreds of thousands of newly landed farmers who gained under the White Revolution. They were a new phenomenon—a petty bourgeoisie who could now market and develop their own goods with state support.[35] Moreover, the shah could also claim to have overseen the creation of better roads, more electricity, and new schools. However, material gains did not automatically translate into political support; a more systemized understanding of what was required for continued patronage was necessary. The regime created no organizational entity to do this—no peasant union, provincial congress, or other institution that could recruit local communities to act as its spokesman or replace the landlords displaced in the Majles with new representatives. Instead, it expected that its anemic multiparty framework would appeal to the rural masses despite that neither the Melliyun nor the "opposition" Mardom parties had much of any grassroots presence in these areas.

When voter apathy resulted in these parties' middling performances in the rigged 1960 elections, regime officials rallied to another party—Iran-Novin (New Iran). Proposed years earlier by Hassan Ali Mansur, a ministerial veteran and another Pahlavi stalwart, New Iran began from a *dowreh* of technocrats and economists.[36] With royal backing, the new party reaped an overwhelming majority in the 1963 Majles elections and again in 1967 and 1971. Following Mansur's assassination in 1965, Prime Minister Hoveyda became party leader, and New Iran replaced the Melliyun party as the "loyalist" party.

However, New Iran was little better in creating a popular following below the elite level. More so than its predecessors, it had an organizational infrastructure that connected local councils and regional committees to a national leadership. Still, it had little programming in rural areas. Though it claimed hundreds of thousands of rural members, most were affiliated by way of membership in agricultural cooperatives, which were required by law to associate with the party.[37] New Iran candidates won Majles elections in these districts because the party could manipulate the electoral process, meaning rural affiliates still had little voice in selecting their representatives. The senior ranks of the national leadership were filled with well-known politicians or aspiring ministers who sought to advance their own careers rather than promote policy debates and national initiatives.[38] As a result, political life in most villages remained moribund, something that fit with the shah's mentality: he feared that a politicized farming class could betray him if led by a subversive lieutenant, a major reason why he dismissed the popular Arsanjani after the 1963 peasant congress.[39] Despite its large size, the peasantry would remain on the margins, even throughout the Iranian Revolution. Fears of a rural insurrection came to naught; but so too was wasted the opportunity for a narrowing dictatorship to acquire and mobilize a new political base.

INDUSTRIALIZATION: SUFFOCATING THE BAZAAR

Urban industrialization pursued the same agenda as land reform: make Iran an economic powerhouse no matter the cost to the regime's old allies, in this case the bazaar. Much as land reforms brought propertied farmers into existence, the White Revolution's state-invested capitalism in the cities would create a new class of wage earners distinctive from preexisting forces. And yet, much like its inaction in rural areas, the state did little to organize industrial labor to replace the bazaar proprietors it was slowly alienating.

Following the template of import-substitute industrialization (ISI), state policies implemented during the 1960s prioritized light enterprises and national commerce as staging grounds for later advanced production. Early returns were impressive, with nonoil sectors like textiles and commodities driving an over 50 percent increase in industrial output from 1963 to 1966 alone.[40] Banking and other financial services grew to accommodate new demands for capital and credit. In this context, the number of industrial firms employing ten or more workers jumped from 1,581 in 1960 to 6,626 in 1972, while industrial employment rose from about 1.7 million to 2.5 million, with manufacturing and construction becoming key sectors.[41]

However, state-directed industrialization was not more effective here than in other developing countries. Familiar structural problems like infrastructural bottlenecks, skill shortages, and restricted competition precluded innovative breakthroughs and scaled growth.[42] Escalating oil revenues after 1973 strengthened the emphasis on creating capital-intensive sectors, which exacerbated urban joblessness. For all its wealth produced, the production of hydrocarbon exports required less than half of one percent of the labor force. Heavy manufacturing sectors had only mild needs for unskilled and semiskilled workers due to the emphasis on capital-intensive goods that could emulate Western industry. For instance, by 1975 the shah could boast of having car factories—but still needed to import labor-intensive inputs like sheet metal. Unemployment statistics illustrate this dilemma. In 1966, economists estimated a 16 percent joblessness rate, of which the majority was illiterate.[43] A decade later, despite historic economic growth, unemployment still measured over 16 percent despite that *rural* joblessness had dropped below that number, implying a far higher urban figure.[44]

The failure of ISI does not make the Pahlavi regime exceptional. What demands attention are the coalitional priorities embodied in its agenda. Bazaar retailers, artisans, workshops, and guilds faced creeping dislocation as industrialization eroded their economic power. They had significant commercial sway, controlling half the handicraft production, two-thirds of retail trade, and three-quarters of wholesale trade.[45] Many did benefit from urban growth and the rise in internal trade that came with industrialization. Large merchants profited greatly, some moving into land speculation and others becoming industrialists themselves. Yet as a class, the bazaar fell under destructive pressure. Much as the Pahlavi court dismissed the value of obstinate landlords, so too was the bazaar deemed an anachronism. The shah and Prime Minister Hoveyda often characterized them as avaricious sharks whose business methods and re-ligious conservativism were incompatible with capitalism.[46]

From 1963 onward, the Ministry of Economy implemented ISI-friendly policies that cut into bazaar profits. Import restrictions designed to pro-tect state-vested enterprises also undermined the bazaar's long-standing commercial monopolies and merchandising methods.[47] New banking laws also favored large loans for industrial projects rather than the small-scale credit needed by shopkeepers. By 1976, the bazaar only accounted for 24 percent of all commercial products. One observer lamented how "the bazaar, which has survived the vicissitudes of invaders, is dying . . . the bazaar as a way of life has come under attack."[48] As oil wealth rose in the 1970s, so too did the regime's plans to overrun the bazaar with struc-tures of glass and steel. In Tehran and other large cities, planners began calling for sprawling malls, state-run supermarkets, and office towers to replace old bazaar districts. Many *bazaaris* saw this "Woolworth mental-ity" as a direct offensive against their livelihoods.[49] Resistance was futile, however. In Mashhad, the second largest city, local outcries could not pre-vent the government from demolishing thousands of shops around a reli-gious shrine in the bazaar during the mid-1970s.[50]

Royal hostilities worsened over time. In September 1975, when warned of hyperinflation and food shortages by royal court chief Asa-dollah Alam, the ruler "blamed the problem entirely on hoarding" and price gouging by the bazaar.[51] As a result, the new state-run hegemonic party, Rastakhiz (Resurgence), began attacking the bazaar. Among other measures, it launched an "anti-profiteering" campaign that handed down punitive sanctions against the bazaar, among them price ceilings, higher taxes, licensing restrictions, and disruptive inspections with an army of ten thousand hired students.[52] The results were devastating. By 1978, the

Rastakhiz-led campaign had handed out 250,000 fines, banned twenty-three thousand merchants and traders from their home districts, and imprisoned eight thousand businessmen, with another 150,000 cases against shops and retailers pending in court.[53]

As these measures emasculated the bazaar, the regime did little to marshal alternative support among the new working class. Despite high unemployment, many wage-earning families indeed gained during the White Revolution. For the first time, many could access modern housing, consumer goods, and higher education. Gender equality also noticeably improved. Yet, much as in rural areas, the regime did little to give this new group any stake in its survival. Labor laws from the post-Mossasdegh period still prevented workers from creating any "solidarity structure" that could result in coordinated action.[54] It controlled all unions and syndicates and set wage levels, while also prohibiting strikes and other collective actions. By the 1970s it had become obvious that labor had no political outlet to express their frustrations about growing urban hardships. For instance, the emphasis on heavy industry meant that in Tehran, regulators favored the operation of a few mechanized factory bakeries over the city's three thousand neighborhood bakeries, many of which were shuttered.[55]

Rising inequality also became problematic as inflation pummeled purchasing power. During the years between 1969 and 1974, by the government's own figures for shares of total household expenditures, the top 20 percent of families accounted for nearly 56 percent, a net increase, whereas the lowest 40 percent accounted for just 17 percent, a net decrease.[56] More visibly, a new echelon of capitalist elites had replaced the Thousand Families as the country's preeminent holders of wealth, among them industrial moguls (including royal cronies and retooled landlords), private investors, and the Pahlavi clan itself. Just 150 families owned 67 percent of all financial establishments and industrial enterprises and sat upon more than a thousand company boards.[57]

Given their isolation from the conditions of everyday life, many officials made tone-deaf gestures that infuriated workers, epitomized by the shah's younger brother's comment on pollution and gridlock: "If people don't like traffic jams, why don't they buy helicopters?"[58] Other evidence regarding the regime-labor disconnect lay in the shah's 1975 directive to privatize government companies, with the goal of demonstrating his benevolence by allowing workers to acquire shares even on credit. Yet what workers desired in this period of inflation and deprivation was not *paper* stock but rather *material* protections against the rising cost of food and fuel, which had outstripped their wage levels.

In short, urban workers lacked any institutional intermediary that could funnel their interests into politics. For instance, by the late 1960s, the New Iran party could claim hundreds of thousands of wage-earners in its membership, but as in rural areas only because unions and syndicates were mandated to associate. Most workers had little contact with any party official or delegate, including their supposed Majles deputies. The party doctored its activity for the press, such as inflating the number of participants or inventing issue-based campaigns that never happened.[59]

This vacuous framework meant that New Iran also did not provide "buy-in" to the other urban beneficiary of the White Revolution—the educated professional class, many of whom were funneled into state employment. The central bureaucracy mushroomed in size, with nonmilitary payrolls jumping from 260,000 in 1963 to 856,000 in 1972 and nearly 1.3 million in 1976.[60] The shah and his advisers assumed economic dependence upon the state alone would capture the bourgeoisie's political loyalties, but in reality most shunned New Iran because it was indistinguishable from the state itself, with no ideology or agenda. For instance, by the early 1970s the Ministry of Interior could state honestly that it no longer screened Majles candidates before elections—instead, New Iran did the job for it, with its officials weeding out its ranks with no less prejudice. With little room for internal contestation, national conventions of New Iran were glorified exercises of praising the shah's policies, with the sole function to update the official platform with royal directives.

DILUTING AND DISMISSING THE ʿULAMA

From the late 1950s, the shah began viewing clerical influences, including the powerful and established ʿulama of Qum, with suspicion.

The clerics presented a formidable obstacle. Cemented through centuries of reciprocal ties with the dynastic center, the clergy's power manifest through its educational, religious, and economic activities. The shah upended those arrangements in stunning fashion, demoting the ʿulama in almost every sphere of influence.

The Amini premiership began this coalitional divorce. Sensing the potentiality of land reforms, in 1959 the Grand Ayatollah Borujerdi preemptively issued a *fatwa* (Islamic legal opinion) against land redistribution by invoking tenets of shariʿa that enshrined the sanctity of property rights.[61] After his death in 1961, other senior ʿulama continued to press the issue. They leveraged their large networks of mosques, schools, and courts to appeal to a wide audience and lead public sermons on the matter. The issue concerned more than the potential loss of their own landed assets. For many, the regime was overstepping its boundaries by violating the clergy's hierocratic domain, a sacral space governed by Islamic jurisprudence and that could not be overrun by temporal mandates. From September 1962 onward, seminarians led protests in Qum against the land program, attracting nearby landlords, bazaar workers, and students.[62] However, land redistribution continued. The government took control of many vaqf lands, renting some out to farmers on ninety-nine-year leases, while transferring other plots to larger producers.[63]

Further friction emerged over the issue of female enfranchisement, another initiative of the White Revolution. Even moderate jurists who seldom spoke on politics began to release fatwas against new laws enhancing women's rights, calling the reform a Western corruption that would destroy Iran's social fabric.[64] Among the most critical was the Ayatollah Seyyed Ruhollah Khomeini. He joined with more conservative jurists in lambasting the White Revolution as violating both Islamic law and the Iranian constitution.[65] Signaling this worsening split with the regime, the ʿulama led a boycott of the January 1963 referendum, with many bazaar shops closing in support. In Qum, Khomeini led a series of vitriolic sermons against the shah and Western imperialism that drew twelve thousand students.[66] More protests and police clashes exploded in March, when SAVAK and army paratroopers battered a demonstration at the Faiziya Seminary, resulting in hundreds of deaths. Further demonstrations culminated in the June 1963 killings, when Khomeini's arrest instigated riots in Tehran and other cities, spurring an army onslaught. However, this marked a pyrrhic victory. Though Khomeini was exiled, the crackdown lionized him as both a leading voice among the ʿulama and major opposition figure against the shah.[67]

After the early 1960s, the Pahlavi regime sought to bring the religious sphere fully under its control through repression and bureaucratization. The shah no longer believed he needed the legitimating approval of the ʿulama or that new laws should abide by their view of Shiʿa doctrine. The police and SAVAK thus began eliminating religious critics, driving them underground or into exile. The regime's religious allergy extended even to nonclerical groups that drew upon Islam for inspiration, such as Ali Shariʿati's intellectual following and Mehdi Bazargan's Liberation Movement.[68] The official press resounded with the acerbic attacks, framing the ʿulama, like the landlords and bazaar, as black medievalists who threatened the enlightening enterprise of the White Revolution.[69] In addition, administrative agencies either curtailed or assumed control over Islamic schools, religious shrines, and other clerical assets. Many closed; the number of seminaries plummeted from 229 in 1963 to just 138 in 1968.[70] It then co-opted a small minority of clerics who assumed quasi-governmental positions and became spokespersons for the "official" Islam desired by the shah—one free of anti-Pahlavi elements and incidentally submissive to state authority. A Religion Corps came about in 1971 modeled after the Literacy Corps, consisting of university graduates charged with propagating this official version of Islam through proselytizing and educational services.

In essence, the autocracy attempted to displace the ʿulama. For the next decade, a predictable pattern of interaction emerged. The regime would decree a new law, against which the ʿulama would dissent with countervailing fatwas that cited Shiʿa doctrine or constitutional law. The shah would plow ahead anyway, ignoring calls for religious exemptions and threatening retribution to any who resisted further. A characteristic effort took place in September 1973, when the Education Ministry—which had already rolled back much religious materials throughout curricula—

decreed that girls in religious high schools could no longer wear the veil. The shah dismissed the clerical outcry, noting "this is not . . . the first time the mullahs have criticized our social reforms" and ordered the statute enforced even if it meant closing all the schools for noncompliance.[71]

However, much like its failure to incorporate landed farmers and urban labor, the regime's desire for unconstrained policy making obscured important trends and opportunities to harness the religious arena as new fount of support. For instance, contrary to expectation that urbanization would secularize Iranian society, the bazaar, industrial workers, and rural migrants generated rising demand for Islamic materials and literature like sermons, translations, and other teachings as the White Revolution proceeded. In addition, informal religious associations for laymen proliferated; after 1965, over 12,300 sprang up in Tehran alone, providing new spaces for wage earners and modest families to engage in religious and political debate.[72]

The shah and his clique also could not see a vital opposition trend—how Khomeini and his followers fostered alliances with formerly moderate jurists offended by the monarchy's anticlerical stances, resulting in an underground network that circulated his writings inside the country and ensured his political relevance. Likewise, the regime's distance from the clergy rendered it unable to combat anti-Pahlavi rhetoric at the doctrinal level, which was where Khomeini's critique of the shah evolved after his exile. His reformulation of Shiʿa doctrine held that it was not so much the Pahlavi crown but instead the secular state itself that threatened the community of Shiʿa believers—a circumstance that could only be rectified with his new theory of *vilayet-e-faqih*, or direct rule by the ʿulama.[73] Similarly, officials could not marshal clerics beyond the few on the government payroll to refute accusations that the Pahlavi monarchy lacked Islamic credentials. Neither could they justify to the urban pious, in theological terms, why religion and politics needed to remain separate, which formed the crux of Khomeini's critique: by neglecting his religious duties, the shah was no longer fit to be a political leader.[74]

The absence of institutional contact between the regime and clerical sector mirrors development in the party system, which continued to play an ancillary role after the 1960s. By 1975, New Iran had ossified even by its own lethargic standards. Further, the shah recognized that the inflationary crisis had created rising social and political tensions, as exemplified by new labor unrest, as well as guerilla attacks by urban militant movements. The solution, concocted by a small group of political advisers, was to remove the mask of electoral competition altogether in favor of one hegemonic party. The result was the Rastakhiz. In theory, Rastakhiz resembled the fascist model of an organic party-state, with every societal group represented in a large corporatist system governed by a single command structure.[75] Designed to be coextensive with the political system, every Iranian over eighteen was required to join. Rastakhiz superseded all of civil society—rural cooperatives, bazaar guilds, labor unions, and so forth.

In practice, however, Rastakhiz became an even hollower royal appendage. Whereas New Iran at least began from a *dowreh*, Rastakhiz was artificially grafted onto the public from the start. Almost overnight, the government installed branches across the country, created a liberal and conservative wing, and even founded a political science college for cadres.[76] Yet Rastakhiz had no ideological content. Despite its fifty thousand claimed cells and bombastic populist rhetoric, the party held few organizational events.[77] Instead of developing a grassroots infrastructure or internal platform, the regime used Rastakhiz to further attack the bazaar. The party often acted like an auxiliary police in many markets. In addition to the antiprofiteering campaign and new regulations, it replaced the trade and craft guilds with business chambers headed by Pahlavi dependables and backed the campaign to replace "flea-infested" bazaar districts with new highways and shopping centers.[78]

Rastakhiz also made the crown's alignment against the ʿulama more explicit. The shah dismissed the possibility of incorporating clerics into the party, despite its all-encompassing role to represent Iranian society: there was still no need for "listening to the clergy, much less making concessions to them."[79] Instead, Rastakhiz declared the shah as the spiritual leader of Iran and among other activities changed the existing Islamic calendar to a more fictitious imperial version. To little surprise, Khomeini and other clerics denounced the party as against Islam and forbade the pious from joining.

The failure of the Pahlavi regime to use Rastakhiz to widen its coalition served as a microcosm of its wider disconnect from Iranian society. The state could fashion all the accoutrements of the industrialized modernity envisioned by the shah—factory plants, land redistribution, political parties, and secular government. Yet it refused to incorporate social forces, whether former enemies, old allies, or new actors, into the institutions of that new order. This would have historic consequences soon enough, when the shockwaves of crisis exposed an emperor—or in this case, a king—with no clothes.

REPRESSION, DETACHMENT, AND AMERICAN EXPECTATIONS, 1963–1979

During the White Revolution, the Pahlavi regime's destruction of its old tripartite coalition of landlords, the bazaar, and ʿulama went hand-in-hand with several other trends that eroded its social foundations. The first was deepening neopatrimonialism. By the mid-1960s, the entire political system revolved around the shah. Despite the large Iranian bureaucracy, major policies originated from him or trusted lieutenants—premiers, ministers, bureaucrats, committee heads, army commanders, and SAVAK officials who reported to him.[80] Such an environment made the Majles a legislative afterthought. As a result, the regime had little grasp of public opinion. For instance, in 1974, economists pleaded with the royal court to exercise fiscal discipline with the incoming flood of oil revenues, for quantum increases in spending would cause hyperinflation and potential social troubles.[81] Yet officials ignored such warnings, insisting that new expenditures for petrochemicals, steel mills, military weapons, and other impressive items would be appreciated by the masses.[82] They believed that citizens were more concerned with Iran's global prestige than material needs at home.

Second, the shah extended patronage as enrichments for *individuals* rather than collective groups. For aspiring politicians, promotions and appointments were treasure. Others received material prizes. While the royal family accumulated $20 billion in private wealth, the quieter operation of the Pahlavi Foundation shows the strongest evidence of individualistic patronage. Created in 1958 to replace the royal office in charge of selling Crown Lands, the Foundation operated publicly as a nonprofit charitable enterprise but privately served as the royal court's investment arm.[83] At various points, it controlled Bank Omran (the fifth largest commercial bank), the National Iranian Tanker Company, agribusinesses, factories, and hotels. All told, the Pahlavi Foundation had shares in 207 companies equating to over $3 billion in assets.[84] This gave the shah enormous resources to channel toward favored personalities. Close associates, for instance, sat on the board of Bank Omran, despite few of them having an understanding of the banking sector. Investor friends received capital injections from the Foundation's coffers. After the 1973 oil boom, the Foundation even started directly paying the pensions of well-liked bureaucrats.

Third, the autocracy continued to see coercion as the most effective method of dealing with opposition. There was no reason to believe otherwise. Authorized to monitor and punish, SAVAK was the warden in one of the Middle East's largest police states. It exploited a huge network of informants supplemented by the latest technologies. It could make dissidents lose their jobs, torture arrested critics, and dole out extrajudicial violence. At any given point, it held thousands of political prisoners, among them religious clerics, bazaar workers, guerrilla fighters, literary scholars, university students, and labor activists.[85] Fear of SAVAK also buttressed censorship laws in sanitizing the media and education. In the 1970s, urban insurgencies by new guerrilla movements like Mojahedin-e Khalq (People's Freedom Fighters) justified, in the eyes of the regime, more brutal campaigns of repression.[86] Elsewhere, the regime also continued to squelch centrifugal forces, such as Kurdish groups and other ethnolinguistic minorities. Likewise, tribal communities were pushed to the brink of extinction, due to gendarmerie policies and pastoral nationalization.[87]

As the ultimate sentinel of the Peacock Throne, the military grew rapidly during the White Revolution. As table 6.1 illustrates, defense spending mushroomed from under $200 million in 1963 to over $1.8 billion in 1973 and nearly $10 billion in 1978—figures that correspond to 26 percent,

22 percent, and 19 percent of government spending. Manpower rose from over two hundred thousand in 1963 to nearly four hundred thousand on the eve of the revolution.[88] Army officers continued to receive training through U.S. exchange programs. Most spending, however, went to arms purchases. In 1973, the shah announced a campaign to upgrade the army and air force, using oil revenues to expand its military as expected by the Nixon Doctrine.[89] The doctrine was conceived when U.S. policy makers, reacting to the Vietnam debacle, began to withdraw further overseas security commitments. However, this stoked another fear—the looming shutdown of Britain's military bases in the Persian Gulf, scheduled for completion by 1971.[90] Its imperial moment gone, London no longer had the resources to preserve what had been two centuries of hegemony over the waterway. Given fears of Soviet intrusion, the Nixon administration called for Iran to fill the post-British vacuum and, alongside a heavily armed Saudi Arabia, maintain collective security in the Gulf. Those "twin pillars" would preserve Western hegemony over its rich oilfields, only this time by proxy.[91]

Such expectations also embodied Iran's continuing importance in Washington's grand strategy. First, industrial expansion engineered by the White Revolution had greatly increased demand for American goods, from wheat shipments and farm tractors to motor engines and drill pumps. By 1965, the United States had become the country's second largest trade partner for civilian goods. The shah's grandiloquent promises of urban modernization led many U.S. policy makers to believe that Iran would soon become one of the largest import markets for American banking and consumer products outside of Europe.[92] Second, the country remained an irreplaceable energy producer, especially after the 1973 oil crisis. At the time, with U.S. domestic oil reserves waning, strategic projections held that by 1975, a hypothetical oil import cutoff would cripple America's ability to run even a skeletal wartime economy.[93] By contrast, the Soviet Union had become one of the world's largest oil producers. Third, Iran still hosted various American intelligence activities dedicated to monitoring the Soviet Union, continued to grant territorial concessions in the form of overflight and landing rights, and maintained amiable ties with Israel—all in line with American geopolitical interests in the region.

TABLE 6.1

IRAN'S GROWING DEFENSE SECTOR IN SELECTED YEARS, 1963–1978
(IN $U.S. MILLIONS, HISTORICAL)

	MILITARY SPENDING*	TOTAL PUBLIC SPENDING	MILITARY AS PERCENTAGE OF TOTAL PUBLIC SPENDING	MILITARY MANPOWER
1963	191	735	26	208,000
1968	604	2,168	27.8	
1971	734	5,198	14.1	255,000
1974	4,731	11,609	40.7	
1975	6,697	28,135	23.8	
1976	7,790	32,899	23.7	390,000
1977	7,958	44,658	17.8	
1978	9,507	50,091	19	400,000+

*Does not include budget allocations for SAVAK and Interior Ministry

Sources: Hurewitz (1982); ACDA (serial); Central Bank of Iran (serial)

Yet the Nixon Doctrine called for Iran to become something else—a military power in its own right. In accordance, the Pahlavi regime began purchasing some of the most advanced aircraft, missiles, and weaponry in the U.S. arsenal. It could do so without congressional oversight, a privilege no other ally enjoyed. From 1973 to 1978, Iran spent over $16 billion for this purpose. As table 6.1 shows, 1974 was an especially expensive year, with defense expenditures consuming nearly 41 percent of the national budget. It also purchased weaponry from Britain in exchange for oil. American military advisers and technicians arrived in droves, charged with implementing new systems and training their Iranian counterparts on the ground. So confident was the shah of his American ties that he even suggested U.S. officers take direct operational roles in his military, although Washington demurred.[94] MAAG continued to play a supervisory role, counseling the shah on military issues, while various officials and private agents connected him to eager U.S. firms hoping to ride the Iranian bonanza. From 1972 to 1976, the number of American residents increased from fifteen thousand to thirty-one thousand, more than half of whom were civilians.[95]

This should not imply that from the early 1960s onward, the United States never criticized Iran. Many diplomats bemoaned the repression and inequality they observed. However, the Iranian lobby had a strong presence in Washington. Iranian officials enjoyed access to the president and secretary of state during every administration, assuring them that America had no surer ally in the region. Based upon his own dealings with the White House, by 1977 the shah had every reason to assume that U.S. support "was unqualified and unquestioning."[96] By contrast, it was support from *Iranian* society that would prove vacuous in the coming years.

THE REVOLUTIONARY CLIMAX

From the first scattered protests of late 1977 to the shah's departure in January 1979, the Iranian Revolution ranks among the most accessible episodes of dictatorial overthrow in Middle Eastern studies. Within a decade of the new Islamic Republic, explanations for the Pahlavi dictatorship's fall abounded: declining economic conditions due to high inflation and relative deprivation; the cultural appeal of Shiʿa Islam as a unifying ideology; the leadership and organizational capacity of the cross-cutting opposition; decision-making paralysis by an overcentralized state; the shah's personal vacillations and illness; and Western pressures against the regime.[97] As Charles Kurzman's more recent account notes, equally vital in understanding the revolution were highly contingent "moments" when subjective perceptions shifted on the ground—that is, when previously apathetic or wavering citizens began feeling that opposing the regime had become a "viable" behavior and was therefore worth doing.[98] The analysis here supplements these thoughtful arguments with the reminder that the revolution's sweeping breadth, which entailed thousands of protests with millions of participants, only became apparent after it had ended. The revolution started as a very minor crisis, and only in late 1978 did observers believe the end was near. The problem was that given its prior coalitional narrowing, the Pahlavi regime aggravated the crisis at every stage due to its inability to find peaceful solutions, creating a self-propelling momentum that produced ever-larger waves of opposition. It not only refused to compromise from the start, it also did not know *how* to do so—that is, how to bargain for survival—because it had never done so in the past.

The first protests in late 1977 gave little clue to the coming tempest. They included intellectual manifestos and student strikes that encompassed just a few hundred participants. They did not call for regime change but instead advanced specific issues of reform such as desires for greater literary freedom and better educational facilities. Tensions rose in January 1978, when the army smashed a clerical gathering in Qum; memorial processions held for those killed resulted in bloodier clashes the next month. For the next year, different groups—clerics, merchants, shopkeepers, students, workers, professionals—held marches and strikes calling for political change. These protests and riots grew larger and more obdurate despite the imposition of martial law. By Black Friday of September 1978, when a huge march numbering over a hundred thousand was bloodily suppressed, the "wall of fear" had been shattered.[99] What began as moderate reformism had hardened into the maximalist goal of unseating the shah. By November and December, Tehran and other cities were witnessing constant protests, with several million demanding the regime's end. With the economy at a standstill and crowds refusing to disband, the shah left Iran on 16 January 1979. A new political order followed not long after.

Why could the regime not stop the crisis from escalating into revolution? For one, having dismembered its coalition without gaining new constituencies, the Pahlavi monarchy had ceded a huge space by which Khomeini and other opposition entrepreneurs could gain followers. Those hurt the most by Iranian state-building were most active in mobilizing. Of nearly 2,500 documented protests, leaders associated with the bazaar and

ʿulama groups led two-thirds.[100] Bazaar markets led mass strikes, distributed information, protected demonstrators, and by virtue of their central locations stood as unifying spaces of dissent. Though less involved early on, the ʿulama came to harness their religious network to coordinate protests, pioneer religious symbolism, and politicize holy days and mourning rites. By the late 1970s, these were not small actors. The bazaar sector encompassed 725,000 workers and owners, or nearly 7 percent of the national labor force.[101] The religious sphere encompassed hundreds of seminaries and over five thousand mosques utilized by ninety thousand clergymen, including fifty jurists holding the rank of Ayatollah, five thousand prayer leaders, and over ten thousand students.[102] They could utilize their social capital to reach other groups, such as teachers, university students, factory workers, and bureaucrats. On the ground, they provided leadership and organization.

By contrast, the White Revolution left no class or group bound to Pahlavi perpetuity. On the one hand, landowners and peasants played little role in the revolution, with the shah making almost no outreach to them. Urban workers, on the other hand, flocked to the opposition. Even if many did not mind Pahlavi rule, there was no organizational framework that could coordinate activity and channel it into opposition strongholds in cities like Tehran, Esfahan, and Mashhad. Rastakhiz's anodyne framework meant that at most, liaisons could call up a few hundred students for short rallies. Most tellingly, Rastakhiz's many branch offices became popular targets of looting because so few members were ever present to defend them. That civil servants were still outside the party's purview became lucid in the fall of 1978, when many public-sector employees joined the opposition, among them electricians, oil workers, journalists, doctors, and postal workers.[103] This hampered many government functions. Finally, the new capitalist elite created by the White Revolution had little political role. They instead funneled considerable wealth out, accounting for much of the $2.5 billion that left Iran during the last three months of 1978.[104]

Consequently, the regime could not counterpunch with supporters. It did not have cadres who would counteract even minor acts of resistance, such as covering graffiti and images with pro-Pahlavi symbols or spearheading university events to explain the shah's position. What it mustered instead, by November 1978, were thousands of police-hired hooligans.[105] Some engaged in pro-shah demonstrations, while others assaulted opposition protesters, bazaar shops, and neighborhoods. However, such violence was opportunistic rather than systematic, and the perpetuating thugs were ill-trained and without leadership.[106] They carried out paid assignments rather than binding political commitments and as a result all but abandoned the regime by December.

At the same time, the Pahlavi monarchy could not demobilize the protests using violence alone. As Benjamin Smith has argued, given his distance from Iranian society, the shah could not " 'reach into' the opposition to assess the scope of demands and respond to them . . . with means other than raw force."[107] The regime was, however, willing and able to repress until the end. SAVAK and the military consistently fired on demonstrators and continuously arrested and maltreated oppositionists. Total casualty estimates of the revolution vary, but at least several thousand people were killed and several times more were maimed. The record is not gorier because by November 1978, when crowds had grown impossibly large, the shah realized that ordering all-out coercion would result in murder on a scale that even the United States could not ignore. Yet had that order come, the coercive apparatus would have carried it out. Likewise, the army did not disintegrate until after the monarchy abdicated.[108] Most enlisted soldiers did not heed Khomeini's call for desertion, and the officer corps remained ready to fulfill directives from above. Simply put, repression did not work because every abuse drove more participants to the opposition and radicalized their demands. Citizens continued protesting *despite* the possibility of coercion.[109] From lyricized slogans to the black humor of body counts, few could claim ignorance about the potential for injury or even death by mobilizing on the street.[110]

Neither did a reformist strategy work. During the summer of 1978, with growing crowds no longer afraid of bullets, the regime tried to bargain its way out. Spirited hunts for scapegoats netted the arrest of high-ranking officials, such as former Prime Minister Hoveyda, and numerous SAVAK officers as evidence that the shah would prosecute those responsible for past deaths. In August, he appointed his trusted deputy Sharif-Emami to the premiership to signal the sudden move toward liberalization. The regime loosened censorship and released political prisoners; increased salaries and housing subsidies for striking workers; closed casinos, night-clubs, and theaters criticized by the clergy and restored the old Islamic calendar; and promised new elections and the closure of Rastakhiz. In November, the shah appeared on television, apologizing for past brutalities and promising democracy.

Clerics and *bazaaris* had little incentive to believe such concessions because they came after not just a year of carnage but decades of estrangement. The bazaar was still smarting from the repercussions of the anti-profiteering campaign. For the ʿulama, initiatives like the Religion Corps signaled that the state could never respect their hierocracy. The shah brought no trustworthiness to the table. Thus the biggest strikes, protests, and riots occurred *after* the shah began making concessions. During Sharif-Emami's three-month premiership, nearly a hundred cities and towns gave rise to antiregime activities, with the largest marches now drawing hundreds of thousands. This surprised the shah and his advisers, who believed that such mollifying tactics would work, and that in just six months normalcy would return.

Finally, American support had little effect. Some analysts have lamented how the United States "lost" Iran by withdrawing its support for the shah.[111] Under the Carter administration's goal to promote human rights, policy principals allegedly refused to give the shah encouragement to exterminate his enemies.[112] In reality, while the Carter White House differed from previous administrations in its liberal rhetoric, in bilateral terms it embraced the Pahlavi regime as warmly as its predecessors. President Carter famously toasted the shah in Tehran on New Year's Day of 1978 and delivered many communiqués that Iran was, as always, the linchpin of U.S. regional interests. During the protests, while liberal voices in the State Department pressed for peaceful negotiations, they were overruled by a White House desiring a strong and stable autocracy led by the shah.[113] In November 1978, National Security Advisor Zbigniew Brzezinski told the shah that he should use whatever means necessary to restore order with Carter's blessing. The ruler was hardly "paralyzed" with fear of offending America: though discouraged with setbacks, he never refrained from violence because of worry about U.S. abandonment.[114]

In truth, the United States did not lose Iran, because its fate was never Washington's to decide in the first place. Given the millions of Iranians mobilized by January 1979, it would have taken something far more than another Operation Ajax to quiet the streets. The Pahlavi regime was trapped by its own choices, confronted by a burgeoning opposition front with neither committed supporters nor the means to defuse the situation peacefully. The shah faced an untenable dilemma: to "either overhaul entirely the structure [he] had so painfully created over nearly four decades or to launch a bloody, repressive campaign. He was unwilling to do either. Instead, he temporized and maneuvered on the margins, hoping for a break that never came."[115]

||||||||||||||||||||||||||||||||||||||||||||||||||||||||||||||||||||||||||||||||||||||||||||||||||||||||||||||||||||||

This chapter investigated the process of state-building in modern Iran. Geopolitical substitution rooted in American intercessions after 1953 resulted in a narrowing coalitional logic that produced exclusionary economic and political institutions. The elimination of communist and nationalist movements had an intoxicating effect: without having to make any concessions to win over enemies, the Pahlavi regime never learned how to bargain with social groups. From the White Revolution to political parties, new institutional investments signaled the ambitious vision of modernization espoused by the shah. However, such initiatives only further detached the Iranian state from its own society. Traditional allies in landowners, bazaar, and ʿulama were greatly harmed by new policies, and their interests discarded by ruling elites. Worse, the autocracy made little effort to reach into society and carve out new ties with constituencies that benefited from its developmental push, from urban workers to rural peasants. Insulated from popular interests and reliant upon violent coercion, the Pahlavi leadership created an increasingly personalistic state that lacked institutionalized ties with social forces.

This climaxed in the Iranian Revolution. As the evidence suggests, the onset of street demonstrations and other urban resistance by 1978 presented the regime with a decisive test of its past coalitional commitments. Had it carried more popular support, it could have more effectively addressed grievances, made reform concessions, and crafted other compromises in order to contain opposition from spreading. Its nonexistent bases of societal loyalty, however, combined with the hollowness of state institutions meant that the dictatorship had neither the social knowledge nor the institutional mechanisms to do so. It still assumed, until far too late, that violent repression and American support would secure its future.

Not all autocracies that become clients of outside powers suffer such remarkable destruction, of course. Often found in other countries that reap foreign support to win domestic conflicts are confounding factors that compel at least *some* coalition to form after leaders stand triumphant over a repressed society. The case of Jordan, delivered in the next two chapters, speaks to this point. In this kingdom, communal tensions around a demographic split generated fear and mistrust that impinged upon the regime's decision-making calculus; this resulted in a modest coalition, a larger marginalized majority, and a costly recipe for longevity.

7

A CONFLICT INTERRUPTED
IN JORDAN

JORDAN EXEMPLIFIES THE third causal pattern encompassed by this book's central theory of authoritarian state-building: that of geopolitical subsidization and tenuous survival. This chapter traces the historical processes and events that culminated in the domestic unrest of the mid-1950s, which nearly ended the rule of its Hashemite regime. The 1948 annexation of the land on the West Bank of the Jordan River, which created a Palestinian majority atop the preexisting population of Transjordanian tribes and communities, represented a watershed moment in Jordanian history. The resulting social and political flux helped stir new urban opposition, among them leftist and Arab Nationalist parties that rose to prominence in parliament and on the streets. Like the Pahlavi monarchy of Iran, King Hussein had nearly lost control until U.S. intervention provided the diplomatic, economic, and military support to regain order in 1957.

However, though Jordan's new cliency relationship with the United States facilitated the defeat of most opposition, it did not extirpate the social roots of instability in the form of communal frictions. By the 1960s, relations between many Palestinians and the regime were not only frayed but even worsening after the reconsolidation of Hashemite power, resulting in Transjordanian fears of subordination and dislocation. Though

not ethnic in the strictest sense, this divide began acquiring some quali-
ties of ethnic conflict, in particular the ways that constructed prejudices
began aggravating conceptions of the "other." Harnessing American assistance, the regime chose to reconfigure its ruling coalition by drawing
its Transjordanian base even closer through promises of *protection*. It also
began creating increasingly exclusionary policies toward most Palestinians. Such a strategy underlay the survival of the monarchy through these
turbulent decades, and also contributed to the 1970 civil war and the ethnocratic state built afterward.

A COLONIAL PROJECT STUMBLES, 1921–1956

The British collusion with the Sharif of Mecca, Hussein bin ʿAli,
during World War I birthed two new regimes. Whereas one son, Faisal,
was put in charge of Iraq, in 1921 elder son ʿAbdullah had to settle for
Transjordan—the section of the British Palestinian Mandate east of the
Jordan River, a desert patch with 225,000 mostly tribal inhabitants. In
the first years, the British managed the domestic and foreign policies of
Emir ʿAbdullah.[1] A combination of seconded British officials, Syrian and
Palestinian administrators, and personal advisers would staff early governments, while the British took responsibility over protecting the new
kingdom's irregular borders. Above all, the British held the purse strings;
fiscal grants composed the budget's largest portion until the late 1920s,
when customs and licensing fees began accruing in reasonable numbers.[2]

Western and Arab histories often portray Jordan as an imperial ap-
parition, created more through British imposition than through local
social relations.[3] Yet Emir ʿAbdullah did not arrive in Amman alone. He
relied upon his "palace group" to initially rule, factotums who circulated
throughout the government and royal court in order to fulfill various
administrative functions. These mandarins hailed from diverse backgrounds, with first Syrian elites and accompanying Sharifian officers from
his father's wartime army and later notables from settled tribal families
like the Majali and Rifaʿi clans dominating their ranks.[4] Certainly, Emir

ʿAbdullah could not have overcome early threats, from the Istiqlal move-ment campaigning for pan-Arab independence to tribal uprisings, with-out British muscle. However, also important were early alliances created with existing Transjordanian forces.

First was a small merchant elite. Though much of this wealthy group originally had Syrian (Damascus) or Palestinian (Nablus) roots, they had flourished on the East Bank for generations; the ʿAsfour and Touqan fami-lies were primary examples.[5] Concentrated in Amman and northern Jor-dan given their proximity to overland trade routes, the Tranjordanian merchant elite constituted a cohesive group held together by commer-cial and interfamilial bonds. Almost as quickly as the Mandate began, the merchants created the Amman Chamber of Commerce (ACC) to organize their interests. Emir ʿAbdullah found them willing allies, for what they desired most was not power but peace—and in particular, favorable poli-cies.[6] The regime could deliver such patronage. New land regulations and retail taxes in the 1930s enriched merchants in various ways from spe-cific statutes, such as the provision to allow mortgage lending, to outright loopholes allowing for the evasion of merchandising and employee taxes. The merchants were hence co-opted early on, although few entered the realm of politics. Though some served in new ministries, most conveyed their interests through personal contacts or associational channels like the ACC.[7]

The ruling coalition's major core, however, derived from the rest of the populace and encompassed the two tribal currents—settled families and nomadic clans. Most settled Transjordanians were Sunni Muslim fel-lahin, village-dwelling peasants with varying tribal affiliations. Their ag-ronomic burdens resembled the impoverished agrarian tenants of Iraq, Syria, or Iran, but their financial subservience did not. Unlike those ar-eas, Transjordan had no extreme landowning inequality, no "pronounced class distinction between peasant and landlord."[8] The weakness of Otto-man law and the prevalence of local tradition meant that most village lands were communally owned rather than held by powerful sheikhs.[9] Their greatest danger, apart from the lack of arable land, came from prop-erty disputes and the periodic raids by Bedouin. The settled populace also included sectarian and ethnic minorities, including about twenty thousand Circassians and a similar number of Arab Christians. By contrast, the nomadic sector encompassed numerous Bedouin confederations and seminomadic tribes of varying size and origin. Led by different sheikhs and intermediary kin, most of these tribal residents engaged in pastoral production ranging from camel herding to limited farming.[10]

Many Transjordanians, especially Bedouin sheikhs, were reluctant to give fealty to a foreign regime imported by British imperialism.[11] Contrary to popular belief, most East Bank tribes had rejected the call of ʿAbdullah's father, Sharif Hussein, to join the Arab Revolt during World War I.[12] Thus, early relations with monarchical authority were tense, punctuated by periodic clashes such as the 1923 Balqaʿ Revolt. Yet, if the new emirate struggled for lack of domestic support, the tribes also faced hardship. This was no land of bounty. The loss of export markets for camel meat and the use of mechanized transportation impoverished many tribal groups in central Jordan, like the Bani Sakhr, a powerful Bedouin confederation.[13] Southern confederations like the Huwaytat were harangued by a combination of Saudi taxes on seasonal grazing grounds and Ikhwan raids from the south. In the late 1920s, the first of several consecutive droughts hit the East Bank, destroying many herds and bringing starvation to Bedouin and fellahin alike.[14] The Great Depression did not help matters, and the general state of scarcity that resulted in the early 1930s drove many tribal communities to send laborers to the coastal towns of Palestine in order to find seasonal income.

The tribal-state alliance began under these conditions of mutual insecurity. The monarchy provided private goods to sheikhs, such as land grants, agrarian subsidies, and tax abatements, to win their support.[15] Land reforms greatly improved the condition of fellahin by recognizing property claims and adjudicating conflicts over titles.[16] They were also protected against Bedouin raids, as the regime encouraged sheikhs to police their communities, often giving financial stipends to those who ensured "good behavior" among tribesmen.[17] Direct rural assistance and employment on public works like the railway also helped reduce the margins of rural poverty.[18] Finally, sheikhs received political representation.

Emir ʿAbdullah began consulting with major tribal leaders, couching his authority in the symbolic language of consultative rule. Favored sheikhs also received positions on the Legislative Council, a mostly symbolic body created in 1928, and pecuniary rewards like financial stipends. Circassian and Christian minorities also attracted attention as reservoirs of support. They were overrepresented on the Council and also tapped as administrative functionaries.[19]

Embodying this new Transjordanian coalition, one knit together by patronage, was Al-Jaysh Al-ʿArabi, the Arab Legion. Rooted in the desert police created in the 1920s, the kingdom's first army was organized, financed, and led by the British.[20] By the late 1940s, the Legion consumed more than half the annual government budget.[21] Such resources ensured that the Legion not only served as a constabulary force within the territory but also as an instrument of tribal co-optation. That process began under British Captain John Bagot Glubb, known as Glubb Pasha, after 1930. Glubb Pasha prioritized Bedouin recruitment, with the Bani Sakhr, Bani Hassan, Sirhan, and Huwaytat confederations contributing the most personnel. Though tribesmen of fellahin background also found acceptance in the military, the nomadic and seminomadic confederations came to contribute the bulk of both enlisted men and officers. Employment provided regular pay as well as entitlements like education, food, and medical care. In poorer areas, a single soldier's benefits could sustain several families. Further, military training gave British officers a powerful venue to invent Jordanian nationalism and, with it, a sense of personal loyalty to the Hashemites.[22] For all these reasons, by the end of World War II, the Legion had become both an economic lifeline to tribes as well as an institutional expression of Bedouin identity.[23]

The Legion encapsulated Britain's interest in the stability of its Mandate. Though World War II had exposed the untenable costs of running a global empire, British policy makers were loath to surrender their hegemony over the Middle East, with military bases stretching the Suez Canal to the Persian Gulf. Most did not wish to accept the "decline to the status of a third-world power" to become "another Belgium."[24] One response was to convert its dependencies into client states. This produced the

Anglo-Jordanian Treaties of 1946 and 1948, which granted independence and transformed the emirate into a kingdom. The final accord called for the British to transfer economic and military grants equaling £12 million annually for twenty years in exchange for territorial concessions, such as basing and overflight rights during war.

DEMOGRAPHIC SHIFTS AND NEW OPPOSITION

The Anglo-Jordanian cliency relationship would not stand long, however. In 1951, 'Abdullah was assassinated during a visit to Jerusalem. Following the abdication of his son, Talal, 'Abdullah's grandson Hussein ascended to the helm in May 1953. King Hussein inherited a changing society. With the Arab-Israeli War in 1948, the kingdom had annexed the West Bank and Jerusalem, whose custodianship represented a source of pride and responsibility for the Hashemites. Though a moral victory for the regime, it also overwhelmed the kingdom with newfound responsibilities. The war added 800,000 Palestinians, including 350,000 refugees, to a preexisting population of 375,000 Transjordanians. It left 40 percent of the West Bank population destitute, and by 1950 nearly a hundred thousand Palestinians had resettled on the East Bank.

The lack of arable land on the East Bank, continuing threats from Israeli incursions on the West Bank, and shortages in refugee housing resulted in large-scale Palestinian migration to Amman, whose population soared from twenty-six thousand in 1946 to 155,000 in 1955. In a time when agriculture still composed a third of the GDP, Jordan's small industrial sector driven by construction, textiles, and other light industries could not cope with new demands for jobs. Thus greater urbanization wrought greater unemployment and material hardships.[25] Compounding the problem, the war cut off access to Palestinian coastal areas that had soaked up seasonal tribal labor. In 1955, economists estimated a 16 percent unemployment rate and nearly 11 percent underemployment rate among *non*-refugees, with those in refugee camps faring far worse.[26] Only British aid and support from the United Nations Relief and Works Agency (UNRWA) preserved the regime's solvency during this time of scarcity; from 1949 to 1956, these constituted more than half of all official revenues.

The demographic shift transformed political life as well. Through World War II, the palace and the British had regularly stamped out incipient opposition party and union activities.[27] Yet now, for the second time in thirty years, the Hashemite monarchy claimed leadership over an Arab society with little desire for its rulership. Though Palestinians had no choice in the matter, notable differences between the two communities emerged early on. Palestinians were generally better educated and more urbanized than their Transjordanian counterparts, whom they did not necessarily see as peers. Indeed, some separatist elements in the Palestinian West Bank rejected the annexation altogether, including communists who served as the precursors of future opposition parties. Economic inequalities were also exacerbated. Whereas poorer refugees either settled in large camps or became urban squatters, more well-to-do Palestinian families simply rented homes and apartments in Amman and other cities, quickly integrating into their new urban environs.[28] In this manner, Palestinians soon comprised the majority of Jordan's wage-earning and professional strata, becoming especially prevalent as teachers and lawyers.

Of course, that social and economic differences existed does not mean that Palestinians and Transjordanians formed diametrically opposing communities predestined for conflict. Such a primordialist view ignores that following 1948 most residents in the newly amalgamated kingdom of Jordan were more preoccupied with the struggle for material security than ethereal debates concerning national identity and belonging.[29] Yet it is undeniable that the merger produced greater uncertainty regarding the direction of the kingdom's policies—and that what followed afterward was the rapid growth of urban opposition that heavily drew upon the Palestinian demographic.

For its part, the regime was ill-prepared to accommodate this demographic situation. Previously, the palace group and tribal sheikhs had announced their pro-Palestinian and anti-Israeli sentiments in the spirit of pan-Arab solidarity.[30] Indeed, Emir ʿAbdullah's original dream after World War I had been for an Arab state under Hashemite rule encompassing the entire Levant, including Palestine. Partly for these reasons, after 1948 Jordan was the only state that granted citizenship to most Palestinian refugees, and in public forums the monarch celebrated the ideal of national unity.[31] Yet signs of reticence for true political equality emerged early on. For instance, King Hussein inherited a liberal constitution crafted by his father, one that legalized political parties and established a bicameral parliament.[32] However, the elected Majlis Al-Nuwab, the Lower House, drew equal seats between the West Bank and East Bank, despite the former's much larger population.

Second, some Palestinian elites did become part of the regime's coalitional base, but they were hardly representative of the West Bank. Most came from wealthy landowning and trading families with preexisting ties to East Bank merchants, and they quickly integrated into Jordanian business networks after the acquisition of new trade licenses and retail permits. The Abu-Ghazaleh and Masri families were two such examples. A handful of West Bank notables also entered public service as bureaucrats and ministers, developing close royal affiliations and becoming part of the palace group.[33]

Third, the Arab Legion was slow to integrate Palestinians, with frontline units like the infantry and most officer positions remaining Bedouin preserves. To defend the frontier border between the West Bank and Israel, the regime instead created a Palestinian National Guard made subordinate to the Legion. National Guard regiments "had little beyond their rifles," were led by Transjordanian officers, and trained in military camps located in the East Bank rather than Palestine.[34] Finally, early enthusiasm to resettle refugees within the largest cities of Amman and Irbid bogged down within years, especially as the predominance of Palestinian labor and bourgeoisie invigorated an explosive wave of urban growth around Amman. Many regime insiders advised King Hussein against encouraging any further repatriation of Palestinians from the West Bank, because it would divert financial resources away from more important development projects.[35]

Atop this uncertainty emerged a swell of new opposition in the early 1950s. Local branches of the Arab Nationalists, communists, Ba'thists,

and other regional parties began recruiting heavily, with most establishing major offices and networks on both banks.[36] Palestinians would represent the majority of their cadres, including those from refugee camps as
well as urban activists from Amman and the West Bank.[37] Another source
of opposition was the labor movement. Remnants of labor unions in the
West Bank were responsible for establishing worker movements in Jordan
by founding branches on the East Bank in 1950.[38] The 1954 founding of
the General Federation of Jordanian Trade Unions marked a milestone,
as organized labor now enjoyed formal recognition for the first time.[39]
Together, these opposition factions would form a broad alliance called
the Jordanian National Movement, which would count among its numbers Transjordanian activists, including many students, teachers, and
writers, and a much larger contingent of Palestinian wage earners and
professionals.[40]

Though not always a united front given their diverse ideologies, the
political parties and civil organizations comprising this growing opposition converged upon a common platform of issues. Above all, they saw the
monarchy as an enduring symbol of Western imperialism whose power
needed to be rolled back. In addition to greater democracy, most also desired the end of Britain's de facto control over the Arab Legion through
Glubb Pasha and other British officers, as well as greater ties with the
Arab Nationalist regimes of Egypt and Syria. In both the West Bank and
Amman, the street gave rise to contentious protests and marches, with
schools and social clubs becoming rich sites of ideological production for
many parties.[41] Starting in October 1954, parliamentary elections also allowed for vigorous campaigning and recruiting, giving another stage for
opposition groups to showcase their resistance.

Though the regime had little tolerance for such public dissent, the
police struggled to contain the largest protests. Riots over the 1954 elections, which were rigged to favor nonparty candidates, necessitated the
Legion's deployment into civil action for the first time.[42] However, that
action backfired. A few dozen officers harbored sympathies for the Arab
Nationalists and soon formed a secret Free Officers faction led by General ʿAli Abu Nuwar.[43] The use of military troops to suppress urban un-

rest aggravated their frustrations, precipitating Abu Nuwar's dismissal of some Bedouin personnel deemed too loyal to the kingship. In late 1955, rumors about Jordan's potential accession into the UK-led Baghdad Pact stoked more angry demonstrations.[44] In December, protests forced the resignation of successive governments led by Sa'id Al-Mufti and Hazza' Al-Majali, two reliable royalists. Calling upon the Legion to quell the violence once more, the regime yielded to popular opinion and rejected the pact. In March 1956, further street agitations compelled the palace to dismiss Glubb Pasha and other British officers from the twenty-three-thousand-strong Legion. This resulted in the appointment of Abu Nuwar as new chief of staff for the renamed Jordanian Arab Army.[45]

Such moves to sever London's vestigial influence emboldened the opposition to seek more aggressive domestic change. In the October 1956 parliamentary elections, they won their greatest victory by capturing more than half the Lower House's forty seats.[46] This marked a turning point. Since May 1953, the king had presided over eight cabinets stacked with trusted subordinates to handle the policy making agenda. Prime ministers came from key constituencies that had been carefully wedded to Hashemite rule during the colonial period: for instance, Hazza' Al-Majali hailed from a prominent southern tribal clan, while Sa'id Al-Mufti was a Circassian notable. King Hussein had little choice but to appoint as prime minister Socialist Party leader Sulayman Al-Nabulsi, which represented the pinnacle of success for opposition parties, many of whose leaders became part of the new government.[47]

Al-Nabulsi's cabinet quickly did what past ones did not: rather than act as the royal mouthpiece and carry out palace directives, it assumed an activist stance and sought to undermine monarchical power in various ways. For instance, while indecisive in terms of economic policies, Al-Nabulsi pursued a new foreign policy that greatly diverged from Jordan's historically pro-Western stance. He enhanced relations with the Arab Nationalist regimes of Egypt and Syria, and frequently criticized Britain for its role in the recent Suez War.[48] Backing the ideological agenda of Arab Nationalism, his administration also encouraged the creation of a pan-Arab federation, even if it meant toppling existing state boundaries and national governments. In support of that ideal, in January 1957 Al-Nabulsi pushed Jordan into inking the Arab Solidarity Agreement, which promised to replace British foreign aid with assistance from Egypt, Syria, and Saudi Arabia.

With much of the Jordanian public endorsing the anti-Western rhetoric of Al-Nabulsi and cheering these moves, King Hussein had little choice but to annul the Anglo-Jordanian Treaty in March 1957, which satisfied one of the core demands of the Jordanian National Movement. This marked the formal end to cliency relations with London and encouraged more aggressive efforts to overturn the monarchical position. For instance, prominent oppositionists publically campaigned against high-ranking royal officials, resulting in the dismissal of the police director. They soon began targeting Bahjat Al-Talhouni, the Chief of the Royal Court and one of the most powerful members of the palace group. If Al-Talhouni left, some thought, then little would stand in the way of directly attacking King Hussein and the Hashemite family.

April 1957 was the cruelest month, as the crisis reached its dénouement. It began when army officers supportive of Al-Nabulsi undertook "Operation Hashim," positioning troops around Amman in order to intimidate the palace.[49] Hussein responded by dissolving Al-Nabulsi's government, but parliamentary outcry prevented the appointment of a more malleable cabinet. On 13 April, Abu Nuwar and several other officers insisted that Hussein reinstate Al-Nabulsi. An ill-coordinated mutiny at a military base in the governorate of Al-Zarqa failed, resulting in the expulsion of Abu Nuwar and other collaborators to Syria. Yet political resistance persisted, with leftist and Arab Nationalist activists continuing to organize rallies and strikes across Amman and the West Bank, including Jerusalem and Ramallah. On 22 April, opposition leaders convened a popular congress in Nablus, calling for Al-Nabulsi's restoration, a new federal union with Egypt and Syria, and various other provisos.[50]

This paralysis exposed the Hashemite regime's inability to regain political control, which stemmed from several sources. There was obvious uncertainty regarding the army's loyalty, which impeded confidence about ordering outright repression. Jordan also suffered a fiscal crisis, thanks to lagging economic growth and military overspending. Though the problem had deep structural origins, it greatly magnified the monarchy's economic vulnerability when the annulment of the Anglo-Jordanian Treaty resulted in the loss of British aid. Lacking natural resource wealth, postcolonial Jordan had inherited little extractive capacity or budgetary discipline from its mandate years.[51] Winning over merchant and tribal loyalties required a dilatory taxation system, while decades of British funding for the Legion had shielded officials from learning how to finance the military through domestic revenues. Predictably, the loss of British aid was catastrophic; from the end of World War II to 1957, Jordan had received £82 million in total grant support from London, with the last subsidy measuring £12.5 million, or $33.6 million.[52] The replacement Arab Solidarity Agreement fizzled out, as just Saudi Arabia made its quarterly payment before backing out. As a result, in April 1957 the Jordanian government had less than $2 million in cash reserves.

Finally, the palace group withered under regional pressures. With the end of British cliency support, King Hussein feared backlash from hostile neighbors if he moved against the Jordanian National Movement. One threat came from foreign troops already inside the country. In late 1956, Al-Nabulsi's government had agreed to multilateral defense arrangements with other Arab countries in the spirit of pan-Arab unity, resulting in a Syrian armored brigade and six thousand Saudi troops being based in the kingdom. In addition, worries about subversive Egyptian interference also abounded. Gamal ʿAbdel Nasser had warmed to Al-Nabulsi, and Cairo continued to stream radio propaganda encouraging anti-Hashemite resistance across the West Bank and Amman. Some Jordanian officials believed that Egyptian contacts were secretly plotting with opposition parties to help overthrow the monarchy.[53]

AMERICAN SUBVENTION AND A RESCUED REGIME, 1957

The outlook for the Jordanian regime appeared no better than its dictatorial peers during the height of social conflict. Had King Hussein conceded to the opposition congress at Nablus in April 1957, the leading leftist and Arab Nationalist parties would not only have reconstituted the government but taken further measures to sideline royal power.

The monarchical response was violent counterattack, a coercive restoration of authoritarianism that could not have occurred without the support of a new great power patron, the United States. On April 25th, King Hussein declared a state of emergency and imposed martial law. The regime then viciously declawed society. Mass arrests decimated the leftist and nationalist opposition in Amman and the West Bank, with high-ranking figures brutalized or forced underground. Two Palestinian members of parliament even saw their political immunity revoked and were given long prison terms due to affiliation with the communists.[54] All political parties were dissolved, parliament was suspended, and the independent press and many civic associations were shuttered. As one indicator, the number of unions dropped from fifty-nine to sixteen between 1955 and 1958.[55] Labor suffocated: the union law of 1960 not only banned unionization in the public sector but also interpreted an enormous range of worker activities as "political."

The military also underwent purging. The new army chief, Habis Al-Majali, arrested at least fifty officers for suspected party ties, restored those tribal personnel sacked by Abu Nuwar, and moved loyal Bedouin-manned brigades into Amman in a show of royal might.[56] Soldiers arrested thousands of leftist and Arab Nationalist activists, with many facing charges in closed tribunals. With political prisons fast filling up, the remaining oppositionists went into exile or underground, their parties eviscerated. When Hussein lifted martial law in December 1958, autocracy ruled once again. The monarchy would never allow civil society and opposition groups to menace its dictatorial supremacy: "not parliament, democracy, or even some abstract and well-meaning notion of constitutionalism was ever again permitted to conflict with the royal 'we.' "[57]

Such a clampdown occurred in Amman but echoed through the policy corridors of Washington. The Eisenhower administration gave unconditional backing for the Hashemite regime to restore order by force. It began with diplomatic shows of sponsorship. Shortly after the onslaught against opposition began, the White House released a public statement declaring Jordan's "independence and integrity" as central to U.S. interests.[58] It pressured Israel not to attack the West Bank, warned Syria against maneuvering its armored brigade, and pushed Saudi Arabia to place its own troops temporarily under Jordanian command. The United States also conducted saber rattling, moving warships from the Sixth Fleet into the eastern Mediterranean and mustering troops at West German bases as if preparing for an airlift.[59] Such minatory diplomacy enhanced the regime's confidence by removing the threat of regional blowback, insulating it from any military reactions from Egypt and Syria.[60] Its timing was crucial, as some journalists in Amman were predicting the revolutionary end by late April: "many a prudent courtier, up on the royal hill, packed himself an overnight bag or memorized a precautionary radical slogan."[61]

In fiscal terms, the United States resolved the crisis. Days after Hussein declared martial law, the Eisenhower administration authorized a $10 million emergency grant to address the near bankruptcy of the government. In June, the United States cleared another $10 million grant for the Jordanian spending budget, with the Pentagon noting that any delay in such aid transfers could result in the kingdom's financial collapse.[62] In a year when the Jordanian state collected only $27.6 million in domestic revenues but spent nearly $37 million on internal policing and the military, such cash infusions were manna. Among other uses, they allowed for the payment of salaries to most civil and military employees.[63] The regime also began receiving American weaponry in order to boost its basic capacity to police society. During that same summer of 1957, the Eisenhower administration announced an initial $10 million arms grant consisting of firearms, spares, and light equipment so that the Jordanian army could plug any immediate material shortages and maintain readiness for deployment given the state of emergency.[64]

Here, the U.S.-Jordanian cliency relationship began. The logic of geopolitical intervention reflected the same Cold War mentality that produced the Iranian operation years earlier. Until the mid-1950s, the United States had only modest ties with Jordan, providing several million dollars in technical assistance, educational support, and refugee services per year. Jordan otherwise had little inherent value apart from its proximity to Israel and the Trans-Arabian Pipeline running through its territory. By 1956, however, CIA officers in Syria and Lebanon had convinced policy principals in Washington that King Hussein's survival was vital to countering Nasser and the forces of Arab Nationalism.[65] Several worked directly for the king, who lacked his own espionage service, by providing intelligence about the Zerqa mutiny and other suspected plots involving opposition elements.[66] Indeed, it was through CIA operatives that Hussein contacted Eisenhower before the April blitz in order to confirm the promise of American support.[67]

New fears about Arab Nationalism fed off of two realities. The first was Britain's fast-fading imperial profile in the Middle East. The dissolution of the Anglo-Jordanian Treaty was the latest in a series of regional setbacks for London that included the 1948 Palestinian partition, the 1951 Mossadegh interlude, and the 1956 Suez War; the 1958 July Revolution in Iraq would extinguish another of London's client states. Expectations were building that the United States would take Britain's place as the paramount power in the region.

The second was the perceived threat of Soviet domination, which reflected early Cold War thinking. Recent events within the Arab world further deepened suspicions that, without continued American interventions, the regional balance of power would soon tilt away from the West. In late 1955, Moscow directed a $250 million weaponry sale from Czechoslovakia to Egypt, thereby breaking the Western arms trade monopoly in the region, and in November 1956 signed another pact of assistance with Syria.[68] Sectarian tensions rumbled through neighboring Lebanon as well, unsettling pro-Western president Camille Chamoun. For some in the Eisenhower White House, the nightmare was taking shape: unchecked, within years the Soviets would sweep into the Arab world, linking up with local communist parties and exploiting Arab Nationalism to mastermind more revolutionary coups and grab the oil-rich Gulf.[69] Further, unlike the West the Soviets carried no colonial baggage from past overseas imperialism, nor did it suffer any guilt by association with Israel. The Arab Nationalist regimes would *choose* to become Soviet clients. "Moscow did not gate-crash," warned one analyst; "it was invited."[70]

Such trepidation came more from paranoia than fact. Soviet influence had indeed spread since the early 1950s, but Moscow's interest in the region was far more modest than often assumed.[71] It saw in Arab Nationalist regimes potential clients to counter Western ascendancy in the eastern Mediterranean but did not envision either territorial annexations or ideological conquests through the spread of communism. Still, the United States decided that "moderate" states like Jordan would be the firebreak to halt the spread of Soviet and Arab Nationalist influence. In March 1957, Congress authorized up to $200 million in aid as well as military protection to any Arab state that acknowledged the threat of communism—that is, ones that aligned against the Soviet Union and leftist-nationalist opposition, and turned toward the West. Under this Eisenhower Doctrine, elected governments like those of Al-Nabulsi became threats to American national security.

The United States expected few concessions from its new client state. It did not need territorial concessions for basing purposes, as its vast naval capabilities and proximity of Turkish NATO facilities provided alternate means to moving military forces into the region. It needed little economically, as Jordan represented a tiny market that produced few exports of value. Still, as in many other client states, the U.S. government engaged in "donor recycling," in which many development projects disbursed through USAID also required the involvement (and thus rewarding) of private American firms. This was especially prevalent regarding aid given to improve transportation, water, and communications infrastructure, where USAID and its partners assumed considerable responsibility in upgrading these public goods.[72]

Washington's preference lay elsewhere. The Eisenhower and future presidential administrations wanted the regime to simply exist—to preserve King Hussein's rule in Jordan, a strategically located country where American interests regarding oil, ideology, and Israel all intersected.[73] In return, they expected Jordanian foreign policy to align unambiguously toward the West. The king did not disappoint, announcing after April 1957 that the recent troubles had all been the responsibility of international communism and its followers, a broad category that included any actor affiliated with the Soviet Union and Arab Nationalism.[74] During his 1959 visit to the United States, he further proclaimed that the Hashemites were not only descendants of the Prophet but also the Muslim leaders best placed to "save Islam in general and the Near East in particular from communism."[75] Jordanian-Soviet relations, by contrast, were tenuous at best. Though they maintained formal diplomatic ties, Moscow's support for Egypt, Syria, and now the postcoup regime of Iraq meant that the two states would seldom cooperate outside of commercial and educational issues.[76]

COMMUNAL TENSIONS AND AMERICAN SUBSIDIES

Despite having demolished its opposition by 1958, the Jordanian regime saw an uncertain future. Some within the palace group still clamored for the resolution of the Palestinian question through the grand Hashemite dream of a pan-Arab state. By the late 1950s, however, regional tensions from what Malcolm Kerr called the "Arab Cold War" muddied this ambition, with Arab Nationalist regimes like Egypt and Syria aligned against pro-Western clients like Jordan and Saudi Arabia.[77] That so many leading oppositionists were West Bank Palestinians also stirred unease, one that dueled with prior optimism for national unity. That some Transjordanians had led the Jordanian National Movement, among them the Free Officers and leftists, was conveniently forgotten. So too was the permeability of the communal divide, as a decade of intermarriage, common schooling, and working-class solidarity encouraged social integration.[78] What emerged after 1957, hence, was gradual abandonment of the earlier vision for a unified Jordan. In its place was a new discourse driven by Transjordanian fears of marginalization should Palestinians attain economic and political influence.

Such imagined fears soon appeared, albeit quietly. Some tribal sheikhs began communicating to the palace their belief that Palestinians, now deemed "newcomers," held responsibility for the recent troubles, either by association with parties and unions or openness to Egyptian and Syrian provocation.[79] Their antipathy to urban opposition already was no secret. Bani Sakhr, for instance, had frequently evinced their loyalty to Hashemite rule, going so far as to march thousands of tribesmen to Amman during the crisis.[80] In his memoirs, Glubb Pasha recounted how "ninety per cent" of Transjordanians living in tribal areas had denounced political parties and opposition ideologies.[81] Within Amman, now under martial statute, strict censorship laws wiped out any vestiges of Palestinian nationalism.

Further, it became dangerous to even mention Al-Kayan Al-Filastini, the Palestinian entity, in public, since that implied a framework for an independent Palestinian state rather than accepting accommodations within the Jordanian state. Those accommodations were now seen as temporary: the monarchy constantly backed UN proposals to resolve the Palestinian dilemma that involved the relocation of most refugees in the East Bank back across the Jordan River. Cabinet appointments continued to be dominated by Transjordanian names, including Circassians and Christians; few efforts were made for greater Palestinian integration. Though Palestinians were occasionally promoted to the cabinet, they had no access to the sovereignty portfolios, in particular the Ministries of Interior, Information, and Foreign Affairs, much less the premiership itself.[82] By the early 1960s, prominent politicians like Wasfi Al-Tall were no longer shy about their abandonment of the ideal for a unified kingdom and vocalized their preference instead for the subordination of Palestinian interests within Jordan.[83]

Communal tensions were magnified by the regional context. In July 1958, the Iraqi revolution shocked Amman by replacing its own Hashemite monarchy with a military regime aligned with Arab Nationalism. This tripped rumors that the United Arab Republic, the federation of Egypt and Syria formed in 1958, was now intent on toppling Hussein.[84] In response, Britain scraped up the resources to dispatch several thousand paratroopers to Jordan. Though just an ostentatious show intended to shore up morale, it was facilitated by U.S. assistance. The British move was conducted in tandem with the American intervention in Lebanon in support of the embattled President Chamoun. American jets escorted British transports through Israeli airspace and later staged aerial maneuvers over Jordan in a display of coercive might. U.S.-Jordanian ties thickened even further in 1959, when the king and his most important lieutenants—the prime minister, the joint chief of staff for the military, and palace officials—visited Washington, beginning an annual pilgrimage designed to reinforce the bilateral relationship, discuss regional security threats and the issue of Israel, and review the latest economic aid and military assistance requests.[85]

On the external front, rival regimes continued to harangue Hussein. The UAR devised several coups and assassinations in Jordan during 1959 and 1960; though one bombing killed Hazzaʿ Al-Majali, Jordanian intelligence managed to foil others, including those with Palestinian elements. Further, Palestinian oppositionists expelled by the crackdown, such as ʿAbdullah Al-Rimawi and Kamal Nasser, continued their activism abroad, creating the Jordanian Revolutionary Council in Damascus dedicated to overthrowing the Hashemite monarchy.[86] The UAR also launched media offensives, portraying the king as a Western stooge and calling for Jordanians to revolt.[87] In April 1963, student demonstrations in Amman and Jerusalem broke out in support of a proposed federal union between Iraq, Syria, and Egypt. The potential for turmoil was enough to make the nervous palace reenact martial law.[88] Rising tensions with Israel and rumors of another Nasserist coup plot compelled Washington to send the Sixth Fleet to the eastern Mediterranean once more, a minatory maneuver that reassured Hussein of U.S. support.

As fear began taking reconfiguring coalitional politics, the Jordanian regime remained reliant upon outside assistance. It became a "semirentier" state, reallocating its foreign aid from outside donors into domestic policies and institutions intended to benefit its Transjordanian base.[89] Though European countries gave some development aid, besides the UNRWA aid earmarked for Palestinian refugees, the United States contributed by far the most fungible resources in terms of budgetary support and development assistance. By relieving the burden of military spending and providing injections of foreign capital for economic development, Washington enabled the regime to chronically overspend. Figure 7.1 shows this impact: during the period from 1958 to 1967, on average Jordan annually

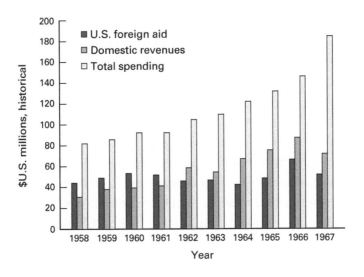

FIGURE 7.1   U.S. foreign aid and domestic revenues in Jordan, 1958–1967

Note: U.S. foreign aid includes grants and loans.

Sources: USAID (serial); Central Bank of Jordan (serial)

collected $50 million of American aid versus $55 million in domestic revenues. Not until 1962 did domestic revenues outpace U.S. aid. In addition to budgetary grants, technical and humanitarian assistance also arrived. Whereas the former meant large-scale upgrades to Jordan's dilapidated infrastructure, the latter meant food. In the late 1950s, a severe drought depressed agricultural yields. American agricultural aid compensated for this adversity, with large wheat shipments ensuring that bread prices remained affordable. From 1958 to 1961, the United States donated over $43 million of food assistance in this manner. Some of these foods were diverted by regime officials for sale or distribution to merchant retailers and tribal leaders. One diplomat recalled how some Jordanian politicos jokingly referred to the U.S. ambassador as Santa Claus given Washington's perceived generosity.[90]

Jordan's coercive apparatus also expanded in ways that tightened the tribal-state compact. In the years between 1958 and 1967 the United States provided $80 million in coercive assistance, compared with $420 million in economic aid. Such help came through not only small-scale arms grants but also indirect financing to help acquire modern British aircraft and vehicles.[91] Another purpose was training, as Jordanian officers enrolled in various American training programs. In 1965, the Johnson administration agreed to sell advanced heavy weaponry requested by Hussein, including fighter jets and battle tanks. Though objections from Israel interrupted the transfer of aircraft, the United States began providing the most advanced tanks Jordan had ever acquired on a part-credit, part-cash basis.[92] The greatest impact flowed from the economic portfolio, as U.S. budgetary and developmental assistance enabled the regime to stay afloat while still spending immensely on its military and police. Table 7.1 outlines this

TABLE 7.1

JORDAN'S COERCIVE COMMITMENTS, 1958–1967 (IN $U.S. MILLIONS, HISTORICAL)

	SECURITY SPENDING*	TOTAL SPENDING	SECURITY SPENDING AS PERCENTAGE OF TOTAL SPENDING	MILITARY MANPOWER
1958	46.5	82.1	56.6	23,000
1959	50.4	86	58.6	
1960	51.5	92	56	
1961	52.4	92.3	56.7	36,500
1962	53.5	105.1	50.9	
1963	58.8	110.2	53.4	
1964	60.5	122.1	49.5	
1965	62.2	131.6	47.3	45,000
1966	47.3	146.5	32.3	
1967	78.7	185.2	42.5	55,000

*Includes expenditures on military and Public Security Directorate, but not General Intelligence Directorate figures, which remain undisclosed.

Sources: Hurewitz (1982); Central Bank of Jordan (serial).

commitment. Military and police spending not only increased almost every year, but such expenditures usually consumed over half the budget.

This had two domestic implications after 1957. First, the army remained a crucial economic institution for many tribal communities, with the Bedouin Bani Sakhr and seminomadic Bani Hassan becoming the most represented confederations on its payroll. Up to 70 percent of the rural populace depended upon the salaries, housing, food, education, and medical care provided to personnel and families.[93] King Hussein also satisfied senior officer requests for bigger budgets and more weaponry, giving them input into discussions about defense priorities.[94] Sensitivity to tribal politics also characterized the custom of distributing command positions and senior promotions on the basis of tribal affiliation (and to a lesser degree, religion), which balanced out privileges.[95] Finally, Palestinians continued to be segregated from major fighting units. In 1965, the regime dissolved the Palestinian National Guard and integrated a third of its members—nearly ten thousand Palestinians—into the army. However, most elite units and officer positions were still dominated by Bedouin. Many Palestinian personnel were funneled to unarmed technical units, and led by Transjordanian officers who often doubted their loyalty.[96]

Second, the regime aimed its harshest repressive measures at areas with the highest concentrations of Palestinians—urban neighborhoods and refugee camps. In July 1958, the Ministry of Interior retooled the civil police as the Public Security Directorate, with expanded policing powers. At the same time, CIA officers provided useful intelligence to the regime, and sometimes much more: from 1957 onward, King Hussein received up to $15,000 in annual cash payments from the local CIA station for his personal use.[97] In 1964, the General Intelligence Directorate (GID), or *mukhabarat*, was created under the stewardship of Muhammad Rasul Al-Kaylani, whose intelligence training in the late 1950s came under American supervision. Recruiting among Transjordanian communities, the mukhabarat exercised untrammeled authority to monitor and eliminate any perceived threat to the monarchy. The GID saw itself as "the guardian, protector, and stronghold" of Hashemite power and saw much of the Palestinian populace as an inherent menace.[98] It also received ample American assistance, not least because Amman had become one of the

CIA's most important stations in the Middle East given the kingdom's strategic location abutting Israel, Syria, and Iraq.[99]

During the 1960s, regional and domestic events aggravated communal tensions, further distancing the monarchy from many Palestinians. On the invitation of Nasser, King Hussein attended the Arab League summit in Cairo in January 1964, which sought to enhance pan-Arab unity. Among other initiatives, that meeting resulted in the establishment of the Palestinian Liberation Organization. Supporting the PLO and its constituent groups, in particular Fatah, was a bold foreign policy gamble for Jordan, one intending to reduce hostilities with regional rivals like Egypt and Syria. However, it put the monarchy in an awkward position at home. Hussein asked the PLO to hold its first legislative congress in Amman, but its leadership refused and insisted on operating from Jerusalem instead. The king eventually conceded, which worried some palace politicians and army officers: it hinted at the possibility that Palestinian citizens would no longer be under the monarchy's sole authority, raising the prospect of a weakened state and dueling sovereignty.[100] If previous years were characterized by dueling interests regarding Palestinian accommodation, now fears of Transjordanian subordination had become prevalent.

The demotion of Palestinian interests became undeniable by the mid-1960s. Whereas Emir ʿAbdullah had celebrated Hashemite stewardship over Jerusalem, by the early 1960s the regime had stopped trumpeting the city's importance. Neither King Hussein nor his lieutenants considered state visits there a priority. Indeed, the only royal edifice planned for Jerusalem was a small palace begun in 1963; it was still unfinished when Israel took the city in the June 1967 war. One tense moment came in January 1963, when Hussein replaced Jerusalem Governor Anwar Nusseibeh, who represented a powerful Palestinian notable family, with a Transjordanian civil servant from Irbid. The dismissal raised local ire, especially when the king visited the city days later with a military escort under orders to shoot any suspected agitators.[101] Gone too were calls to make Jerusalem a second capital by transferring ministries and even parliament there, a refrain repeated during the 1950s. Now, nothing "would detract from the status of Amman" as the epicenter of power.[102] In addition, the regime stymied PLO efforts to attain more organizational autonomy, such as blocking the imposition of a special tax on Palestinians to finance its operations. Periodic dragnets, such as an April 1966 campaign that arrested a hundred suspected dissidents, were motivated not only by antipathy to the old opposition but also the desire to uncover incriminating PLO connections.[103] By January 1967, the regime closed the PLO's Jerusalem office altogether and arrested its staff.

In response, the monarchy promoted its tribal base even further. One institutional change involved the ascension of Bedouin leaders into ministerial positions, an area previously reserved for notables from the more settled families and small tribal clans who had become part of the palace group. Signifying this was the appointment of ʿAkif Al-Fayez, a respected Bani Sakhr leader, as Minister of Agriculture in the first post-April 1957 government. The royal court itself, the Diwan, helped maintain good relations with tribal communities by facilitating elite-level contacts. Not only did the Diwan serve as a parallel government to the official cabinet, it also held a special tribal liaison office that helped the king consult with tribal representatives, resolve rural disputes, and present gifts to key sheikhs.[104]

Another sign of this solidifying Transjordanian compact was the modest incorporation of another actor, the Muslim Brotherhood. Founded during World War II, the Jordanian branch of the Brotherhood had backed King Hussein during the April crisis.[105] It had little enthusiasm for the secular parties of the Jordanian National Movement, particularly since the icon of Arab Nationalism, Gamal ʿAbdel Nasser, had demolished the Brotherhood in Egypt. Then with a mostly Transjordanian membership, the Brotherhood was the only major sociopolitical association to escape the gutting of civil society that followed the 1957 crisis. In the 1960s, through ministerial appointments and royal liaisons, the Brotherhood in Jordan would begin gaining more influence over religious affairs and educational policies.

The fracturing of state institutions extended into the economy. The 1958–1967 period exhibited impressive growth. Jordan's GNP more than doubled from $245 million to over $630 million in this decade, much of it due to the Five-Year Plan launched in 1962.[106] However, though oriented toward national development, many policies exhibited bias in favor of Transjordanian constituencies. The state itself grew to become an employment sponge for East Bank workers and professionals. By 1961, civil service payrolls counted nearly twenty-four thousand employees, or nearly one-quarter of the nonagricultural labor force.[107] Redundancy and inefficiencies within administrative organs, of course, were of little concern. The more than 50 percent doubling of military manpower by 1967 also served to soak up tribal labor, especially those of Bedouin and lower-income backgrounds.

Industrialization also skewed eastward. The Ministry of National Economy, the predecessor to the future Ministry of Industry and Trade, allocated enormous capital to expand the largest public shareholding firms in heavy industries like phosphate mining and petroleum refining. Protected by tax leniency and import barriers, these heavy industries grew by 16 percent annually from 1959 to 1966, providing further enclaves of preferential Transjordanian employment.[108] In total, civil employment, military expansion, and public enterprises helped propel Jordan's economic boom, producing a 4 to 5 percent unemployment rate among the non-refugee (that is, mostly Transjordanian) population by 1966.[109]

Meanwhile, the West Bank received little industrial financing and remained dependent upon subsistence agriculture and tourism. By 1966, the territory accounted for half the national population but contributed just one-third of the GNP. Joel Migdal has argued such institutional policies reflected a deliberate strategy "to prevent the growth of a West Bank infrastructure," one that could facilitate the formation of new opposition or any coherent Palestinian identity separate from Hashemite rule.[110] The government also encouraged Palestinians to migrate to other countries for work, an easy task given that the Interior Ministry and GID controlled the distribution of travel permits.[111] In the decade before the 1967 Arab-Israeli War, between fifteen and fifty thousand Palestinians left every year, most to other Arab countries or the West.[112]

Economic institutions also reflected elite interests, as the wealthiest Transjordanian merchants, now supplemented by Palestinian business-persons, prospered. Working with ministry technocrats, many of these old and new elites invested in state-oriented firms and sat on their gov-

A CONFLICT INTERRUPTED IN JORDAN

erning boards, hence becoming the kingdom's first industrialists.[113] An iconic example rests in the Shoman family, whose patriarch ʿAbdul Hameed Shoman founded Arab Bank in Jerusalem in 1930. After its relocation to Amman in 1948, Arab Bank became one of the region's largest private financial houses through retail banking and commercial loans and by the 1960s helped seed new industries like potash, cement, and food processing. Such state-allied industrialists also worked with the Central Bank and Industrial Development Bank to ensure the regulatory environment would not hinder their commercial interests.[114] Finally, East Bank infrastructure received considerable attention. With the help of USAID, state planners upgraded technical projects begun in the mid-1950s and improved roads, dams, hospitals, and schools throughout the East Bank.[115] By contrast, the economic priority for the West Bank was promoting tourism, which by 1960 had become one of its leading sources of income.[116] Transjordanians also benefited from supposedly "national" projects. For instance, the East Ghor Canal project was an enormous USAID-supported effort to reclaim and maintain fertile land within the Jordan Valley that took place between 1958 and 1967. Through land redistribution and expanded irrigation, the project aimed to create a flourishing community of farmers that could reduce local poverty and make Jordan a more competitive agricultural exporter.[117] Instead, the regime gave much of this new land away as gifts to tribal sheikhs, upon which Palestinian refugees were then brought in to work as sharecroppers. By the 1967 war, these landless tenants farmed over half of all arable estates, producing uncompetitive yields of fruits and vegetables.[118] UNRWA aid, too, was victim of corruption. Though assigned for Palestinian refugees, regime officials siphoned off significant volumes of those payments and materiel for redistribution among their own communities.[119]

All told, by the mid-1960s the Jordanian state was fracturing around a communal split within society. However provoked or invented, fears of communal marginalization to Palestinian interests influenced powerful voices within the monarchy's original East Bank social base, despite the advent of U.S. patronage that rescued the autocracy in April 1957. Despite the defeat of urban opposition groups, many regime elites believed that their autocracy still suffered from insecurity, with threats emanating from both demographic reality and regional pressures. The Hashemite leadership hence had a strong incentive to backtrack from previous efforts to unify the country, and instead deepen coalitional linkages with Transjordanian constituencies through new economic and political institutions that would protect their dominance. Subsidizing this coalitional shift was Washington. After the 1958 July Revolution in Iraq, the United States became the paramount power in the region, with the British sphere of influence contracting to the Persian Gulf and the French mired in Algeria. Jordan became one of Washington's closest client states, a consummate "moderate" Arab ally.

Such evidence runs against narratives of Jordanian politics during this time period that explain the Hashemite monarchy's endurance in two words: King Hussein, whose legions of biographers (and hagiographers) portray as an adaptable, shrewd, and iron-willed survivor. While all regimes reflect the proclivities of their rulers, greater forces in Jordan influenced the coalitional choices and institutional decisions made by the royal autocracy through the mid-1960s — demographic flux, urban mobilization, regional pressures, and U.S. intervention. Like Iran, American support facilitated the continuity of an endangered dictatorship; but unlike Iran, it did not result in that dictatorship dismantling its own social foundations in favor of reliance upon external protection. Communal tensions instead pushed the regime onto a middle-range pathway of cultivating a more selective coalition, one that would soon be tested by civil conflict.

8

RECURRENT TENSIONS AND TENUOUS SURVIVAL UNDER HASHEMITE RULE

I N PREVAILING INTERPRETATIONS of Jordanian history, political rupture between Palestinians and Transjordanians did not occur until after 1970, when the civil war poisoned relations between these two overlapping communities. However, the previous chapter showed that communal relations began degrading far earlier, not long after the United States enabled King Hussein to crack down on urban opposition in April 1957. The regime's shift away from a truly national coalition in favor of bolstering its Transjordanian core gave rise to new economic and political institutions that increasingly excluded Palestinians from the state, a strategy bankrolled by continuing U.S. aid and assistance.

These rising tensions, intensified by the creation of the PLO, would pave the way for the 1970 civil war of Black September, which pitted Palestinian militant groups against the Hashemite regime. The monarchy would barely survive this conflict thanks to the institutionalized loyalty of its Transjordanian base as well as timely American assistance. Afterward, as this chapter illustrates, the regime's formula for survival was to reproduce the familiar, deepening the logic of ethnocratic rule by directly suppressing many Palestinians while protecting key Transjordanian supporters, such as tribal communities. Even political liberalization undertaken in response to the 1989 financial collapse, a crisis that kindled the worst violence since Black September, would not shake this strategy of tenuous survival. The reforms undertaken starting in the 1990s continued to protect Transjordanian constituencies. The United States continued to subsidize this strategy given the magnitude of Jordan to its Middle East grand strategy. Yet, while ethnocratic state-building has enabled the Hashemite monarchy to persist, its survival has been tenuous. The regime has not abandoned its belief that existential threats lurk deeply within society, creating an atmosphere of endemic insecurity that necessitates holding large coercive and political reserves while awaiting the next crisis.

REPRESSION, INSTABILITY, AND DISORDER

By the 1967 Arab-Israeli War, the structure of decision making within the Hashemite regime had coalesced around predictable patterns. Authoritarian power was less centralized than in sultanistic Iran under the shah but more unified than in the dynastic model of Kuwait. Though formally executed by the appointed cabinet government, most major policies emanated from the palace, where various players made their influences known upon King Hussein — the Diwan (royal court), prime minister and other senior cabinet officials, senior military officers, the General Intelligence Directorate (GID), tribal leaders, and trusted family members, such as his brother and Crown Prince Hassan.[1] Given this closed network of mostly Transjordanian elites, only through appointment to a ministry or the Diwan could Palestinian politicians gain access to royal power.

This political framework is crucial in understanding the deterioration of communal relations after 1967 and after the 1970 civil war. When the 1967 Arab-Israeli War began, Jordan counted within its confederal territory over half of the 2.35 million Palestinian Arabs residing in the Middle East. The conflict was a catastrophe for Nasser of Egypt and was the death knell for the pan-Arab basis of the Arab Nationalist movement. Much like the 1948 war, it also transformed Jordan. With the loss of the West Bank, two hundred thousand more refugees entered the East Bank due to Israeli expulsion, such that Palestinians comprised over half of the kingdom's population. Economic damages were crippling. The Israeli occupation of the West Bank meant that Jordan lost a quarter of its cultivable land, most tourism revenues, and substantial productivity—in all, around 40 percent of national economic output.[2] The military took nearly seven thousand casualties and lost its entire air force, most armored units, and much of its artillery. The Johnson administration also sided with Israel and cut off most U.S. aid to its Arab client states, though it assured King Hussein that this would not endanger the kingdom's long-term ties to Washington. Still, the public about-face meant Jordan's economic aid dropped from $45.5 million in 1967 to almost nothing in 1970.

Filling the gap was multilateral Arab aid; at the 1967 Arab League summit in Khartoum, the three countries of Libya, Kuwait, and Saudi Arabia pledged $112 million of annual financial assistance to Jordan. These payments enabled the regime to rebuild its military and recover from economic damages after the war.[3] But this bailout also put the regime in a straitjacket by setting implicit conditions regarding the treatment of Palestinian interests. King Hussein had to maintain an official stance of support for the Palestinian cause—and thus allow the PLO to operate freely, despite the antipathy of many Transjordanian elites that had accumulated since 1957. For instance, Wasfi Al-Tall and other politicians pronounced the loss of the West Bank as a territorial defeat but also a cultural and political gain for Jordan, since now all the kingdom's resources could focus upon the East Bank.[4] Still, the regime allowed Palestinian nationalists to conduct activities once more within the kingdom, which raised another flashpoint of conflict. When PLO members like Yasir ʿArafat's Fatah organization relocated to Amman, they also brought with them the *fidaʾiyin*, their armed wings. These commandos had created some headaches before; in November 1966, for instance, they clashed with Israeli troops in the West Bank village of Al-Samuʿ, which forced the Jordanian army to intervene.[5] At this point, however, they began launching guerilla strikes into Israel from the East Bank itself. From the June 1967 ceasefire through 1968, Israel reported 920 acts of violence from Jordan-based commandos.[6] Escalation was inevitable: because most attacks provoked Israeli retaliation, the Jordanian army was repeatedly drawn into skirmishes to defend East Bank areas against Israeli forces.

No matter how sympathetic to the Palestinian cause that King Hussein appeared to Jordan's aid donors, it became clear that the fida'iyin were disrupting the regime's domestic authority. When the Jordanian army began halting their incursions into Israel in 1968, the fida'iyin moved their main bases to Amman. The new Popular Front for the Liberation of Palestine emerged and soon competed with Fatah for influence. A surfeit of smaller outfits formed, so that by September 1970 ten fida'iyin organizations operated in the East Bank, each with their own network of training camps and educational centers. They steadily eroded legal order; among other activities, they intimidated the police, extracted fines, arrested residents, and confiscated property.[7] Army units could not respond despite often being provoked, an order that left many Bedouin troops smoldering. An apocryphal story holds that, during one royal inspection by King Hussein, Transjordanian officers fluttered brassieres from the antennas of their tanks to express their frustrations.[8] The fida'iyin also began targeting agents of the state itself. In September 1967, Fatah lambasted the GID and its director, Muhammad Al-Kaylani, for their discouraging of fida'iyin raids into Israel and ominously called for the liquidation of such "collaborators."[9]

Some historical accounts find that because the fida'iyin came from *outside* Jordan, these domestic troubles had little to do with Palestinians *within* the kingdom.[10] However, these organizations could not have operated effectively without local support. The fida'iyin never represented all Palestinians, but neither were they rebels operating in hostile territory. While the most affluent Palestinian businessmen, like their Transjordanian counterparts, remained on the political sidelines, the larger middle-class stratum of salaried Palestinians was split. Many did not take sides. Other households, however, did sympathize with their cause and so contributed funds and other materiel to various PLO factions.[11] The 1969 national conference for the General Union of Palestinian Students in Amman also made clear that strong sympathetic sentiments swirled throughout many schools and universities.

Further, many refugee camps became strongholds of fida'iyin activity. Hundreds of thousands of Palestinians lived in these neglected areas, and though not all residents became involved, those who did donated important resources.[12] Certain neighborhoods served as residences for fida'yin, arms and ammunition caches, and safe zones to keep hostages and captives.[13] Another resource was manpower, which along with some Transjordanian volunteers accounted for the rapid growth of the fida'iyin. By September 1970, fida'iyin groups could muster twenty-five thousand armed fighters and seventy-five thousand civilian affiliates, an immense increase from the ten thousand total membership estimated two years earlier.[14] Indeed, so synonymous had the camps become with lawlessness and fida'iyin activity that by 1969 Wasfi Al-Tall and other officials suggested bulldozing them and resettling the refugees elsewhere.[15]

The fida'iyin also reached out for grassroots support, not just among Palestinians but also the remnants of the Jordanian National Movement. They made various ideological appeals along leftist lines, including continuing the promise of Jordanian democracy that suffocated in 1957.[16] The national labor confederation, the GFJTU, was dominated by Palestinian membership and articulated solidarity with the cause. Taking advantage of this brief opening, some leftist and Arab Nationalist activists emerged from underground to announce a new opposition current in 1967, Al-Tajammu' Al-Watani (National Gathering).[17]

Finally, the regime's own responses suggest that Palestinian commando groups, far from being a nuisance, represented a major threat to power given their social foundations. For instance, by 1968, hardliners like Sharif Nasser bin Jamil, King Hussein's uncle and army chief, had resorted to creating "shadow" fida'iyin groups that, on the army and GID payroll, would abuse Palestinians in Amman in order to corrode local support for the real fida'yin.[18] In 1969, the regime also quickened the pace of its military rebuilding program by raising recruitment salaries and increasing promotion opportunities for tribal personnel.[19] By then, the United States urged Hussein to begin checking fida'iyin activities, not least because of rowdy Palestinian demonstrations around the U.S.

Embassy that transpired in August 1969, which dispersed only when Jordanian soldiers threatened to open fire.

THE CIVIL WAR OF BLACK SEPTEMBER

The creation of the fida'iyin "state within a state" paved the way for civil war. By the spring of 1970, a palpable sense of disorder pervaded the streets of Amman. In April, several hundred students and fida'iyin members marched to prevent a controversial visit by senior American official Joseph Sisco, storming the U.S. Embassy and forcing the withdrawal of Ambassador Harrison Symmes soon after.[20] Now, some in the PLO and other factions began calling for the deposal of King Hussein and the monarchy altogether.[21] As they could not retake the West Bank given their current strength, fida'iyin leaders reasoned, the East Bank could be a major staging ground for the national movement to gain more adherents and resources. While Jordan was not a surrogate Palestinian state, the road to Jerusalem nonetheless ran through Amman.

For their part, Hussein and his palace group understood that the fida'iyin activities had become intolerable. In June 1970, Yasir 'Arafat told an American reporter that Fatah now controlled Amman, which state officials saw as a mockery of Hashemite authority. Regime hardliners like Al-Tall and Sharif Nasser called for their complete eradication. The palace, however, was hamstrung by two uncertainties. First, King Hussein considered his bordering rival states of Syria and Iraq as dangerous as Palestinian commandos at home. Given the friction with the United States caused by Jordan's participation in the 1967 war, the king harbored some uncertainty whether Washington would intervene to prevent the Syrian and Iraqi militaries from interfering in any domestic showdown with the fida'iyin.[22]

Second, some advisers to the king feared not just fida'iyin resistance but wider backlash within the Palestinian refugee camps and certain Palestinian neighborhoods in the cities if the monarchy ordered any crackdown.[23] As a result, the king adopted a cautiously conciliatory tone early on. For instance, when GID chief Al-Kaylani enacted harsh new security measures in February 1970, Palestinian leaders successfully lobbied for his sacking. A failed assassination attempt on Hussein followed in June, along with five days of street battles between fida'iyin and army units that left almost two hundred dead.[24] Yet Hussein continued to accede to fida'iyin demands to dismiss hardliners with anti-Palestinian views, including not only Sharif Nasser but another royal relative within the army's commanding ranks, Zeid bin Shakir.

The civil war transpired in September, which began with another assassination attempt against the king and further outbursts of street fighting. The degradation of central authority became irrefutable with the Dawson's Field hijacking incident, followed by a general strike declared by the GJFTU on September 14th. Only at this moment did King Hussein and his confidantes—among them Al-Tall, Sharif Nasser, Bin Shaker, and Diwan Chief Zeid Al-Rifaʿi—decide to clamp down with force. On September 16th, the regime declared martial law, and the army soon besieged fida'iyin bases in major cities as well as Palestinian refugee camps. An unexpected twist came from the north, when Syrian tanks crossed the border to support the commandos. Jordanian forces repelled the incursion, however, and within a week had decimated most local resistance. Fida'iyin areas, including refugee camps and populated neighborhoods in cities, came under intense bombardment, resulting in mass civilian casualties.[25] After a week of intense urban fighting, the Palestinian Red Crescent estimated 3,650 dead and 11,500 wounded, almost all of them Palestinian.[26] In July 1971, the army eliminated the last fida'iyin enclaves in the north. By then, the regime claimed to hold over twenty thousand Palestinian detainees, and the Palestinian national groups no longer had any political presence.[27]

The Hashemite regime's survival stemmed from its Transjordanian base and, to a lesser extent, its cliency ties with the United States. The latter has historically garnered the most attention. When the fighting began in mid-September, the United States deployed an array of "low-key diplomatic and military measures" designed to boost Jordanian morale.[28] This included implying retaliation against Syria and Iraq if they intervened by readying troops at overseas bases and repositioning Sixth Fleet warships closer to Lebanon.[29] When such minatory tactics failed to deter Syria, the Nixon White House pressed Israel to intercede under the premise that it was better off with the Hashemite autocracy than a Palestinian commando state on its eastern flank. It promised economic aid, arms transfers, and protection against Egyptian and Soviet retaliation, which the Israeli government accepted.[30] Israeli aircraft then undertook warning flights over Syrian forces while Israeli troops mobilized on the nearby occupied Golan Heights; plans for more direct intervention came to naught, however, as the conflict tilted in Jordanian favor. Within days, the Jordanian air force had destroyed a Syrian tank column and ended the northern threat, allowing the army to continue assaulting fida'iyin in the cities. In December 1970, the Nixon administration also authorized emergency arms shipments to replenish the Jordanian army's exhausted stocks. Among the transferred items were tanks, spare parts, and sixteen thousand new M16 automatic rifles—the last of which Hussein insisted on, arguing that his troops were unprepared for the AK-47s carried by the fida'iyin.[31]

As in the 1957 crisis, strategic interests underlay the provision of U.S. support to its client state. Policy principals, particularly Secretary of State Henry Kissinger, argued that the collapse of Hussein's rule would not only endanger Israel but also hurt American standing far outside the region by coming across as a perceived Soviet victory.[32] They also believed that a fida'iyin triumph over a U.S.-backed client would diminish American leverage in other arenas of superpower engagement, such as the SALT I talks and the Vietnam War.[33] As in past interventions, such opinions were highly tinged by the urgency of recent regional crises. By Black September, the British had all but conceded their former imperial position, as they were finalizing their withdrawal from the Gulf and becoming a non-factor in regional affairs.[34] Coming after the most recent Arab-Israeli war, coups in Iraq, Sudan, and Libya during 1968 and 1969 also reinforced the perception of regional volatility and danger. During the summer of 1970, the Jordanian conflict coincided with two Soviet moves elsewhere. The first was the consolidation of the Marxist regime in South Yemen, which

benefited from Soviet patronage. The second was the War of Attrition between Egypt and Israel, a series of clashes that saw the number of Soviet
"advisers" in Egypt swell to twenty thousand.[35] Given this regional context, any prospective Soviet entry into Jordan through its client states like
Syria or on invitation from a triumphant fida'iyin government was anathema. In fact, two years earlier in 1968 the Johnson administration had resumed its tank and aircraft sales to Amman despite stringent Israeli objections, out of concern that King Hussein might seek arms from Moscow.[36]

While the United States counteracted a hostile regional environment,
it is important to not overplay its influence and ignore the regime's coalitional constituencies at home. The king proceeded throughout the
heaviest fighting in September with the assumption that the United States
would *not* intervene militarily. Though CIA personnel relayed Washington's efforts to protect Jordan from external attack, the Nixon administration never promised to provide direct coercive support, such as airlifting
troops or bombing fida'iyin bases.[37] Western media outlets also did little
to shore up the image of a sinking autocracy; at one point, *Newsweek* erro-
neously reported the government had surrendered to the fida'iyin.[38] Progress in the field until the end of September was inconsistent, with the entire northern city of Irbid at one point being declared a "liberated" zone
by the commandos. Several times, Hussein and his inner circle considered
the option of a humiliating truce to avoid total defeat. By mid-September,
the GID was shredding numerous files to cover its tracks as well, given the
possibility of the regime's overthrow.[39]

Yet institutionalized ties of Transjordanian support allowed the regime
to ultimately prevail over the fida'iyin. Like all civil wars, communal
boundaries blurred during Black September. Thousands of Palestinians
served in the Jordanian army, albeit mostly in noncombat units, while the
fida'iyin counted among their ranks numerous Transjordanian volunteers,
including veterans of the old Jordanian National Movement.[40] Nonetheless, the success of the operation partly stemmed from the cohesion of the
Bedouin-dominated army. The tribal composition of frontline units made
them effective in combat, with just a handful of defections among the officer corps and the rank and file.[41] Other Transjordanian actors mobilized

support for King Hussein as well. The Muslim Brotherhood included few Palestinians in its ranks at the time, and its spokespersons rejected the appeal of the fida'iyin groups, even if it agreed with the underlying call to resist Israel.[42]

In addition, commando entreaties failed to gain traction in many Transjordanian communities. Throughout the summer of 1970, sheikhs from the Bani Sakhr tribes, the 'Adwan confederation, and several smaller groupings held congresses in rural areas to discuss the Palestinian "problem" and reiterate their desire to eject the fida'iyin.[43] Though such meetings trafficked in discourse bordering on xenophobic racism, they demonstrated how the fida'iyin never made substantial inroads into most tribal communities that lay outside urban areas. Across the rural south, for instance, townspeople and police were able to disarm and defeat some local fida'iyin units well before military operations began.[44]

This recalcitrant autocracy would not have survived had it suffered massive defections from its social base and political institutions. The coalitional calculus during Black September was costly but, if sheer survival was the yardstick of achievement, successful: in the simplifying eyes of royal observers, reliable Transjordanian defenders had destroyed unruly opposition drawing upon the Palestinian majority, with some help from Washington. This provoked an unprecedented degree of nationalistic prejudice against Palestinians in the aftermath of the civil war and pushed the Jordanian state to become even more ethnocratic and segmented during the 1970s and 1980s—again, with some moderate assistance from the United States.

DEEPENING ETHNOCRACY WITH U.S. SUPPORT, 1971–1980

With Black September, the Hashemite regime reaped what it had begun sowing more than a decade earlier. Even so, neither King Hussein nor other decision makers within the palace felt it urgent to reverse their approach and begin a fresh course of action to reach out and incorporate Palestinian segments into state institutions. Doing so would risk alienating Transjordanian supporters who associated Hashemite rule with protection; there was little incentive to entertain drastic changes given the very fact that the regime had weathered yet another storm. However, neither could it expel the Palestinians altogether from Jordan. Most were citizens and many had resided in the kingdom for decades. Expelling them would incur the vitriol of other Arab states given Hussein's prior commitments to the Palestinian cause. The only pathway left was to make East Bank constituencies even more dependent upon the monarchy, ensuring their support during any future crisis.

The monarchy understood that Transjordanian loyalty was never unconditional: Bedouin sheikhs, established families, merchant elites, religious leaders—these voices all could find shortcomings with their king. Coalitional accountability to these groups meant hearing not only affirmations but also being open to their demands, grievances, and objections within the framework of existing state institutions. The royal wager, however, was that fear of "Palestinization" would discourage any truly threatening opposition from coalescing within Transjordanian communities, especially tribal constituencies. Indeed, from 1971 onward, the regime would encourage key political voices to look upon Black September and realize that "the problem was not merely the fedayeen organizations, but rather the whole of the [Palestinian] population in the East Bank."[45]

The next two decades of Jordanian political development thus deepened the cleaved coalition and fractured state-building process begun earlier, with the regime manipulating its economic and political institutions to strengthen ties with East Bank supporters. While the Palestinian business elite would continue working with Transjordanian capital in exercising wide economic influence, most other Palestinians would remain on the margins of a burgeoning state—one defined by a renewed discourse of Transjordanian nationalism on the political side and an economy driven by a public sector designed to primarily benefit East Bankers.

External capital from the United States in the early 1970s and later Arab donors helped finance these decades of ethnocratic deepening. Black September caused considerable economic harm, not only from the physical destruction of the fighting but also because Libya and Kuwait halted their half of the $112 million annual Khartoum payments in protest of the violence against Palestinians.[46] For the next decade, the United States would plug this gap by revitalizing its fiscal and coercive aid flows to the kingdom, a renewed stance motivated by old anti-Soviet concerns in the region as well as recognition that the kingdom's stability was crucial to Israel's security. U.S. economic aid jumped from almost nothing in 1970 to nearly $60 million in 1972. From that point through 1980, it would average close to $70 million per year, equivalent to a quarter of the Jordanian government's domestic revenues. Jordan's lack of participation during the 1973 Arab-Israeli War allowed for the uninterrupted flow of these American aid dollars. As in the past, much consisted of unrequited cash grants that meant the difference between solvency and bust for the regime's fiscal planners. During one U.S. visit, King Hussein and Prime Minister Zeid Al-Rifaʿi highlighted this dependence by reminding Kissinger that interrupting even a $10 million tranche of scheduled budgetary aid would force them to "declare bankruptcy" within a single quarter.[47] Other American assistance given included numerous infrastructural and technical projects, as well as agricultural assistance in the form of wheat transfers to ensure low bread prices.

U.S. assistance was soon overtaken by pan-Arab aid, which came in two waves. The first came with the 1974 Arab League summit in Rabat, when King Hussein extracted a promise of $300 million in annual assistance from Saudi Arabia, Kuwait, and other oil exporters in return for recognizing the PLO as the sole legitimate representative of the Palestinian people—a controversial move in itself, since that mandate also theoretically applied to the millions of Palestinians residing within the kingdom as Jordanian citizens. The 1978 Arab League meeting in Baghdad went further; by rejecting the Camp David peace process between Egypt and Israel, Jordan secured a promise of $1.25 billion in annual financial support, mostly from the Gulf states like Kuwait and Saudi Arabia riding high on record oil prices.[48] As figure 8.1 shows, by 1979 foreign aid outpaced domestic revenues by nearly two to one, allowing for record government expenditures. Further, because Arab aid usually consisted of outright grants rather than conditional loans, Jordan's Central Bank could treat

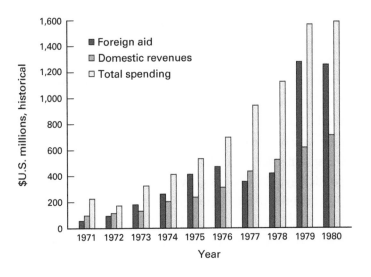

FIGURE 8.1 Recovering Jordan, 1971–1980

Note: Foreign aid includes grants and loans from the United States and European and Arab states.

Sources: World Bank (serial); Central Bank of Jordan (serial)

these monies as fungible cash going straight to the treasury, much like U.S. budgetary aid grants.[49] Various regime lieutenants also skimmed considerable funds from these payments for their own use, often requiring the Central Bank to invent bogus accounts and funds to obscure this corruption.[50] Few noticed: in the end, the kingdom was flooded by external financing, which allowed for pinnacle economic growth stimulated by massive public spending. During the decade from 1971 to 1980, the GDP soared from $640 million to nearly $4 billion.

The state, as well as related institutions like public enterprises, remained the largest employer of Transjordanian labor. Natural population growth and increased sedentarization of the Bedouin produced greater demand for public employment. With the loss of pastoral and agricultural income, tribal families began generating a rising supply of unskilled and semiskilled workers needing secure jobs and pensions.[51] State-owned heavy industries grew to absorb some of these workers, and as a secondary goal produce products for exports like phosphates and cement.[52] Developmental policies also targeted rural areas through the extension of physical infrastructure and creation of light industries like textiles and food processing. As one indicator of such investments from above, annual rates of gross fixed capital formation rose dramatically from just $71 million in 1970 to nearly $1.4 billion by 1980.

The same logic of economic protection drove the expansion of the civil service and state agencies, which kept many East Bank professionals tethered to public payrolls. Counting civil jobs, government firms, and the military, by 1975 the public sector employed half the nonrefugee labor force of 328,000.[53] That proportion held for the next decade, such that by the late 1980s nearly 75 percent of the entire Transjordanian workforce received a public salary in some form.[54] As a result, after military and security spending, the second largest expenditure within the national budget—typically, a quarter or more—went to public salaries and pensions. Periodic salary increases, price controls over consumer products, and subsidized housing further defrayed living costs.[55]

Protecting the growing number of Transjordanian households of modest means, however, came at the cost of constraining the interests of the old merchant elite, who saw their political status slowly ebb. By the early 1970s, Palestinians had displaced Transjordanians as the predominant group represented on the Amman Chamber of Commerce (ACC). More than this, however, a split emerged between the old guard and a newer class of entrepreneurial retailers, traders, and investors who had entered the commercial stratosphere during the halcyon decade of the 1970s, when the availability of state financing expanded the boundaries of business.[56] Between 1970 and 1982 the number of registered companies rose from 2,305 to 12,439, while from 1976 to 1980, 670 medium-sized private firms acquired new operating licenses from the state.[57] That generational gap between established wealth and new money created internal bickering that weakened the organizational cohesion of the ACC, which reduced its influence upon state policies.

As a result, the ACC was unable to prevent the formation of the Ministry of Supply in 1974, which gave the government unprecedented regulatory control. The ministry instituted price controls for fuel, food, and other basic necessities, creating a baseline level of affordability for many East Bank families dependent upon modest civil and military salaries. Among other consequences, such state interventionism reduced profits for private suppliers and cut other merchant distributors out of the import chain.[58] The Ministry of Commerce and Industry in 1976 also bypassed the ACC in removing restrictions on foreign businesses operating in Jordan such as customs fees, further eroding the protectionism that enabled earlier generations of the wealthy merchant families to prosper.

This was not a frontal assault upon the coalitional alliance with Palestinian and Transjordanian business elites so much as a necessary tradeoff in order to widen protections for other East Bankers. The merchants could still amass large profits within areas of the economy not monopolized by the state, in particular banking and retail.[59] Further, not all economic policies aligned against them. For instance, the Central Bank raised the exchange rate of the Jordanian dinar in 1973 and 1978, a deliberate overvaluing that favored import consumption—and hence profited the old commercial houses that dominated trade in finished products, luxury items, and capital goods—all areas where planning ministries such as the Ministry of Supply had little say.[60]

THE SCOPE OF ECONOMIC AND POLITICAL EXCLUSION

In contrast to these institutional protections for Transjordanians, citizens of Palestinian descent faced a greater degree of exclusion. Following Black September, Wasfi Al-Tall led efforts to uproot hundreds of Palestinian civil servants from their positions, a process justified by new Transjordanian nationalists as *ardanna*, or Jordanization.[61] However constructed before, now the Palestinian-Transjordanian divide was reproduced with everyday economic and political practices. New forms of systematic discrimination all but foreclosed most Palestinians from gaining a foothold within the state's administrative echelons. Well-educated

Palestinians from bourgeois backgrounds often had a far more difficult time obtaining civil service appointments than did lesser qualified East Bankers, especially those whose relatives and tribal kin already worked in the public sector or within security institutions. This hardened the implicit division of labor within the national political economy, one that still largely defines Jordan today. While Palestinian wage-earners and professionals dominated the private sector, Transjordanians operated the public sector.[62]

One implication was that Palestinians continued to study and work abroad, which the GID and Interior Ministry expedited since they controlled the distribution of labor permits and exit visas. During the 1970s, around 200,000 Palestinians left to work in the affluent oil-based Gulf economies, from where they remitted billions of dollars back to their families. At its peak in 1984, Jordan received $1.24 billion in remittances, equivalent to 67 percent of its export earnings. Those remittances were vital in supplementing household incomes in urban areas like Amman, as well as helping to circulate fresh currency within banks and money houses.[63] For those who stayed in Jordan, however, political restrictions gutted one field that Palestinian activists had directed before: unionization. The post–Black September arrests thinned the ranks of labor activists and union leaders. A 1976 law fixed the number of national unions at just seventeen, which resulted in the dissolution or merger of numerous associations while also banning unionization in new industries. This limited the mobilizational capacity of workers to advance political demands, much less bargain with private employers who enjoyed little regulatory oversight from the state.[64]

Above all, the coercive apparatus continued to institutionalize the tribal-state alliance. After Black September, the army and Interior Ministry cleaned house by discharging thousands of Palestinian personnel regardless of their conduct. The advent of national conscription in 1976 increased the proportion of Palestinians in the military from 10 to 30 percent. However, Palestinian conscripts were discouraged from seeking careers beyond their minimum service and were sequestered into menial tasks and noncombat positions that had little contact with the regular tribal-dominated army structure.[65] The rank and file stayed the preserve of *abna' al-'asha'ir*—tribal sons, who were still praised in educational and political discourse as holding the most prestigious of all occupations.[66] Though salaries were modest, the prospect of lifetime employment—that is, of a guaranteed salary, social services, and pension—made them coveted vessels of economic security. In addition, tribal affiliations continued to influence the distribution of officer positions, with King Hussein carefully using senior promotions to balance out representation between major tribal groupings.[67]

Enlarged payrolls and more arms imports created a swelling defense budget. Annual military and security expenditures more than quadrupled from $107 million in 1970 to an average of over $454 million during the 1970s, averaging over 43 percent of total government spending. Even these gargantuan figures underestimate because, by the late 1970s, the regime devoted much of its Arab aid grants to purchasing advanced arms from the United States and Western European suppliers through "off-book" acquisitions, and so were not counted in official registers.[68] Jordan also received almost $900 million in U.S. military assistance from the Nixon, Ford, and Carter administrations, most as arms credits and with some funds dedicated to services like officer training and technical assistance. In the political arena, Palestinians as a whole experienced greater institutionalized denigration. From 1970 through 1989, the regime inundated Palestinian-prevalent urban areas with repression and surveillance, as martial law was in continuous effect. The Ministry of Information curtailed or disbanded many weeklies and newspapers, establishing in 1971 the Jordanian Press Foundation and its semiofficial *Ra'y* newspaper. While the foundation held a monopoly over journalism, the 1974 Publications and Press Law formalized new censorship rules and gutted whatever media independence remained. The *mukhabarat* kept tight reins over civil society activity, deploying a large network of informants to monitor and extirpate critics. Professional associations and student groups were kept on a tight leash.[69] Public security forces did not hesitate to quell disturbances with force, as in the bloody 1986 student protest at Yarmouk University.[70] Though King Hussein continued to pay lip service to the

197

Palestinian cause in his foreign policy, at home the regime was complicit in fomenting chauvinistic nationalism that treasured Transjordanian and especially Bedouin "values" as the authentic cultural linchpin of the Hashemite kingdom.[71]

While parliament remained dormant with the previous national elections having been held in 1967, Jordanian autocracy still gave Transjordanian constituencies symbolic forms of political representation. Overall Palestinian representation among ministerial offices, never high before, dropped to even lower levels; now, not just the sovereignty portfolios but most mid-level positions remained beyond reach. After 1970, only one Jordanian of Palestinian origin would ever rise to the premiership. Tribal sheikhs continued to utilize the Diwan to speak with King Hussein through his liaisons, and many argued that the entire Palestinian populace had become a threat to national stability.[72] Hussein also undertook personal interventions to preserve good relations with major tribal confederations and minority communities. The palace or the GID would often confer direct payments, such as cash and material gifts, to favored sheikhs.[73] Circassians and Christians continued to be tapped for political service, with the ministerial ranks populated by a disproportionately high number of these small minority groups. In addition, although its rank-and-file membership was gradually becoming more urban, Palestinian, and middle-class, the Muslim Brotherhood retained considerable influence over religious and educational policies.[74] For instance, ʿAbdul Latif ʿArabiyyat served as the Ministry of Education's secretary general from 1982 to 1985 and would utilize such political experiences to help launch the Brotherhood's political party in 1993, the Islamic Action Front.[75]

With the shuttering of parliament and ongoing prohibition on parties restricting potential mobilization of opposition, the regime experimented with new organizational structures that catered instead to Transjordanian interests. One was the National Union. Created in 1971 by Wasfi Al-Tall, the Union celebrated Hashemite rule and Jordanian identity through party-like activities such as national conventions, committee meetings, and local councils, which also allowed Hussein to monitor and circulate East Bank luminaries close to the throne.[76] Despite its name, its Transjordanian inclination surfaced quickly. It was especially active in tribal areas including the rural north, but struggled to recruit members from the Palestinian-dominant urban neighborhoods, and its executive committee was stacked with Transjordanian political elites from the palace group.

The Union fizzled out, partly due to Al-Tall's assassination in November 1971 and partly because of its incongruous existence. It was, for all intents and purposes, a party designed to mobilize Transjordanians for elections that would never be held.[77] Another organizational effort to serve the East Bank coalition came in 1978, when the king launched the National Consultative Council. This advisory assembly had sixty appointed seats, which represented another way to implant Transjordanian elites into a political organization close to royal power.[78] Though the council did not last long, it demonstrated yet another institutional commitment by the monarchy to provide symbolic voice and political proximity to supporters.

Having rebuilt the Jordanian state around its coalition after Black September, the Hashemite monarchy had reason to look forward to the 1980s with optimism. Huge levels of Arab foreign aid and a decade of repressive closure created a new era of stability. That coalitional formula would be tested by the economic crisis of 1988–89.

FINANCIAL CRISIS AND REEQUILIBRIUM, 1980S AND 1990S

The collapse in oil prices that buffeted Kuwait and the other Gulf states by the mid-1980s acutely affected Jordan by preventing the fulfillment of the pan-Arab aid grants stipulated by the Baghdad agreement. By 1985, every Arab donor save Saudi Arabia had reneged on its economic support payments.[79] At the same time, as the Gulf economies contracted, remittances from Palestinians working there declined. In 1988, the last year of the Baghdad agreement, the Central Bank estimated receipts of just $417 million of foreign aid, the lowest since 1977, and $895 million of remittances, the lowest since 1980. It had no contingency for such unexpected shortfalls, as it had long assumed that the

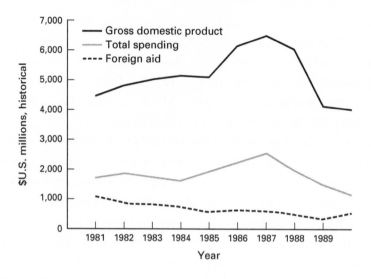

FIGURE 8.2 Economic boom and bust in Jordan, 1981–1990

Note: Foreign aid includes grants and loans from the United States and European and Arab states.

Sources: World Bank (serial); Central Bank of Jordan (serial)

Gulf states had deep reserves to weather oil price fluctuations. Incapable of extracting greater tax revenues to compensate, but resistant to abandoning its institutionalized commitments to Transjordanian protection by reducing public-sector and military spending, the government turned to concessional and then commercial loans. Figure 8.2 graphs this contradictory state of affairs: as aid monies decreased, spending still increased until the bubble burst in 1987. Debt servicing charges whittled down cash reserves, resulting in currency runs and the devaluation of the Jordanian dinar in late 1988. The government was starved of cash.

As the economy teetered on collapse, Arab oil exporters could provide just modest assistance. Saudi Arabia, Kuwait, Oman, and Iraq pledged $300 million of aid in June, and a subsequent Saudi grant measured $200 million—generous donations, but far from the billions needed to balance the budget and restore confidence in the currency. The American response was negligible, as the United States had reduced its foreign aid to Jordan since the mid-1980s under the mistaken assumption that Arab grants would sustain the kingdom. Hussein hence received messages of sympathy but no bailout; in 1989, the first Bush administration provided just $16 million in economic aid. As inflation surged, the foreign debt reached $8 billion, or twice the GDP. As Jordan neared default, the World Bank and IMF agreed to intervene. Like other structural adjustment programs, the bailout loans given by these multilateral lending agencies came with pressure to implement neoliberal reforms, in particular the reduction of public spending starting with price subsidies on basic goods like fuel.

Such fiscal moves resulted in social agitation. The sudden hike in fuel prices spurred truck drivers in the southern town of Maʿn to protest. Demonstrations spread to other tribal areas, where thousands of participants attacked public institutions, marched on central streets, and overwhelmed local police. Palestinian-dominated areas, in particular Amman and Irbid, remained quiet. The removal of subsidies affected salaried urbanites less than modest tribal communities reliant upon public wages, while the previous decade of repression left few activists willing to directly challenge the regime. In the countryside, however, the army was forced to contain the largest display of civil violence since Black September. Such rioting in tribal areas electrified the international media by exposing a newfound weakness of the Hashemite monarchy: its own bastions of loyalty were now revolting against it.

To be sure, many in the palace were surprised at the extent to which tribal Jordanians were willing to voice their anger through the street through such spontaneous mobilization. However, their coalitional ties helped curb any potential for radicalization and escalating among protesters, allowing the crisis to be quickly contained. This occurred in three ways. First, demonstrations congregated around a highly limited set of goals. Most protesters desired not changes within the rulership but the dismissal of Prime Minister Zeid Al-Rifaʿi, under whose watch the austerity measures had been implemented and who was perceived as a corrupt "old guard" politician, despite his family's history of service to the Hashemites. Regime change was beyond the realm of imagination; policy shifts were the call of the day. Indeed, public security forces charged with keeping order until the army arrived reported that participants shouted slogans of support for King Hussein while denouncing the politicians surrounding him. That many protesters had relatives working in the public sector meant that a revolutionary campaign would demolish the very state structure designed to benefit them but that had temporarily failed. That vested stake limited the horizon of potential radicalization.

Second, the regime's social ties and political credibility allowed it to defuse unrest in many tribal areas, which minimized the need to mete out violent punishments. The riots caused a considerable spate of destruction, including torched police stations, vandalized government buildings, and damage from firearms. Eight were killed and more than a hundred injured in clashes with public security and military units. However, the violence could have been far worse had army liaisons and political officials not sought out local representatives and persuaded them to discourage any more protests.[80] Those efforts to circulate calls for calm among familial and tribal networks helped deescalate tensions in small towns like Maʿn that contained a high number of unregistered firearms. Upon returning from a visit to the United States, King Hussein redoubled these efforts by personally reaching out to tribal sheikhs. These tribal-state interactions reveal how proximate ties between coalitional partners allow for strategies of opposition management that need not require systemic coercion. By contrast, if thousands of Palestinians in the refugee camps or Amman had decided to riot, the official response would have been far more repressive. "We could not be too violent. . . . These were our brothers and cousins, and we naturally showed restraint. It was like scolding family members."[81]

Finally, the palace undertook a surprising concession after the end of the violence. Unable to reverse the $100 million cuts in subsidies now that structural adjustment was under way, it launched a process of political liberalization in the ultimate bargain to its coalition—more democracy in place of lessening material benefits and welfare provisions. From the summer of 1989 to 1993, the regime successively released political prisoners, held elections for a new parliament, ratified a national charter, abrogated martial law, legalized political parties, and lifted some press censorship.[82] Civil society underwent a rapid revival, with hundreds of new nongovernmental associations appearing within years.[83] That national charter, in particular, came after extensive dialogues held with various civil society groups and communities across the kingdom, including Palestinian voices.

At the time, the charter was interpreted by many scholars as a desperate effort by a flailing regime to expand its base of popular support, because the old ruling formula was no longer sustainable in this new era of economic privation.[84] In retrospect, such assessments were too optimistic. Liberalization during the 1990s was no entrée to democratization. By 1999, when King Hussein's son, ʿAbdullah, assumed the throne upon his father's death, it had become obvious that the levers of royal autocracy remained as secure as ever. Despite the provision of greater civil liberties, restoration of parliamentary elections, and other pluralizing concessions granted under the national charter, the palace still held executive primacy over all policy making as well as ironclad control over the coercive apparatus.[85]

Political liberalization after 1989 was still significant, however. Far from signifying any coalitional expansion as many observers predicted, liberalization instead reflected the regime's renewed commitment to *maintain* its ethnocratic strategy of tenuous survival—to shelter and protect Transjordanian interests while foreclosing any Palestinian empowerment. Fear that the Palestinian majority could exploit any democratic opening and make inroads into the state remained regnant. Hence, liberalization reproduced preexisting patterns of exclusion for many Palestinians.

Critical to this new form of subordination was the 1988 disengagement from the West Bank. For two decades after the 1967 Arab-Israeli War, the Jordanian regime still considered the West Bank as part of its confederal territory—only under Israeli occupation. In July 1988, however, the monarchy decided to withdraw all administrative claims from the territory, thereby tacitly accepting the PLO's counterclaim of owning ultimate responsibility over these lands. Regime insiders had also been disheartened by the outbreak of the intifada the previous year, which worsened relations with Israel and further weakened the lethargic economy.[86] While framed as a concession to the PLO and hence a victory for Palestinian interests, in reality the disengagement also removed major financial and legal burdens from the state. For instance, almost eighteen thousand civil servants on the West Bank who had previously received some support from the Jordanian government, such as teachers and health workers, were retired overnight. In this context, many royal elites interpreted the move from the perspective of Transjordanian nationalism and applauded the withdrawal.[87] They "saw no moral problem in the de facto demotion of Palestinian-Jordanians who were supposed to be fellow citizens."[88]

Before the 1989 elections, royal officials also laid down two caveats. First, the elected Lower House of parliament would no longer have any Palestinian constituencies in the West Bank due to the 1988 disengagement. Second, electoral districts would be drawn with different voting magnitudes, such that in rural areas far fewer votes would be needed to elect a deputy than in urban districts.[89] The result was grotesque malapportionment that discriminated against Palestinians in the three largest cities—Amman, Irbid, and Zarqa—while overrepresenting sparsely populated tribal communities. For instance, a deputy from the small town of Ma'n represented 5,600 voters, but a parliamentarian from Amman's Second District represented 24,333.[90]

Another institutional mechanism that transmitted coalitional bias against the Palestinian majority was the balloting system. In August 1993, the government amended the electoral law by changing the existing block vote system to the more obscure single nontransferable vote (SNTV). This change exerted its intended result in the November general elections, when loyalist tribal and conservative candidates running on independent platforms trounced opposition parties, whose aspirants found it difficult to woo voters under the SNTV system. Among those groups was the Muslim Brotherhood's Islamic Action Front.[91]

The Brotherhood had grown more distant from the palace starting in the 1980s, representing a subtle shift on the margins of the monarchy's social foundation. Secular ideological threats that facilitated Islamist cooperation with the regime, such as communism and Arab Nationalism, had vanished in the post–Cold War era. In addition, demographic and structural changes meant that the majority of the Brotherhood's membership now consisted of middle-class Palestinians. Though the Islamist leadership adopted a moderate stance in calling for reforms and never revolution, they increasingly diverged from the regime over contentious issues like the 1994 Israeli peace treaty and fiscal austerity programs. When the Islamic Action Front boycotted the 1997 elections, tribal deputies and conservative independents became the parliamentary majority, along with a high number of Christian deputies.

A COSTLY FORMULA FOR SURVIVAL

The worsening split between the Brotherhood and the palace underscored the importance of sustaining Transjordanian support, which the newly liberalized political system facilitated. Thanks to a combination of malapportioned districts combined with SNTV, the new arena of parliamentary life helped fulfill this prerogative. Formally, parliament had the responsibility of crafting laws and checking the monarchy.[92] In practice, the Jordanian legislature had little law-making ability and no capacity to monitor the palace or the coercive apparatus. Its practical function was to merely promulgate laws that had already been written, debated, and ordered by the cabinet government working under the king. However, parliament became another means of redistributing economic and social goods to Transjordanian communities. Elected deputies received not only hefty salaries but also the newfound ability to lobby the state to more directly help their communities through development projects and direct funding.[93] Much like Kuwait, tribal primaries allowed for extensive coordination between sheikhs and front runners in many districts, leaving minimal suspense on the day of elections.

Providing new benefits for tribal groups through liberalized politics was consonant with a desperate rearguard action to preserve the greatest sources of East Bank employment—public-sector payrolls and the military. Jordan's economic recession lasted until the mid-1990s. In addition, after the 1991 Gulf War the return of nearly 300,000 Jordanian expatriates, most of whom were Palestinian, saturated domestic labor markets and forced the government to extend new social services; atop lost remittances, the cost of reabsorbing these expatriates was estimated to exceed $3 billion.[94] Though inflation returned to single digits by 1996 and the economy had stabilized, the kingdom still struggled with high unemployment and a poverty level as high as 40 percent. In August 1996, another round of austerity measures under structural adjustment resulted in the lifting of wheat subsidies, which doubled the price of bread and resulted in small-scale protests.

Still, the regime managed to maintain its economic commitments to its coalitional core. Following the Gulf War, both the Arab Gulf states and the United States cut off most of their aid promises to punish Jordan for backing Iraq. However, this cliency relationship would recover with the 1994 Israeli peace accords, which rehabilitated Jordan's Western image and resulted in a flood of new foreign aid by the late 1990s.[95] Until then, the regime managed to maintain its coalitional commitments. For instance, prior to the Israeli peace treaty, the government promulgated a general sales tax in a deliberate attempt to raise domestic revenues indirectly, rather than pursue the politically risky project of implementing a new income tax system.[96] In 1996, Finance Minister Basil Jardaneh raised pay for all public sector workers despite the atmosphere of fiscal austerity, which cost $160 million, or nearly 7 percent of all government expenditures. IMF objections were overcome with a blunt explanation by Jordanian liaisons: if civil servants did not come to work, then the kingdom could not keep its peace with Israel, maintain a secure border with Iraq and Syria, and perform other functions crucial for regional peace.[97]

Given its strategic value to Western donors, Jordan thus exited multilateral structural adjustment programs with little fiscal discipline to show for it. As a percentage of GDP, taxes collected scarcely rose from 14.4 percent in 1989 to 15.9 percent in 1999, while income and business tax revenues actually fell from 4.3 percent to 2.7 percent.[98] As another example, in 1989 military manpower reached a hundred thousand, a record high. During the 1990s, it remained steady at that level despite the end of conscription in 1992 and continual IMF pressures to reduce the defense and security budget, which still exceeded a third of total government spending. If there were fiscal austerity measures in Jordan, the coercive apparatus never felt it.

The result of these maneuvers in the 1990s was an extension of life for the regime's costly strategy of tenuous survival through the 2000s under a new king, Abdullah. More regional turbulence would come after 9/11, including the Iraq War and homegrown terrorism. The constant throughout these events was the predictable Transjordanian coalition backing Hashemite rule and the persistent marginalization of many Palestinians from political life. Most of all, the GID and palace continued to see their futures as conditioned by not only external forces but more poignantly the fate of their Palestinian majority, many of whom had resided in Jordan for so long that they would not likely return to the West Bank and Gaza Strip even if Palestinian statehood materialized. For this reason, the autocracy's longevity since its inception has not equated to long-term stability, which would require a creative institutional settlement with its Palestinian populace that might finally allow the monarchy to drop its repressive guard.

|||||||||||||||||||||||||||||||||||||||||||||||||||||||||||||||||||||||||||||||||||||||||||||||||||||||||||||||||||||||

This chapter traced how Jordan continued along its pathway of geopolitical subsidization and tenuous survival, analyzing new periods of social tension and economic trouble. Extending the postconflict dynamics first seen after 1957, including worsening abrasion between the Palestinian majority and Transjordanian minority, historical evidence showed how the ruling autocracy continually reconfigured the budding Jordanian state by mobilizing an ethnocratic coalition with the dual purpose of protecting Transjordanian supporters and suppressing Palestinian interests. The 1964 entry of the PLO and the 1967 Arab-Israeli War accelerated this process while also creating more Palestinian opposition to the regime, which came to a head during the 1970 Black September civil war. Since then, a costly pattern of tenuous survival has taken hold, one subsidized by international (and usually American) support motivated by the strategic value of preventing revolution and uprising in a kingdom strategically sandwiched between Israel, Syria, Iraq, and Saudi Arabia.

Such costly persistence stands apart from cases of regime durability in an important way. While the autocracies of Kuwait and Jordan have both endured since the 1950s, the Hashemite monarchy has done so by incurring far more costs in terms of violence and destruction. In Jordan, this does not preclude changes in the future. However, while coalitional broadening is possible, it is unlikely given not only the continued availability of external support but also the prohibitive cost of reversing institutionalized policies of communal protection. The economic structures and political institutions that have long protected Transjordanian interests constitute the fabric of the state itself, and the authoritarian regime would risk alienating its staple East Bank support base should it drastically veer off the very coalitional trajectory that helped create political order in the first place. It would take a major crisis threatening to overturn monarchical power, combined with the withdrawal of international assistance from the United States and other foreign patrons, for the Jordanian leadership to seriously consider reconfiguring its coalitional strategy and inducing a new ruling bargain. Until another such critical juncture arrives, the Hashemite monarchy will most likely continue to rule in the tenuous manner that has characterized its modern reign: it may survive but it will seldom truly feel secure.

9

THE GEOPOLITICAL ORIGINS OF
DURABLE POLITICAL ORDER

THE THEORY ADVANCED through historical case studies of
Kuwait, Iran, and Jordan in the preceding chapters may
be encapsulated in this thesis: the *depth* of external penetration shaped the *breadth* of regime coalitions which in turn explains
the *durability* of political order. Paying close attention to how hegemonic
interventions by great powers influenced the course of early social conflicts, it has explained why equally ambitious autocrats in the postcolonial
Middle East met such unequal fates. By exploring the historical origins of
authoritarian state-building, this book has underscored the decisive importance of geopolitical circumstance. Geopolitical seclusion in Kuwait
produced regime durability; geopolitical substitution in Iran resulted in
revolutionary turmoil; and geopolitical subsidization in Jordan facilitated tenuous survival.

Process tracing within each case highlighted every step of this causal
framework, marshaling empirical evidence to account for the behavior of
key actors and the unfolding of major events. The analysis corroborated
that by giving weak autocrats the confidence and capacity to subdue opposition without compromise, geopolitical mediation often changed the
course of history. It did so by transforming the incentives of authoritarian
leaders regarding their winning coalitions. When outside assistance was

available, besieged rulers could forgo the crafting of bargains with contentious social groups in order to secure domestic peace. They could consolidate their dominion over society without sacrificing much, thereby exiting periods of conflict and unrest with uncontested authority. When secluded from such external support, however, regime incumbents were forced to negotiate for their survival. They had to broaden their ruling coalitions by sharing power and resources with not only their former foes but also new sectors of support within society. This marked the beginnings of more inclusionary rule.

These coalitional choices had lasting legacies on subsequent statebuilding. They shaped the design and purpose of the institutions built by these regimes in their efforts to modernize the national economy and centralize political power. Economic programs and political structures expressed coalitional preferences and preserved them over time. Institutions, in sum, were utilized in various ways. Through the provision of patronage and protection to targeted supporters, they could knit together broad coalitions and keep rulers close to societal interests. Equally, by excluding and marginalizing wide swathes of society they could also enforce the absolutist supremacy of leaders over any demands from below. In turn, these institutional investments help explain the performance and fate of these authoritarian regimes decades later, when they faced major economic crises that catalyzed new opposition and threw routine politics into uncertainty.

The case of Kuwait shows the upshot of one historical pathway. The ruling Sabah dynasty's experiences during the 1980s and 1990s revealed that the wider the regime's societal coalition and more inclusive its ruling institutions, the more likely political order would remain stable in the face of new challenges. Broad-based coalitions meant that opposition elites had a smaller audience from which to recruit. They gave rulers a high degree of credibility in offering reforms in return for demobilization and provided a repertoire of nonviolent tools of engagement that enabled state officials to reach out to protesting groups and attempt to strike compromises. These strategies ensured that emergent opposition would remain modest, moderate, and malleable, allowing for the seamless continuity of this nondemocratic regime with virtually no bloodshed or violence. Such experiences present an enduring lesson: long-term stability requires that states turn citizens into constituents by giving them some enduring stake in defending political order.

By contrast, autocracies that ruled through economic and political institutions that excluded large societal groups faced grave danger when crises engendered unrest. They had far fewer means to contain dissent and demobilize opposition peacefully. The case of Iran illustrates the result of another causal-historical trajectory of state-building. Decades of relative autonomy from society meant that the Pahlavi dictatorship confronted demonstrations and resistance without deep or extensive ties of loyalty with potentially supportive groups. What began as scattered protests mushroomed into a national uprising that eventually overwhelmed the regime despite the use of ruthless repression and ongoing American support. The leadership lacked effective engagement strategies that could defuse tensions, hold dialogues with opposition, and offer credible reforms to buy time.

Such revolutionary collapse differs from the Jordanian case, which occupies a middle ground between Iran and Kuwait. Like its Pahlavi peer, the Hashemite monarchy benefited from U.S. intervention during early social conflict that enabled the establishment of authoritarian power. However, the kingdom also had a structural obstacle that considerably changed the coalitional calculus—a demographic transformation that brought communal tensions between a growing majority and an increasingly fearful minority. Driven by fear and predicated upon protection, this mostly tribal minority became the backbone of the state apparatus and public sector economy. The effect of institutionalizing such ethnocracy over time was instability, civil conflict, and endemic mistrust. The Jordanian autocracy's survival has been tenuous at best, dependent upon continued Western support and maintaining those selective loyalties at home.

This new argument about the geopolitical origins, coalitional choices, and institutional lineaments of authoritarian state-building integrates ideas from several different areas of scholarship and emerges through careful comparative-historical analysis. It is comprehensive enough to account for three different causal pathways, integrated enough to tie those trajectories back into a unified understanding of coalitional politics and state-building, and still specific enough to divulge the actors and events operating in each national context. The result is a new theory that generalizes across the postcolonial Middle East. However, generalization is not universalization. Applying this theory systematically to additional cases from other regions may uncover new causal twists in the logic or necessitate creative revisions in the argument. As this book was devoted to qualitatively generating theory rather than mechanically testing it, that task is better left to other researchers.

On this merit, the conclusions posited here brandish potent implications for scholarship and theory across several fronts, as well as contemporary debates in U.S. foreign policy.

DICTATORIAL DIVERGENCE

First, this study affirms that authoritarianism is not only about coercion but also about coalitions—and thus, about choices. Its results validate the paradoxical adage that dictators last longest and enjoy the most stability when they are less autonomous from society and constrain their absolutist impulses the most. Accountability exists for authoritarian regimes, too; it just does not manifest through regular electoral contestation open to all. Rather, nondemocratic regimes can make themselves accountable through economic and political institutions that encage their iron fists in silk gloves.

Yet, if certain institutional arrangements are so important, why do not *all* autocrats pursue them? Why do some make manifestly bad decisions? Even more curious than such an intuitive puzzle is that this particular finding—namely, that self-restraint rather than unbridled absolutism is more likely to induce long-term stability by encouraging close state-society relations—is hardly a secret. Such advice can be found in a vast corpus of knowledge stretching back centuries, as written by philosophers, jurists, and counselors. Seneca's *De Clementia* (56 A.D.), Nizam al-Mulk's *Siyasatnama* (1091), and Machiavelli's *The Prince* (1532) are ageless examples.

Today, social science provides similar advice. For instance, economic modeling has mapped out the decision-making process for welfare-maximizing politicians, essentially showing would-be tyrants how to hypothetically eliminate rivals, reward supporters, extract wealth, and manipulate information in the most mathematically efficient way.[1] Scholars of postcolonial politics, such as Joel Migdal, have likewise identified why "rule-maximizing" forms of governance that emphasize societal compromises, popular mobilization, and inclusive institutions are superior to merely "rule-satisfying" leaders, who seem to do the bare minimum of crushing pluralism.[2] Even those with little patience for academic jargon can read self-styled "dictator handbooks" that give direct and lucid instructions on how to craft successful autocracies from scratch.[3]

The point is not that leaders should read classical Latin texts or learn game theory. Rather, it serves as a reminder that political rulers are human actors—and so when faced with the possibility of their own demise, they will pursue whatever option is perceived to best assure their survival. By traveling backward in time and interrogating the challenges facing early state-builders in the Middle East, this book has shown that dictators made decisions in the heat of conflict that seemed consonant with their overarching goal of keeping power. Only with the gift of hindsight does the distinguishing factor come into focus: autocrats made dissimilar choices that led them onto diverging pathways because they faced different geopolitical and domestic circumstances.

COALITIONS AND INSTITUTIONS

Second, the central role played by coalitional politics throughout this analysis should not detract from the prevailing emphasis on institutions that characterize the study of authoritarianism specifically and political regimes more broadly. Instead, the key insight is that economic structures and political organizations do not magically appear when convenient, gifted by the historical gods. Scholars must study not just their effects but also their origins. In postcolonial regions like the Middle East, this work has shown how coalitional politics came *prior* to the construction of new state institutions tasked with the mission of expanding authoritarian power and transforming society. Institutions, then, can be studied as carriers of coalitional preferences. Without fully understanding from where those preferences stem, any explanation of institutional development will be truncated.

In short, institutional outcomes have coalitional causes. This also clarifies the often muddled problem of comparability. Authoritarian institutions take varying forms across the economy and political arena. Land redistribution programs and royal parliaments may both qualify as institutional structures, but they seem to share little else in common. The findings here, however, suggest that what makes them and so many other institutions comparable are the coalitional interests embedded within their design and function. Institutions that channel patronage to supporters or protect endangered constituencies may be no more economically efficient or politically transparent than those that do not; but only the former help mobilize support for the incumbent regime and keep leaders more connected to the ideological trends and social currents running throughout the populace. Institutions under nondemocratic governments may appear extremely different, but they can encompass the same generic logic of coalitional politics.

GEOPOLITICS AND SYSTEMIC CONCERNS

Third, the analysis here underscores the continuing importance of linking domestic and international factors together when explaining national outcomes, especially in regions defined by frequent foreign interventions like the Middle East. The list of geopolitical variables that can possibly influence politics within any country is long and will not be found in this book. The emphasis instead falls on a particular type of external event in the Middle East—hegemonic interventions by great powers in support of regimes—that left long-term legacies upon state-building. Those legacies can be told through the analytic lens of cliency, which accounts for why great power patrons seek to support client regimes as well as how diplomatic, fiscal, and coercive resources can tip the balance of power between client regimes and their societal rivals.

From a historical perspective, parsing out the implications of such interventions many decades ago has illustrated how the international system constrained state formation in the Middle East and other postcolonial regions. Western powers like the United States attained their global power through a costly but necessary process that took centuries: resolving domestic conflicts without constant meddling from some distant empire. No foreign patron mediated the Civil War, infusing the Union or Confederacy with foreign aid. Ironically, the hegemonic products of geopolitical seclusion have often prevented newer states from enjoying the same evolutionary conditions. Founding conflicts were seldom allowed to unfold without interference from above. In this sense, Middle East state-building was interrupted, and its effects still reverberate throughout the region today.

OIL AND COERCION

Fourth, the argument here connects to two extremely popular explanations invoked when discussing the persistence of authoritarianism in the Middle East: oil and coercion. While these cannot be ignored when evaluating the long-term stability of any country, this work highlights a subtler point that reinforces the theme linking coalitions to institutions. The effects of oil wealth and the scope of coercion are never monolithic but instead reflect prior coalitional interests. Thus, they must be analyzed in the close context of antecedent events and interactive forces, not thrown around with a laundry list of other competing variables in an imaginary tussle for causal relevance. By laying out different sequences of state-building, the case studies showed that while oil and coercion "matter" in an elemental sense, *how* they matter is just as significant.

Economic development and political centralization in oil-rich Kuwait and Iran, for instance, occurred through the creation of large-scale institutions. However, institutional creation did not occur until after these regimes began accruing oil revenues, which in turn occurred after leaders had also resolved social conflicts with contentious opposition. Oil affected each authoritarian system differently because rulers had very different strategies of governance. Unlike the detached despotism showed by the Pahlavi regime, Kuwait's strategy of popular incorporation required that hydrocarbon resources be used to institutionalize a cross-cutting and wide coalition of support, which in turn obviated the need for pervasive repression against society. Had Mubarak al-Sabah, the forerunner of the modern Kuwaiti regime, discovered endless wealth prior to his family's struggles against merchant opposition, this principality would have developed in a very different way, and Kuwait might have more resembled Iran.

Timing and context also influence how coercion is evaluated. The punishment puzzle attracts attention given its often contradictory outcomes. Sometimes, very violent and repressive states can overcome crises, eliminate opposition, and cow society into obedience, whereas other times—as deposed dictators can well attest—no degree of violent brutality can hold back revolutionary crowds storming the palace gates. The findings here navigate this indeterminacy by showing that, while most autocracies create some security apparatus, these policing and military organs are seldom constructed in the same way. In Iran, the Pahlavi monarchy had every reason to believe that coercive instruments like detention, torture, exile, and execution were central to its future. Consider its experience in the 1950s: the shah's inability to destroy urban opposition led to near deposal in 1953, whereas the total repression of that opposition afterward thanks to revitalizing U.S. support gave his regime its first taste of uncontested domination over society. Coercion rescued the crown. The picture would look very different had the shah been forced to bargain with opposition and share power due to an absent American intervention.

THE LIMITS OF HEGEMONIC SUPPORT

The study of geopolitical mediation, coalitional strategies, and cliency relationships are central to understanding the historical dynamics of state-building and authoritarianism in the Middle East. It also holds relevance to U.S. foreign policy nearly a decade and half after 9/11. The rise of the Islamic State group and the breakdown of political order in countries as varied as Libya, Yemen, and Afghanistan send a stern warning. However impressive their moral mandate or bombastic their ambitions, leaders who take the reins of government over conflict-ridden societies must find new ways to mobilize popular support that can legitimate and stabilize their rule. This especially applies to countries where the United States has engaged in nation-building and so is directly responsible for the establishment of new regimes following the destruction of old ones, namely Iraq and Afghanistan. For years, American diplomatic, financial, and military assistance flowed freely and almost unconditionally to these new postwar governments. Despite their hollow democratic pretensions and sectarian fragility, few in Washington wished to see the fruits of their controversial invasions and occupations spoil.

The reverse has happened. More than a decade after the ousting of previous dictatorships, state-building in Iraq and Afghanistan has failed because U.S.-supported leaders never felt enough pressure to bargain, compromise, and negotiate settlements. They had little incentive to share power and resources with domestic enemies for peace when the most powerful hegemon in world history, the United States, all but guaranteed their existence through the provision of diplomatic, economic, and military assistance.

Combining the historical record of the Middle East with the contemporary failures of new U.S. client states, the lesson is clear. Policy makers should think twice when intervening abroad to support favored client governments besieged by opposition. Giving rulers the ability to overcome societal challengers can sabotage the future by encouraging them to make narrow coalitional and institutional choices that may secure their immediate existence but leaves them highly vulnerable to future opposition from their societies. If Washington wishes to keep even its most unsavory allies in weak states in power, it should get out of the way and support them *less*. Helping hurts.

NOTES

1. THE ARGUMENT AND THE CASES

1. Samuel Huntington, *Political Order in Changing Societies* (New Haven: Yale University Press, 1968), 7.
2. By institutions, I mean organizational structures that govern relations between actors. Kathleen Thelen and Sven Steinmo, "Historical Institutionalism in Comparative Analysis," in *Structuring Politics: Historical Institutionalism in Comparative Analysis*, ed. Sven Steinmo, Kathleen Thelen, and Frank Longstreth (New York: Cambridge University Press, 1992), 1–29.
3. Anna Grzymala-Busse, "Time Will Tell? Temporality and the Analysis of Causal Mechanisms and Processes," *Comparative Political Studies* 44, no. 9 (2011): 1267–97.
4. Paul Pierson, *Politics in Time: History, Institutions, and Social Analysis* (Princeton: Princeton University Press, 2004), 48–53; and Giovanni Capoccia and R. Daniel Kelemen, "The Study of Critical Junctures: Theory, Narrative, and Counterfactuals in Historical Institutionalism," *World Politics* 59, no. 3 (2007): 341–69.
5. Charles Tilly, *Big Structures, Large Processes, Huge Comparisons* (New York: Russell Sage Foundation, 1984); and James Mahoney and Dietrich Rueschemeyer, "Comparative-Historical Analysis: Achievements and Agendas," in *Comparative Historical Analysis in the Social Sciences*, ed. James Mahoney and Dietrich Rueschemeyer (New York: Cambridge University Press, 2003), 3–40.
6. Competitive autocracies operate democratic institutions that formally regulate political contestation, but incumbent leaders so frequently violate these rules that the playing field for opposition is grossly unfair. They often combine elements

of coercion, fraud, and intimidation with regular elections, independent media, constitutional courts, and other democratic organs. Such "soft" authoritarianism has proliferated in the post–Cold War era. See further Larry Diamond, "Thinking about Hybrid Regimes," *Journal of Democracy* 13, no. 2 (2002): 21–35; Andreas Schedler, ed., *Electoral Authoritarianism: The Dynamics of Unfree Competition* (Boulder, CO: Lynne Rienner, 2006); Marc Morjé Howard and Philip Roessler, "Liberalizing Electoral Outcomes in Competitive Authoritarian Regimes," *American Journal of Political Science* 50, no. 2 (2006): 365–81; and Steven Levitsky and Lucan Way, *Competitive Authoritarianism: Hybrid Regimes After the Cold War* (New York: Cambridge University Press, 2010).

7. Canonical examples include Joel Migdal, *Strong Societies and Weak States: State-Society Relations and State Capabilities in the Third World* (Princeton: Princeton University Press, 1988); David Waldner, *State Building and Late Development* (Ithaca, NY: Cornell University Press, 1999); and Dan Slater, *Ordering Power: Contentious Politics and Authoritarian Leviathans in Southeast Asia* (New York: Cambridge University Press, 2010).

8. Dan Slater and Daniel Ziblatt, "The Enduring Indispensability of Controlled Comparison," *Comparative Political Studies* 46, no. 10 (2013): 1301–27.

9. For a sampling of this vast literature: John Waterbury, "Democracy without Democrats? The Potential for Political Liberalization in the Middle East," in *Democracy without Democrats? The Renewal of Politics in the Muslim World*, ed. Ghassan Salamé (London: I. B. Tauris, 1994), 277–311; Augustus Richard Norton, ed., *Civil Society in the Middle East*, vols. 1 and 2 (Leiden, the Netherlands: Brill, 1995, 1996); Rex Brynen, Bahgat Korany, and Paul Noble, eds., *Political Liberalization and Democratization in the Arab World*, vols. 1 and 2 (Boulder, CO: Lynne Rienner, 1995, 1998); Daniel Brumberg, "The Trap of Liberalized Autocracy," *Journal of Democracy* 13, no. 4 (2002): 56–68; Marsha Pripstein Posusney and Michele Penner Angrist, eds., *Authoritarianism in the Middle East: Regimes and Resistance* (Boulder, CO: Lynne Rienner, 2005); Lisa Anderson, "Searching Where the Light Shines: Studying Democratization in the Middle East," *Annual Review of Political Science* 9 (2006): 189–214; Oliver Schlumberger, ed., *Debating Arab Authoritarianism: Dynamics and Durability in Nondemocratic Regimes* (Stanford: Stanford University Press, 2007); and Holger Albrecht, ed., *Contentious Politics in the Middle East: Political Opposition under Authoritarianism* (Gainesville: University Press of Florida, 2010).

10. The scholarship on the Middle East as a regional subsystem within international relations is enormous. For a slice: L. Carl Brown, *International Politics and the Middle East: Old Rules, Dangerous Game* (Princeton: Princeton University Press, 1984); Bahgat Korany and Ali E. Hillal Dessouki, "The Global System and Arab Foreign Policies: The Primacy of Constraints," in *The Foreign Policies of Arab States: The Challenge of Change*, ed. Bahgat Korany and Ali E. Hillal Dessouki (Cairo: American University in Cairo Press, 1984), 18–39; Fawaz Gerges, *The Superpow-*

ers and the Middle East: Regional and International Politics, 1955–1967 (Boulder, CO: Westview, 1994); Michael Hudson, ed., The Middle East Dilemma: The Politics and Economics of Arab Integration (New York: Columbia University Press, 1998); F. Gregory Gause III, "Systemic Approaches to Middle East International Relations," International Studies Review 1, no. 1 (1999): 11–31; Bassel Salloukh and Rex Brynen, eds., Persistent Permeability? Regionalism, Localism, and Globalization in the Middle East (Aldershot, UK: Ashgate, 2004), 81–104; Fred Halliday, The Middle East in International Relations: Power, Politics and Ideology (Cambridge: Cambridge University Press, 2005); and Tareq Ismael and Glenn Perry, eds., The International Relations of the Contemporary Middle East: Subordination and Beyond (New York: Routledge, 2014).

11. Jason Brownlee, Authoritarianism in an Age of Democratization (New York: Cambridge University Press, 2007), 202.

12. Fawaz Gerges, "The Study of Middle East International Relations: A Critique," British Journal for Middle Eastern Studies 18, no. 2 (1991): 211.

13. Jonathan Adelman, ed., Superpowers and Revolution (New York: Praeger, 1986).

2. COALITIONS, STATE-BUILDING, AND GEOPOLITICAL MEDIATION

1. Hisham Sharabi, A Theory of Distorted Change in Arab Society (New York: Oxford University Press, 1988); and Niklas Potrafke, "Islam and Democracy," Public Choice 151, no. 1 (2012): 185–92.

2. Mohammed Ayoob, "The Muslim World's Poor Record of Modernization and Democratization: The Interplay of External and Internal Factors," in Modernization, Democracy, and Islam, ed. Shireen Hunter and Huma Malik (Norwalk, CT: Greenwood Press, 2005), 186–202; and Amaney Jamal and Mark Tessler, "Attitudes in the Arab World," Journal of Democracy 19, no. 1 (2008): 97–110.

3. Gordon Richards, "Stabilization Crises and the Breakdown of Military Authoritarianism in Latin America," Comparative Political Studies 18, no. 4 (1986): 449–85; and Stephan Haggard and Robert R. Kaufman, The Political Economy of Democratic Transitions (Princeton: Princeton University Press, 1995).

4. Daron Acemoglu and James Robinson, Economic Origins of Dictatorship and Democracy (New York: Cambridge University Press, 2006).

5. Victor Lavy and Eliezer Sheffer, Foreign Aid and Economic Development in the Middle East: Egypt, Syria, and Jordan (Westport, CT: Praeger, 1991); Alan Richards and John Waterbury, A Political Economy of the Middle East: State, Class, and Economic Development, 3rd ed. (Boulder, CO: Westview, 2008); and Clement Moore Henry and Robert Springborg, Globalization and the Politics of Development in the Middle East (New York: Cambridge University Press, 2010).

6. Benjamin Smith, "Rethinking the Economic Origins of Dictatorship and Democracy: The Continuing Value of Cases and Comparisons," American Political Science Association—Comparative Politics Newsletter 19, no. 1 (2008): 16–20.

2. COALITIONS, STATE-BUILDING, AND GEOPOLITICAL MEDIATION

7. Hossein Mahdavy, "The Patterns and Problems of Economic Development in Rentier States: The Case of Iran," in *Studies in the Economic History of the Middle East: From the Rise of Islam to the Present Day*, ed. Michael Cook (London: Oxford University Press, 1970), 428–67; H. Beblawi, "The Rentier State in the Arab World," in *The Arab State*, ed. Giacomo Luciani (London: Routledge, 1990), 85–98; Giacomo Luciani, "The Oil Rent, the Fiscal Crisis of the State, and Democratization," in *Democracy without Democrats: The Renewal of Politics in the Muslim World*, ed. Ghassan Salamé (London: I. B. Tauris, 1994), 130–55; and Michael Ross, "Does Oil Hinder Democracy?" *World Politics* 53, no. 3 (2001): 325–61.

8. Kiren Aziz Chaudhry, *The Price of Wealth: Economies and Institutions in the Middle East* (Ithaca, NY: Cornell University Press, 1997); Thad Dunning, *Crude Democracy* (New York: Cambridge University Press, 2008); Pauline Jones Luong and Erika Weinthal, *Oil Is Not a Curse: Ownership Structure and Institutions in Soviet Successor States* (New York: Cambridge University Press, 2010); and Steffen Hertog, *Princes, Brokers, and Bureaucrats: Oil and the State in Saudi Arabia* (Ithaca, NY: Cornell University Press, 2011).

9. Benjamin Smith, *Hard Times in the Lands of Plenty: Oil Politics in Iran and Indonesia* (Ithaca, NY: Cornell University Press, 2007).

10. Sean L. Yom, "Oil, Coalitions, and Regime Durability: The Origins and Persistence of Popular Rentierism in Kuwait," *Studies in Comparative International Development* 46, no. 2 (2011): 217–41.

11. Mark Irving Lichbach, *The Rebel's Dilemma* (Ann Arbor: University of Michigan, 1995); and Antonio Giustozzi, *The Art of Coercion: The Primitive Accumulation and Management of Coercive Power* (New York: Columbia University Press, 2011).

12. Nazih Ayubi, *Over-stating the Arab State: Politics and Society in the Middle East* (London: I. B. Tauris, 1995); Eva Bellin, "The Robustness of Authoritarianism in the Middle East: Exceptionalism in Comparative Perspectives," *Comparative Politics* 36, no. 2 (2004): 139–57; and Michael Albertus and Victor Menaldo, "Coercive Capacity and the Prospects for Democratization," *Comparative Politics* 44, no. 2 (2012): 151–69.

13. Christian Davenport, "State Repression and Political Order," *Annual Review of Political Science* 10 (2007): 1–23; and Abel Escribà-Folch, "Repression, Political Threats, and Survival under Autocracy," *International Political Science Review* 34, no. 5 (2013): 543–60.

14. Atül Kohli, *State-Directed Development: Political Power and Industrialization in the Global Periphery* (New York: Cambridge University Press, 2004); and James Mahoney, *Colonialism and Postcolonial Development: Spanish America in Comparative Perspective* (New York: Cambridge University Press, 2010).

15. Lisa Anderson, *The State and Social Transformation in Tunisia and Libya, 1830–1980* (Princeton: Princeton University Press, 1986); and Tuong Vu, *Paths to Development in Asia: South Korea, Vietnam, China, and Indonesia* (New York: Cambridge University Press, 2010).

16. Michael Hudson, *Arab Politics: The Search for Legitimacy* (New Haven: Yale University Press, 1977).

17. Victor Menaldo, "The Middle East and North Africa's Resilient Monarchs," *Journal of Politics* 74, no. 3 (2012): 707–22; and Zoltan Barany, "Unrest and State Response in Arab Monarchies," *Mediterranean Quarterly* 24, no. 2 (2013): 5–38.

18. Sean L. Yom and F. Gregory Gause III, "Resilient Royals: How Arab Monarchies Hang On," *Journal of Democracy* 23, no. 4 (2012): 74–88; and Jason Brownlee, Tarek Masoud, and Andrew Reynolds, *The Arab Spring: Pathways of Repression and Reform* (New York: Oxford University Press, 2015).

19. Lisa Anderson, "Absolutism and the Resilience of Monarchy in the Middle East," *Political Science Quarterly* 106, no. 2 (1991): 1–15.

20. Michael Herb's work remains one of the few to explain different outcomes among only monarchies. It presents the practice of familial power-sharing as the guarantor against internal threats, such as jealous relatives and military conspiracies. However, this does not account for situations in which the *masses* revolt, which broadly confronts all autocracies. Michael Herb, *All in the Family: Absolutism, Revolution, and Democracy in the Middle Eastern Monarchies* (Albany: State University of New York Press, 1999).

21. Samuel Huntington and Clement Henry Moore, eds., *Authoritarian Politics in Modern Society: The Dynamics of Established One-Party Systems* (New York: Basic, 1970); Amos Perlmutter, *Modern Authoritarianism: A Comparative Institutional Analysis* (New Haven: Yale University Press, 1981); and David Art, "What Do We Know about Authoritarianism after Ten Years?" *Comparative Politics* 44, no. 3 (2012): 351–73.

22. Barbara Geddes, "What Do We Know about Democratization after Twenty Years?" *Annual Review of Political Science* 2 (1999): 115–44; Beatriz Magaloni, *Voting for Autocracy: Hegemonic Party Survival and Its Demise in Mexico* (New York: Cambridge University Press, 2006); and Jason Brownlee, *Authoritarianism in an Age of Democratization* (New York: Cambridge University Press, 2007).

23. Ellen Lust-Okar, *Structuring Conflict in the Arab World: Incumbents, Opponents, and Institutions* (New York: Cambridge University Press, 2005); Jennifer Gandhi, *Political Institutions under Dictatorships* (New York: Cambridge University Press, 2008); and Carles Boix and Milan W. Svolik, "The Foundations of Limited Authoritarian Government: Institutions, Commitment, and Power-Sharing in Dictatorships," *Journal of Politics* 75, no. 2 (2013): 300–16.

24. Thomas Pepinsky, "The Institutional Turn in Comparative Authoritarianism," *British Journal of Political Science* 44, no. 3 (2014): 11–14.

25. For more on this endogenous view of institutions, see further Barry Ames, *Political Survival: Politicians and Public Policy in Latin America* (Berkeley: University of California Press, 1987); and Peter Hall and Rosemary C. R. Taylor, "Political Science and the Three New Institutionalisms," *Political Studies* 44, no. 5 (1996): 936–57.

26. On the case for exploring preinstitutional origins of institutional structures, see Benjamin Smith, "Life of the Party: The Origins of Regime Breakdown and Persistence under Single-Party Rule," *World Politics* 57, no. 3 (2005): 421–51.

27. Manfred Halpern, *The Politics of Social Change in the Middle East and North Africa* (Princeton: Princeton University Press, 1963), 58–60.

28. William Riker, *The Theory of Political Coalitions* (New Haven: Yale University Press, 1962), 32–46.

29. Bruce Bueno de Mesquita et al., *The Logic of Political Survival* (Cambridge, MA: MIT Press, 2005), 51–60.

30. David Waldner, *State Building and Late Development* (Ithaca, NY: Cornell University Press, 1999), 28–29.

31. Martin Shefter, *Political Parties and the State: The American Historical Experience* (Princeton: Princeton University Press, 1994), 6–7.

32. Barbara Geddes, *Politician's Dilemma: Building State Capacity in Latin America* (Berkeley: University of California Press, 1994), 13.

33. Dan Slater, *Ordering Power: Contentious Politics and Authoritarian Leviathans in Southeast Asia* (New York: Cambridge University Press, 2010).

34. Smith, "Life of the Party."

35. Kenneth Jowitt, "Inclusion and Mobilization in European Leninist Regimes," *World Politics* 28, no. 1 (1975): 69–96.

36. Anna Grzymala-Busse, *Rebuilding Leviathan: Party Competition and State Exploitation in Post-Communist Democracies* (New York: Cambridge University Press, 2007).

37. Alfred Stepan, *Rethinking Military Politics: Brazil and the Southern Cone* (Princeton: Princeton University Press, 1988); and Lucan Way, "Authoritarian State Building and the Sources of Regime Competitiveness in the Fourth Wave: The Cases of Belarus, Moldova, Russia, and Ukraine," *World Politics* 57, no. 2 (2005): 231–61.

38. Steven Heydemann, *Authoritarianism in Syria: Institutions and Social Conflict, 1946–1970* (Ithaca, NY: Cornell University Press, 1999), 30–54.

39. Waldner, *State Building*, 34–41.

40. Patronage is tailored to recipient groups. Thus for rural classes like small cultivators, patronage could entail redistributive reforms resulting in land grants, new lines of financial credit, subsidized inputs, and trade protections.

41. Lloyd Rudolph and Susanne Hoeber Rudolph, "Authority and Power in Bureaucratic and Patrimonial Administration: A Revisionist Interpretation of Weber on Bureaucracy," *World Politics* 31, no. 2 (1979): 195–227.

42. Slater, *Ordering Power*, 47–50.

43. W. Howard Wriggins, *The Ruler's Imperative: Strategies for Political Survival in Asia and Africa* (New York: Columbia University Press, 1969), 207–20.

44. Peter Gourevitch, "The Second Image Reversed: The International Sources of Domestic Politics," *International Organization* 32, no. 4 (1978): 881–912.

45. Laurence Whitehead, ed., *The International Dimensions of Democratization: Europe and the Americas* (New York: Oxford University Press, 1996); Jon Pevehouse, *Democracy from Above: Regional Organizations and Democratization* (New York: Cambridge University Press, 2005); Wade Jacoby, "Inspiration, Coalition, and Substitution: External Influences on Postcommunist Transformations," *World Politics* 58, no. 4 (2006): 623–51; Steven Levitsky and Lucan Way, *Competitive Authoritarianism: Hybrid Regimes after the Cold War* (New York: Cambridge University Press, 2010); and Valerie Bunce and Sharon Wolchik, *Defeating Authoritarian Leaders in Postcommunist Countries* (New York: Cambridge University Press, 2011).

46. Theda Skocpol, *States and Social Revolutions: A Comparative Analysis of France, Russia, and China* (New York: Cambridge University Press, 1979); Skocpol, "Reflections on Recent Scholarship about Social Revolutions and How to Study Them," in *Social Revolutions in the Modern World*, ed. Theda Skocpol (New York: Cambridge University Press, 1994), 301–44; Jack Goldstone, "Toward a Fourth Generation of Revolutionary Theory," *Annual Review of Political Science* 4 (2001): 139–87; and Jeff Goodwin, *No Other Way Out: States and Revolutionary Movements, 1945–1991* (New York: Cambridge University Press, 2001).

47. Charles Tilly, *Coercion, Capital, and European States, AD 990–1992* (Cambridge, MA: Blackwell, 1990); Brian Downing, *The Military Revolution and Political Change: Origins of Democracy and Autocracy in Early Modern Europe* (Princeton: Princeton University Press, 1992); and Thomas Ertman, *Birth of the Leviathan: Building States and Regimes in Medieval and Early Modern Europe* (New York: Cambridge University Press, 1997).

48. Barrington Moore, *Social Origins of Dictatorship and Democracy: Lord and Peasant in the Making of the Modern World* (Boston: Beacon, 1966).

49. Victoria Tin-Bor Hui, *War and State Formation in Ancient China and Early Modern Europe* (New York: Cambridge University Press, 2005).

50. Eiko Ikegami, *The Taming of the Samurai: Honorific Individualism and the Making of Modern Japan* (Cambridge, MA: Harvard University Press, 1995).

51. Joel Migdal, *Strong Societies and Weak States: State-Society Relations and State Capabilities in the Third World* (Princeton: Princeton University Press, 1988).

52. Tuong Vu, "Studying the State through State Formation," *World Politics* 62, no. 1 (2010): 148–75.

53. Miguel Angel Centeno, *Blood and Debt: War and the Nation-State in Latin America* (University Park: Pennsylvania State University Press, 2002).

54. This excludes the Communist bloc, where individual political and economic systems were uniquely prefigured by a single center of geopolitical domination—Moscow. See further Jan F. Triska, ed., *Dominant Powers and Subordinate States: The United States in Latin America and the Soviet Union in Eastern Europe* (Durham, NC: Duke University Press, 1986).

55. Stephen Krasner, *Sovereignty: Organized Hypocrisy* (Princeton: Princeton University Press, 1999); David Lake, *Hierarchy in International Relations* (Ithaca, NY:

Cornell University Press, 2009); and Ja Ian Chong, *External Intervention and the Politics of State Formation: China, Indonesia, and Thailand, 1893–1952* (New York: Cambridge University Press, 2012).

56. Israel's acquisition of the West Bank and Gaza Strip is exceptional in this regard. In the Middle East, Egypt, Jordan, and Syria represent rare losers of claimed and populated territory to a foreign belligerent during the postcolonial era. Ian Lustick, "The Absence of Middle Eastern Great Powers: Political 'Backwardness' in Historical Perspective," *International Organization* 51, no. 4 (1997): 653–83.

57. Jeffrey Ira Herbst, *States and Power in Africa: Comparative Lessons in Authority and Control* (Princeton: Princeton University Press, 2000); and Rolf Schwarz, *War and State Building in the Middle East* (Gainesville: University Press of Florida, 2012).

58. Steven Heydemann, "War, Institutions, and Social Change in the Middle East," in *War, Institutions, and Social Change in the Middle East,* ed. Steven Heydemann (Berkeley: University of California Press, 2000), 1–32; and Deborah Bräutigam, *Taxation and State-Building in Developing Countries: Capacity and Consent* (New York: Cambridge University Press, 2008).

59. Steven David, "Explaining Third World Alignment," *World Politics* 43, no. 2 (1991): 233–56; and Mohammed Ayoob, *The Third World Security Predicament: State Making, Regional Conflict, and the International System* (Boulder, CO: Lynne Rienner, 1995).

60. Peter Mangold, *Super Power Intervention in the Middle East* (New York: St. Martin's, 1978), 12.

61. Laurie Brand, *Jordan's Inter-Arab Relations: The Political Economy of Alliance Making* (New York: Columbia University Press, 1995), 302.

62. Yair Evron, "Great Military Intervention in the Middle East," in *Great Power Intervention in the Middle East,* ed. Milton Leitenberg and Gabriel Sheffer (New York: Pergamon, 1979), 22–23.

63. Richard Rose, "Dynamic Tendencies in the Authority of Regime," *World Politics* 21, no. 4 (1969): 604.

64. Beatriz Magaloni, "Credible Power-Sharing and the Longevity of Authoritarian Rule," *Comparative Political Studies* 41, nos. 4–5 (2008): 715–41.

65. Thomas Pepinsky, *Economic Crises and the Breakdown of Authoritarian Regimes: Indonesia and Malaysia in Comparative Perspective* (New York: Cambridge University Press, 2009), 14–20.

66. Slater, *Ordering Power,* 211–25.

67. Smith, "Life of the Party," 51.

68. Jeff Goodwin and Theda Skocpol, "Explaining Revolutions in the Contemporary Third World," *Politics and Society* 17, no. 4 (1989): 489–509; and Timothy P. Wickham-Crowley, *Guerrillas and Revolution in Latin America: A Comparative Study of Insurgents and Regimes since 1956* (Princeton: Princeton University Press, 1992).

69. Goodwin, *No Other Way Out,* 47.

70. John Foran, *Taking Power: On the Origins of Third World Revolutions* (New York: Cambridge University Press, 2005, 21–22.

71. John Ravenhill, *Collective Clientelism: The Lomé Conventions and North-South Relations* (New York: Columbia University Press, 1985); and Christopher Carney, "International Patron-Client Relationships: A Conceptual Framework," *Studies in Comparative International Development* 24, no. 2 (1989): 42–55.

72. Mark Gasiorowski, *U.S. Foreign Policy and the Shah: Building a Client State in Iran* (Ithaca, NY: Cornell University Press, 1991), 2–7.

73. Steven Krasner, "Sharing Sovereignty: New Institutions for Collapsed and Failing States," *International Security* 29, no. 2 (2004): 85–120.

74. Lake, *Hierarchy*; and David Sylvan and Stephen Majeski, *US Foreign Policy in Perspective: Clients, Enemies and Empire* (London: Routledge, 2009).

3. CONFLICT AND COMPROMISE IN KUWAIT

1. Sabri Falih Al-Humeidi, *Al-Kuwayt: nushuʾha wa tatawwurha, 1760–1871* (London: Dar Al-Hikma, 2005), 151–59.

2. This mirrored many other eastern Arabian tribes. As with mediated societies, the absence of centralized institutions made political authority extremely diffuse. Majlis councils arose out of pragmatic necessity, not cultural inevitability. See James Onley and Sulayman Khalaf, "Shaikhly Authority in the Pre-oil Gulf: An Historical-Anthropological Study," *History and Anthropology* 17, no. 3 (2006): 189–208; and Yusuf Bin ʿIsa Al-Qinaʾi, *Safahat min taʾrikh al-kuwayt* (Kuwait: n.p., 1968): 9–10.

3. Suhail Shuhaiber, "Social and Political Developments in Kuwait Prior to 1961," in *Kuwait: The Growth of a Historic Identity*, ed. Ben J. Slot (London: Gulf Museum Consultancy, 2003), 100–102.

4. Rosemarie Said Zahlan, *The Making of the Modern Gulf States: Kuwait, Bahrain, Qatar, the United Arab Emirates, and Oman* (London: Ithaca, 1998), 95–96.

5. Harold R. P. Dickson, *Kuwait and Her Neighbors* (London: Allen and Unwin, 1956), 82–107.

6. Sayf Marzuq Shamlan, *Min taʾrikh al-kuwayt* (Kuwait: n.p., 1986), 85–87.

7. Musa Ghadban Al-Hatim, *Taʾrikh al-shurta fiil-kuwayt* (Kuwait: Dar al-qirtas lil-nashr, 1999), 16–19.

8. Ghanim Al-Najjar, "The Challenges of Security Sector Governance in Kuwait" (Working Paper 142, Geneva Centre for the Democratic Control of Armed Forces, 2004), 3.

9. Anthony Toth, "Tribes and Tribulations: Bedouin Losses in the Saudi and Iraqi Struggles over Kuwait's Frontiers, 1921–1943," *British Journal of Middle Eastern Studies* 32, no. 2 (2005): 149.

10. Y. S. F. Al-Sabah, *The Oil Economy of Kuwait* (London: Kegan Paul, 1980), 16–17.

11. Ibrahim Al-Sharqawi, *Al-Kuwayt wa al-luʾluʾ*, 2nd ed. (Kuwait: n.p., 1998).

12. Muhammed Al-Ghanim Rumaihi, "The Mode of Production in the Arab Gulf before the Discovery of Oil," in *Social and Economic Development in the Arab Gulf*, ed. Tim Niblock (London: Croom Helm, 1980), 53–57.

13. The Asil are the Ghanim, Hamad, Khalid, Khurafi, Marzouq, Mudhaf, Nisf, and Saqr families.

14. Eran Segal, "Merchants' Networks in Kuwait: The Story of Yusuf Al-Marzuk," *Middle Eastern Studies* 45, no. 5 (2009): 712–15.

15. J. R. L. Carter, *Merchant Families of Kuwait* (London: Scorpion, 1984), 174–98.

16. Jill Crystal, *Oil and Politics in the Gulf: Rulers and Merchants in Kuwait and Qatar* (New York: Cambridge University Press, 1990), 37–39.

17. Jill Crystal and Abdallah Al-Shayeji, "The Pro-Democratic Agenda in Kuwait: Structures and Context," in *Political Liberalization and Democratization in the Arab World*, vol. 2, ed. Rex Brynen, Bahgat Korany, and Paul Noble (Boulder, CO: Lynne Rienner, 1998), 109.

18. Mohammed Alhabib, "The Shia Migration from Southwestern Iran to Kuwait: Push-Pull Factors during the Late Nineteenth and Early Twentieth Centuries" (MA thesis, Georgia State University, 2010), 70–72.

19. Laurence Louër, *Transnational Shia Politics: Religious and Political Networks in the Gulf* (New York: Columbia University Press, 2008), 45–49.

20. Rivka Azoulay, "The Politics of Shi'i Merchants in Kuwait," in *Business Politics in the Middle East*, ed. Steffen Hertog, Giacomo Luciani, and Mark Valeri (London: Hurst, 2012), 72–73.

21. Frederick Anscombe, *The Ottoman Gulf: The Creation of Kuwait, Saudi Arabia, and Qatar* (New York: Columbia University Press, 1997), 91–112.

22. J. E. Peterson, "Britain and the Gulf: At the Periphery of Empire," in *The Persian Gulf in History*, ed. Lawrence G. Potter (New York: Palgrave Macmillan, 2009), 278–83.

23. Ahmad Hijazi, "Kuwait: Development from a Semitribal, Semicolonial Society to Democracy and Sovereignty," *American Journal of Comparative Law* 13, no. 3 (1964): 429–32.

24. Richard Schofield, *Kuwait and Iraq: Historical Claims and Territorial Disputes*, 2nd ed. (London: Royal Institute for International Affairs, 1993), 24–47.

25. Ahmad M. Abu Hakima, *The Modern History of Kuwait, 1750–1965* (London: Luzac, 1983), 132–34.

26. Farah Al-Nakib, "The Lost 'Two-Thirds:' Kuwait's Territorial Decline between 1913 and 1922," *Journal of Arabian Studies: Arabia, the Gulf, and the Red Sea* 2, no. 1 (2012): 19–37.

27. Jacqueline Ismael, *Kuwait: Dependency and Class in a Rentier State*, 2nd ed. (Gainesville: University of Florida, 1993), 46–52.

28. Mary Ann Tétreault, "Autonomy, Necessity, and the Small State: Ruling Kuwait in the Twentieth Century," *International Organization* 45, no. 4 (1991): 570–75.

29. Dhafir Muhammad Nasir Al-ʿAjami, *Jaysh al-kuwayt fii ʿasr mubarak al-sabah* (Kuwait: n.p., 2000), 187–231.

30. James Onley, *The Arabian Frontier of the British Raj: Merchants, Rulers, and the British in the Nineteenth-Century Gulf* (Oxford: Oxford University Press, 2007), 14–28.

31. J. G. Lorimer, *Gazeteer of the Persian Gulf, Oman, and Central Asia*, vol. 1 (Calcutta, India: Superintendent Government Printing, 1915), 1039.

32. Ben Slot, *Mubarak Al-Sabah: Founder of Modern Kuwait, 1896–1915* (London: Arabian Publishing, 2005), 296–317.

33. Salwa Alghanim, *The Reign of Mubarak Al-Sabah: Shaikh of Kuwait, 1896–1915* (London: I. B. Tauris, 1998), 135–41.

34. Muhammad Nayif Al-ʿAnazi, *Dirasat fii-taʾrikh al-kuwayt al-hadith wa al-muʿasir* (Kuwait: Matbaʿ al-fajr al-kuwaytiyyah, 2004), 46–51.

35. Lorimer, *Gazeteer*, 1047–48.

36. ʿAbd Al-ʿAziz Al-Rushayd, *Taʾrikh al-kuwayt* (Beirut: Maktabat al-hayat, 1971), 190–97.

37. Eran Segal, "Formal and Informal Political Participation in Kuwait: Diwaniya, Majlis, and Parliament," *Journal of Arabian Studies: Arabia, the Gulf, and the Red Sea* 2, no. 2 (2012): 131–32.

38. Toth, "Tribes and Tribulations," 150–60.

39. M. W. Khouja and P. G. Sadler, *The Economy of Kuwait: Development and Role in International Finance* (London: Macmillan, 1979), 22–23.

40. Ismael, *Kuwait: Dependency*, 73–77.

41. Andrew Loewenstein, " 'The Veiled Protectorate of Kowait:' Liberalized Imperialism and British Efforts to Influence Kuwaiti Domestic Policy during the Reign of Sheikh Ahmad Al-Jaber, 1938–50," *Middle Eastern Studies* 36, no. 2 (2000): 107–9.

42. Najat ʿAbd Al-Qadir Al-Jasim, *Al-Tatawwur al-siyasi wa al-iqtisadi lil-kuwayt baina al-harbayni* (Kuwait: n.p., 1997), 163–67.

43. Khalid Sulayman Al-ʿAdsani, *Muthakirrat khalid sulayman al-ʿadsani, sikritir majlis al-umma al-tashriʿ al-awwal wa al-thani* (Kuwait: n.p., 1939).

44. Kamal Osman Salih, "The 1938 Kuwait Legislative Council," *Middle Eastern Studies* 28, no. 1 (1992): 76–83. For more on the council's regulation of social spaces, see Farah Al-Nakib, "Public Space and Public Protest in Kuwait, 1938–2012," *City: Analysis of Urban Trends, Culture, Theory, Policy, Action* 18, no. 6 (2014): 726–27.

45. Jill Crystal, "Public Order and Authority: Policing Kuwait," in *Monarchies and Nations: Globalisation and Identity in the Arab States of the Gulf*, ed. Paul Dresch and James Piscatori (London: I. B. Tauris, 2005), 161–62.

46. This argument resonates with many royals today. HRH Sheikh Salim Jabir Al-Ahmad Al-Sabah, personal interview with author, Kuwait, March 24, 2007.

47. Segal, "Formal and Informal," 135.

48. Loewenstein, "Veiled Protectorate," 110–12.

49. Fakhri Shehab, "Kuwait: A Super-Affluent Society," *Foreign Affairs* 42, no. 3 (1964): 462.

50. H. V. F. Winstone and Zahra Dickson Freeth, *Kuwait: Prospect and Reality* (New York: Crane and Russak, 1972), 111–18.

51. Schofield, *Kuwait and Iraq*, 66–76.

52. David Mclean, "Finance and 'Informal Empire' before the First World War," *The Economic History Review* 29, no. 2 (1976): 304.

53. Al-Jasim, *Al-Tatawwur al-siyasi*, 179–81.

54. Majid Khadduri and Edmund Ghareeb, *War in the Gulf, 1990–91: The Iraq-Kuwait Conflict and Its Implications* (New York: Oxford University Press, 1997), 38–40.

55. Crystal, *Oil and Politics*, 50.

56. Paul Rich, *Creating the Arabian Gulf: The British Raj and the Invasions of the Gulf* (Lanham: Lexington, 2009), 215.

57. Alan Rush, *Al-Sabah: History and Genealogy of Kuwait's Ruling Family, 1752–1987* (London: Ithaca, 1987), 39–40.

58. Michael Herb, *All in the Family: Absolutism, Revolution, and Democracy in the Middle Eastern Monarchies* (Albany: State University of New York Press, 1999. 73.

59. Robert Jarmon, *Sabah Al-Salim Al-Sabah, Amir of Kuwait, 1965–1977: A Political Biography* (London: London Center for Arab Studies, 2002), 21–22.

60. Rush, *Al-Sabah*, 58.

61. Salih, "1938 Kuwait Legislative Council," 85–87.

62. Azoulay, "Politics of Shiʻi Merchants," 77.

63. Dickson, *Kuwait and Her Neighbors*, 450–51.

64. Ragaei El-Mallakh, *Economic Development and Regional Cooperation: Kuwait* (Chicago: University of Chicago, 1968), 6–7.

65. Keith McLachlan, "Oil in the Persian Gulf Area," in *The Persian Gulf States: A General Survey*, ed. Alvin Cottrell et al. (Baltimore: Johns Hopkins University Press, 1980), 212–16.

66. El-Mallakh, *Economic Development*, 41.

67. Khouja and Sadler, *Economy of Kuwait*, 26.

68. Yacoub Al-Homaizi, personal interview with author, Kuwait, March 6, 2007.

69. Zahlan, *The Making of the Modern Gulf States*, 40.

70. Ash Rossiter, "Britain and the Development of Professional Security Forces in the Gulf Arab States, 1921–71: Local Forces and Informal Empire" (PhD diss., University of Exeter, 2014), 152–53.

71. Hassan Ali Al-Ebraheem, *Kuwait and the Gulf: Small States and the International System* (London: Croom Helm, 1984), 42–47.

72. Ghanim Al-Najjar, "Decision-Making Process in Kuwait: The Land Acquisition Policy as a Case Study" (PhD diss., University of Exeter, 1984).

73. Isam Al-Taher, *Kuwait: The Reality* (Pittsburgh: Dorrance, 1995), 130–32.

74. Talcott Seelye, personal interview with Charles Kennedy, September 15, 1993, in *Frontline Diplomacy: The Foreign Affairs Oral History Collection of the Association for Diplomatic Studies and Training* (Washington, D.C.: Library of Congress, 2007).

75. International Bank for Reconstruction and Development, *The Economic Development of Kuwait* (Baltimore: Johns Hopkins Press, 1965), 72–74.

76. Crystal, "Public Order," 162.

77. Shuhaiber, "Social and Political Developments," 106.

78. Herb, *All in the Family*, 76–79.

79. Abdullah Khalifah Al-Shayeji, "Democratization in Kuwait: The National Assembly as a Strategy for Political Survival" (PhD diss., University of Texas at Austin, 1988), 75–77.

80. George Lenczowski, *Oil and State in the Middle East* (Ithaca, NY: Cornell University Press, 1960), 20.

81. Malcolm Yapp, "British Policy in the Persian Gulf," in *The Persian Gulf States: A General Survey*, ed. Alvin Cottrell et al. (Baltimore: Johns Hopkins University Press, 1980), 96.

82. Al-Sabah, *Oil Economy*, 39–44.

83. Simon Smith, *Kuwait, 1950–1965: Britain, the Al-Sabah, and Oil* (Oxford: Oxford University Press, 1999), 16–35.

84. William Roger Louis, "Britain and the Middle East after 1945," in *Diplomacy in the Middle East: The International Relations of Regional and Outside Powers*, ed. L. Carl Brown (London: I. B. Tauris, 2004), 21–58.

85. Rupert Hay, *The Persian Gulf States* (Washington, D.C.: The Middle East Institute, 1959), 101–2.

86. Rossiter, "Britain and the Development," 158.

87. Smith, *Kuwait, 1950–1965*, 93.

88. Saba George Shiber, *The Kuwait Urbanization: Documentation, Analysis, Critique* (Kuwait: Kuwait Government Printing, 1964).

89. Falah Al-Mdairis, "The Arab Nationalist Movement in Kuwait from its Origins to 1970" (PhD diss., University of Oxford, 1987).

90. Gawain Bell, *Shadows on the Sand: The Memoirs of Sir Gawain Bell* (London: Hurst, 1983), 244–46.

91. Miriam Joyce, *Kuwait, 1945–1996: An Anglo-American Perspective* (London: Cass, 1998), 40–44. For instance, when thousands of protesters turned out after Nasser's call for a general strike in August 1956, with some carrying placards of his likeness in defiance of Sabah rulership, public security forces responded with "staves" and shut down the National Cultural Club, a center of Arab Nationalist opposition, for just two days. Al-Nakib, "Public Space and Public Protest," 728–29.

92. Smith, *Kuwait, 1950–1965*, 70–78.

93. Jarmon, *Sabah Al-Salim Al-Sabah*, 50.

94. Joyce, *Kuwait, 1945–1996*, 54–55.

95. Mary Ann Tétreault, *Stories of Democracy: Politics and Society in Contemporary Kuwait* (New York: Columbia University Press, 2000), 70.

96. ʿAbdullah Bishara, personal interview with author, Kuwait, March 11, 2007.

97. Joyce, *Kuwait, 1945–1996*, 51–63.

98. Abdul-Reda Assiri, *Kuwait's Foreign Policy: City-State in World Politics* (Boulder, CO: Westview, 1990), 20.

99. Khadduri and Ghareeb, *War in the Gulf*, 63–67.

100. Nigel John Ashton, "A Microcosm of Decline: British Loss of Nerve and Military Intervention in Jordan and Kuwait, 1958 and 1961," *The Historical Journal* 40, no. 4 (1997): 1073.

101. Rosemary Hollis, "Great Britain," in *The Powers in the Middle East: The Ultimate Strategic Arena*, ed. Bernard Reich (New York: Praeger, 1987), 193.

4. INCLUSION AND STABILITY IN A POPULIST AUTOCRACY

1. Ragaei El-Mallakh, *Economic Development and Regional Cooperation: Kuwait* (Chicago: University of Chicago, 1968), 43–46.

2. In regional context, in 1970 Saudi Arabia, Kuwait, Bahrain, Qatar, the United Arab Emirates, and Oman collected $4.96 billion in oil proceeds; in 1980, they recorded $248.37 billion. Roger Owen and Sevket Pamuk, *A History of Middle East Economies in the Twentieth Century* (Cambridge, MA: Harvard University Press, 1999), 267.

3. Y. S. F. Al-Sabah, *The Oil Economy of Kuwait.* (London: Kegan Paul, 1980), 51–67.

4. Khaldun Al-Naqib, *Siraʿ baina al-qabaliyyah wa al-dimuqratiyyah: halat al-kuwayt* (London: Dar Al-Saqi, 1996), 85–113.

5. International Bank for Reconstruction and Development, *The Economic Development of Kuwait* (Baltimore: Johns Hopkins Press, 1965), 44–45. As British Ambassador G. N. Jackson noted in 1964, "If a mysterious plague killed off every Kuwaiti tomorrow the economy would continue very much as it does at present." Smith, *Kuwait, 1950–1965*, 137.

6. Shamlan Alessa, *The Manpower Problem in Kuwait* (London: Kegan Paul, 1981), 89.

7. Abdulkarim Dekhayel, *Kuwait: Oil, State and Political Legitimation* (Reading, UK: Ithaca, 2000), 92–94.

8. Pete Moore, *Doing Business in the Middle East: Politics and Economic Crisis in Jordan and Kuwait* (New York: Cambridge University Press, 2004), 86.

9. Sula Al-Naqeeb, "The Question of Citizenship and Integration in Kuwait: Looking at the Bidoun as a Case Study" (MA thesis, The School of Oriental and African Studies, University of London, 2006), 12–13.

10. Dekhayel, *Kuwait*, 96.

11. Smith, *Kuwait, 1950–1965*, 140–41.

12. Sulaiman Al-Onaizi, personal interview with author, Kuwait, March 13, 2007.

13. Lori Plotkin Boghardt, *Kuwait Amid War, Peace and Revolution: 1979–1991 and New Challenges* (New York: Palgrave Macmillan, 2006), 22.

14. Crystal, "Public Order," 168–70.

15. Fred Halliday, *Arabia without Sultans* (London: Penguin, 1974), 437.

16. Hasan Qayed, "Press and Authorities in the Arab World: The Case of Kuwait," *Arab Affairs* 1, no. 9 (1989): 94–108.

17. Kjetil Selvik, "Elite Rivalry in a Semi-Democracy: The Kuwaiti Press Scene," *Middle Eastern Studies* 47, no. 3 (2011): 481–82.

18. Shafeeq Al-Ghabra, "Voluntary Associations in Kuwait: The Foundation of a New System?" *Middle East Journal* 45, no. 2 (1991): 202–3.

19. Robert Jarmon, *Sabah Al-Salim Al-Sabah, Amir of Kuwait, 1965–1977: A Political Biography* (London: London Center for Arab Studies, 2002), 213–17.

20. Neil Hicks and Ghanim Al-Najjar, "The Utility of Tradition: Civil Society in Kuwait," in *Civil Society in the Middle East*, vol. 1, ed. Augustus Richard Norton (Leiden, the Netherlands: Brill, 1995), 196.

21. Al-Sabah, *Oil Economy*, 76–79.

22. Abdul-Reda Assiri, *Kuwait's Foreign Policy: City-State in World Politics* (Boulder, CO: Westview, 1990), 37–53.

23. Miriam Joyce, *Kuwait, 1945–1996: An Anglo-American Perspective* (London: Cass, 1998), 156–58.

24. Hassan Ali Al-Ebraheem, *Kuwait and the Gulf: Small States and the International System* (London: Croom Helm, 1984), 62–63.

25. An account of this comes from Brandon H. Grove, personal interview with Thomas Stern, November 14, 1994, in *Frontline Diplomacy: The Foreign Affairs Oral History Collection of the Association for Diplomatic Studies and Training* (Washington, D.C.: Library of Congress, 2007).

26. J. B. Kelly, *Arabia, the Gulf, and the West* (New York: Basic, 1980), 172.

27. Dekhayel, *Kuwait*, 167–70.

28. Fawzi Al-Sultan, *Averting Financial Crisis—Kuwait* (Washington, D.C.: World Bank, 1989), 35.

29. Moore, *Doing Business*, 47–57.

30. Carter, *Merchant Families*, 133.

31. Abdullah Khalifah Al-Shayeji, "Democratization in Kuwait: The National Assembly as a Strategy for Political Survival" (PhD diss., University of Texas at Austin, 1988), 421–23.

32. Ghanim Al-Najjar, *Madkhal lil-tatawwar al-siyasii fiil-kuwayt* (Kuwait: Dar al-qirtas lil-nashr, 1996), 71–73.

33. Jassim Muhammad Khalaf, "The Kuwait National Assembly: A Study of Its Structure and Function" (PhD diss., State University of New York at Albany, 1984).

34. Naseer Aruri, "Kuwait: A Political Study," *The Muslim World* 60, no. 4 (1970): 338–43.

35. Abdul-Reda Assiri and Kamal Al-Manoufi, "Kuwait's Political Elite: The Cabinet," *Middle East Journal* 42, no. 1 (1988): 49.

36. Abdo Baaklini, "Legislatures in the Gulf Area: The Experience of Kuwait, 1961–1976," *International Journal of Middle East Studies* 14, no. 3 (1982): 365–66.

37. Anh Nga Longva, "Nationalism in Pre-modern Guise: The Discourse on Hadhar and Badu in Kuwait," *International Journal of Middle East Studies* 38, no. 2 (2006): 172–76.

38. Shafeeq Al-Ghabra, "Kuwait and the Dynamics of Socio-Economic Change," *Middle East Journal* 51, no. 3 (1997): 365–67.

39. Farah Al-Nakib, "Revisiting Hadar and Badu in Kuwait: Citizenship, Housing, and the Construction of a Dichotomy," *International Journal of Middle East Studies* 46, no. 1 (2014): 14–23.

40. Al-Ghabra, "Kuwait and the Dynamics," 364.

41. Al-Taher, *Kuwait: The Reality*, 172–74.

42. I am grateful to Bandar Al-Shimmari for clarifying this. Personal interview with author, Kuwait, March 7, 2007.

43. Nicolas Gavrielides, "Tribal Democracy: The Anatomy of Parliamentary Elections in Kuwait," in *Elections in the Middle East: Implications of Recent Trends*, ed. Linda L. Layne (Boulder, CO: Westview, 1987), 160–61.

44. Al-Homaizi, personal interview. Al-Homaizi served on the Constituent Assembly.

45. Gavrielides, "Tribal Democracy," 185.

46. Al-Naqib, *Sira'*, 136–41.

47. Kamal Osman Salih, "Kuwait Primary (Tribal) Elections, 1975–2008: An Evaluative Study," *British Journal of Middle Eastern Studies* 38, no. 2 (2011): 142–54.

48. Crystal and Al-Shayeji, "The Pro-Democratic Agenda," 103.

49. Azoulay, "Politics of Shi'i Merchants," 78–82.

50. *Dimuqratiyyah al-shuyukh: Asrar al-hayat al-siyasiyyah fiil-kuwayt* (Kuwait: Dar Al-qirtas lil-nashr, 1986), 30–32.

51. Jasem Karam, "Kuwait National Assembly—1992: A Study in Electoral Geography," *GeoJournal* 31, no. 4 (1993): 391.

52. Al-Ghabra, "Kuwait and the Dynamics," 368.

53. Rola Dashti, personal interview with author, Kuwait, February 27, 2007, emphasis mine.

54. Mohammad Abdul Rahman Al-Yahya, *Kuwait: Fall and Rebirth* (London: Kegan Paul, 1993), 34–36.

55. Al-Sultan, *Averting Financial Crisis*, 10–25.

56. Owen and Pamuk, *History of Middle East Economies*, 267.

57. Khouja and Sadler, *Economy of Kuwait*, 196–208.

58. Dekhayel, *Kuwait*, 192.

59. Yousif Al-Ebraheem, personal interview with author, Kuwait, February 28, 2007.

60. Al-Sultan, *Averting Financial Crisis*, 28.

61. K. Celine, "Kuwait Living on Its Nerves," *Middle East Research and Information Project Reports* 130 (1985): 11.

62. Yahya Sadowski, *Scuds or Butter? The Political Economy of Arms Control in the Middle East* (Washington, D.C.: Brookings Institution Press, 1993), 12.

63. Assiri, *Kuwait's Foreign Policy*, 157–60.

64. Ibid., 64–69.

65. Boghardt, *Kuwait Amid War*, 34–35.

66. Azoulay, "Politics of Shiʻi Merchants," 79–81.

67. Boghardt, *Kuwait Amid War*, 71–101.

68. Al-Ghabra, "Voluntary Associations," 206–209.

69. In fact, many royals were suspicious of Islamism, although they were pressured by the emir and other senior relatives to avoid publicly criticizing Islamist groups. Khaled Al-Mutairi, personal interview with author, Kuwait, March 7, 2007.

70. Fahd Al-Sharekh, personal interview with author, Kuwait, February 24, 2007.

71. Falah ʻAbdullah Al-Mudayris, *Al-haraka al-dusturiyyah fiil-kuwayt* (Kuwait: Dar al-qirtas lil-nashr, 2002), 22–33.

72. Crystal, "Public Order," 171.

73. Khaled Al-Mutairi, personal interview with author, Kuwait, March 7, 2007.

74. Tétreault, *Stories of Democracy*, 76–208.

75. Shafeeq Al-Ghabra, *Al-Kuwayt: dirasa fiil-aliyat al-dawla al-qutriyyah wa al-sulta wa al-mujtamaʻ* (Cairo: Ibn Khaldun Center for Development Studies, 1995), 157–82.

76. Steve Yetiv, "Kuwait's Democratic Experiment in Its Broader International Context," *Middle East Journal* 56, no. 2 (2002).

77. U.S. Embassy Political Officer (confidential), personal interview with author, Kuwait, March 21, 2007.

78. Al-Ebraheem, *ʻAjz al-mizaniyyah—awdhaʻ al-maliyyah al-ʻama fiil-kuwayt: al-waqiʻ, al-ihtimal, wa subul al-muwajahah* (Kuwait: Maktabat dar al-qirtas, 1995), 10–24.

79. Al-Naqib, *Siraʻ*, 217–47.

80. For an excellent overview of this renewal of liberal opposition, see ʻAbdullah Yusif Jamal, *Al-Muʻaradha al-siyasiyyah fiil-kuwayt* (Kuwait: Dar al-qirtas lil-nashr, 2004), 265–72.

81. Kuwait Economic Society, *Kuwaiti Public Opinion Survey Report* (Kuwait: KES, 2005), 9–11.

82. Al-Nakib, "Revisiting Hadar and Badu," 24–25.

83. Selvik, "Elite Rivalry," 483–88.

84. Kamal Osman Salih, "Parliamentary Control of the Executive: Evaluation of the Interpellation Mechanism, Case Study Kuwait National Assembly, 1992-2004," *South Asian and Middle Eastern Studies* 29, no. 3 (2006): 36–69.

85. Abdullah Al-Remaidhi and Bob Watt, "Electoral Constituencies and Political Parties in Kuwait: An Assessment," *Election Law Journal: Rules, Politics, and Policy* 11, no. 4 (2012): 521–22.

86. Mary Ann Tétreault and Mohammad Al-Ghanim, "The Day after 'Victory': Kuwait's 2009 Election and the Contentious Present," *Middle East Report Online* (2009), accessed October 13, 2010, http://www.merip.org/mero/mero070809.

87. Paul Salem, "Kuwait: Politics in a Participatory Emirate," in *Beyond the Façade: Political Reform in the Arab World*, ed. Marina Ottaway and Julia Choucair-Vizoso (Washington, D.C.: Carnegie Endowment for International Peace, 2008), 224–30.

5. CLIENCY AND COERCION IN IRAN

1. M. Reza Ghods, "Iranian Nationalism and Reza Shah," *Middle Eastern Studies* 27, no. 1 (1991): 35–45.

2. Stephanie Cronin, *Tribal Politics in Iran Rural Conflict and the New State, 1921–1941* (London: Routledge, 2007), 40–87.

3. Farhad Kazemi and Ervand Abrahamian, "The Nonrevolutionary Peasantry of Modern Iran," *Iranian Studies* 11, no. 1 (1978): 267–75.

4. S. Rezazadeh Shafaq and J. D. Lotz, "The Iranian Seven Year Development Plan," *Middle East Journal* 4, no. 1 (1950): 103.

5. Nikki Keddie, ed., *Iran: Religion, Politics, and Society, Collected Essays* (London: Cass, 1980), 159–65.

6. Ahmad Ashraf, "Historical Obstacles to the Development of a Bourgeoisie in Iran," *Iranian Studies* 2, no. 2 (1969): 59–70.

7. Homa Katouzian, *State and Society in Iran: The Eclipse of the Qajars and the Emergence of the Pahlavis* (London: I. B. Tauris, 2000), 25–54.

8. Nikki Keddie, "The Roots of Ulama Power in Modern Iran," in *Scholars, Saints, and Sufis: Muslim Religious Institutions in the Middle East Since 1500*, ed. Nikki Keddie (Los Angeles: University of California Press, 1972), 579–98.

9. Ahmad Ashraf, "Bazaar-Mosque Alliance: The Social Basis of Revolts and Revolutions," *International Journal of Politics, Culture and Society* 1, no. 4 (1988): 538–67.

10. Shahrough Akhavi, *Religion and Politics in Contemporary Iran Clergy-State Relations in the Pahlavi Period* (Albany: State University of New York Press, 1980), 6–16.

11. Mohammad Faghfoory, "The Impact of Modernization on the Ulama in Iran, 1925–1941," *Iranian Studies* 26, no. 3 (1993): 277–312.

12. Zahra Shaji'i, *Namayandagan-i majlis-i shura-yi milli dar bist-o-yak dowrah-yi qanun-guzari* (Tehran: Institute for Social Studies and Research, 1965), 249.

13. F. Eshraghi, "The Immediate Aftermath of Anglo-Soviet Occupation of Iran in August 1941," *Middle Eastern Studies* 20, no. 3 (1984): 336–46.

14. Eckart Ehlers and Willem Floor, "Urban Change in Iran, 1920–1941," *Iranian Studies* 26, no. 3 (1993): 267–71.

15. G. Hossein Razi, "Genesis of Party in Iran: A Case Study of the Interaction between the Political System and Political Parties," *Iranian Studies* 3, no. 2 (1970): 71–79.

16. Sepehr Zabih, *The Communist Movement in Iran* (Berkeley: University of California Press, 1966), 123–65.

17. L. P. Elwell-Sutton, "Political Parties in Iran, 1941–1948," *Middle East Journal* 3, no. 1 (1949): 46.

18. Ervand Abrahamian, "The Crowd in Iranian Politics 1905–1953," *Past and Present* 41 (1968): 204–6.

19. Sussan Siavoshi, "The Oil Nationalization Movement, 1949–1953," in *A Century of Revolution Social Movements in Iran*, ed. John Foran (Minneapolis: University of Minnesota, 1994), 106–34.

20. Ronald Ferrier, "The Anglo-Iranian Oil Dispute: A Triangular Relationship," in *Musaddiq, Iranian Nationalism, and Oil*, ed. James Bill and William Roger Louis (London: I. B. Tauris, 1988), 171.

21. Mary Ann Heiss, *Empire and Nationhood: The United States, Great Britain, and Iranian Oil, 1950–1954* (New York: Columbia University Press, 1997), 15–76.

22. Majid Yazdi, "Patterns of Clerical Political Behavior in Postwar Iran, 1941–53," *Middle Eastern Studies* 26, no. 3 (1990): 285–89.

23. Misagh Parsa, *Social Origins of the Iranian Revolution* (New Brunswick, NJ: Rutgers University Press, 1989), 95–98.

24. Daniel Yergin, *The Prize: The Epic Quest for Oil, Money, and Power* (New York: Simon and Schuster, 1991), 458–63.

25. Homa Katouzian, *Mussaddiq and the Struggle for Power in Iran* (London: I. B. Tauris, 1990), 121–25.

26. Ervand Abrahamian, *Iran Between Two Revolutions* (Princeton: Princeton University Press, 1982), 272–73.

27. Mohammad Majd, "The 1951–53 Oil Nationalization Dispute and the Iranian Economy: A Rejoinder," *Middle Eastern Studies* 31, no. 3 (1995): 449–59.

28. N. Marbury Efimenco, "An Experiment with Civilian Dictatorship in Iran: The Case of Mohammed Mossadegh," *Journal of Politics* 17, no. 3 (1955): 400.

29. Abbas Milani, *The Shah* (New York: Palgrave Macmillan, 2011), 141–70.

30. Julian Bharier, *Economic Development in Iran, 1900–1970* (London: Oxford University Press, 1971), 46–49.

31. Richard Cottam, "The United States, Iran, and the Cold War," *Iranian Studies* 2, no. 1 (1970): 10–13.

32. Osamu Miyata, "The Tudeh Military Network during the Oil Nationalization Period," *Middle Eastern Studies* 23, no. 3 (1987): 324–27.

33. Stephen Kinzer, *All the Shah's Men: An American Coup and the Roots of Middle East Terror*, 2nd ed. (New York: Wiley, 2008), 85–141.

34. Donald N. Wilber, *Clandestine Service History: Overthrow of Premier Mossadegh of Iran, November 1952–August 1953* (Langley, VA: Central Intelligence Agency, 1969); Mark Gasiorowski, "The 1953 Coup D'état in Iran," *International Journal of Middle East Studies* 19, no. 3 (1987): 261–86; Moyara De Moraes Ruehsen, "Operation 'Ajax' Revisited: Iran, 1953," *Middle Eastern Studies* 29, no. 3 (1993): 467–86; and Fariborz Mokhtari, "Iran's 1953 Coup Revisited: Internal Dynamics versus External Intrigue," *Middle East Journal* 62, no. 3 (2008): 457–88.

35. Habib Ladjevardi, "The Origins of US Support for an Autocratic Iran," *International Journal of Middle East Studies* 15, no. 2 (1983): 225–39.

36. Thomas Ricks, "US Military Missions to Iran, 1943–1978: The Political Economy of Military Assistance," *Iranian Studies* 12, no. 3 (1979): 173–77.

37. Steve Marsh, "Continuity and Change: Reinterpreting the Policies of the Truman and Eisenhower Administrations toward Iran, 1950–1954," *Journal of Cold War Studies* 7, no. 3 (2005): 91–92.

38. Francis Gavin, "Politics, Power, and US Policy in Iran, 1950–1953," *Journal of Cold War Studies* 1, no. 1 (1999): 81–87.

39. Central Intelligence Agency, "The Tudeh Party: Vehicle of Communism in Iran," National Intelligence Estimate ORE 23-49, 18 July 1949, 5.

40. John Campbell, *Defense of the Middle East: Problems of American Policy* (New York: Harper, 1958), 131–32.

41. Ivar Spector, "Soviet Cultural Propaganda in the Near and Middle East," in *The Middle East in Transition: Studies in Contemporary History*, ed. Walter Laqueur (New York: Praeger, 1958), 378–87.

42. Richard Herrmann, "The Role of Iran in Soviet Perceptions and Policy, 1946–1988," in *Neither East nor West: Iran, the Soviet Union, and the United States*, ed. Nikki Keddie and Mark Gasiorowski (New Haven: Yale University Press, 1990), 64–70.

43. Maziar Behrooz, "Tudeh Factionalism and the 1953 Coup in Iran," *International Journal of Middle East Studies* 33, no. 3 (2001): 376–78.

44. George Lenczowski, "United States' Support for Iran's Independence and Integrity, 1945–1959," *Annals of the American Academy of Political and Social Science* 401 (1972): 52.

45. Benjamin Smith, *Hard Times in the Lands of Plenty: Oil Politics in Iran and Indonesia* (Ithaca, NY: Cornell University Press, 2007), 50–51.

46. Homa Katouzian, *The Political Economy of Modern Iran, 1929–1979* (New York: New York University Press, 1981), 192–95.

47. Amin Saikal, *The Rise and Fall of the Shah* (Princeton: Princeton University Press, 1980), 63–65.

48. Zabih, *Communist Movement in Iran*, 209.

49. One apocryphal story holds Mohammad Reza toasting Kermit Roosevelt Jr., the lead CIA officer in Tehran who was in charge of Operation Ajax and grandson of Theodore Roosevelt: "I owe my throne to God, my people, my army—and to you." Douglas Little, "Mission Impossible: The CIA and the Cult of Covert Action in the Middle East," *Diplomatic History* 28, no. 5 (2004): 666.

50. James Bill, *The Eagle and the Lion: The Tragedy of American-Iranian Relations* (New Haven: Yale University Press, 1988), 113–20.

51. Heiss, *Empire and Nationhood*, 201–19.

52. Hugh Wilford, *America's Great Game: The CIA's Secret Arabists and the Shaping of the Modern Middle East* (New York: Basic, 2013), 166.

53. Mark Gasiorowski, *U.S. Foreign Policy and the Shah: Building a Client State in Iran* (Ithaca, NY: Cornell University Press, 1991), 105–6.

54. United States Agency for International Development, *US Economic Assistance to Iran, 1950–1965* (Washington, D.C.: USAID, 1965), 12–13.

55. Ibid., 76–81.

56. Farhad Daftary, "The Balance of Payment Deficit and the Problem of Inflation in Iran, 1955–1962," *Iranian Studies* 5, no. 1 (1972): 13.

57. Saikal, *Rise and Fall*, 51–52.

58. National Security Council, "Report on Iran, NSC 5703/1," 8 October 1958.

59. Nikki Keddie, *Modern Iran: Roots and Results of Revolutions*, 3rd ed. (New Haven: Yale University Press, 2006), 137–38.

60. United States Agency for International Development, *Technical Aid: An Investment in People: The Point Four Program in Iran* (Provo, UT: Brigham Young University Press, 1960), 8.

61. Bill, *Eagle and the Lion*, 125–26.

62. Ricks, "US Military Missions," 177–8.

63. International Cooperation Administration, *Programs of the International Cooperation Administration under the Mutual Security Program* (Washington, D.C.: Department of State, 1959), 10.

64. Saikal, *Rise and Fall*, 54.

65. Hurewitz, *Military Dimension*, 286.

66. Gasiorowski, *US Foreign Policy*, 115–18.

67. Bill, *Eagle and the Lion*, 401–2.

68. National Security Council, "Report on Iran," 7–8.

69. Dilip Hiro, *Iran under the Ayatollahs* (New York: Routledge, 1985), 302.

70. Gholam Afkhami, *The Iranian Revolution: Thanatos on a National Scale* (Washington, D.C.: Middle East Institute, 1985), 203.

71. Richard Cottam, *Iran and the United States: A Cold War Case Study* (Pittsburgh, PA: University of Pittsburgh, 1988), 119.

72. Smith, *Hard Times*, 70.

73. Cottam, *Iran and the United States*, 113.

74. Ali Ansari, *Modern Iran since 1921: The Pahlavis and After* (London: Longman, 2003), 132–35.

75. T. Cuyler Young, "Iran in Continuing Crisis," *Foreign Affairs* 40, no. 2 (1962): 289.

76. Abrahamian, *Iran Between Two Revolutions*, 421.

77. Bill, *Eagle and the Lion*, 99.

78. Akhavi, *Religion and Politics*, 91–99.

79. Leonard Binder, *Iran: Political Development in a Changing Society* (Berkeley: University of California Press, 1962), 223–24.

80. Ervand Abrahamian, *A History of Modern Iran* (New York: Cambridge University Press, 2008), 130.

81. Binder, *Iran: Political Development*, 297.

6. EXCLUSIONARY POLITICS AND THE REVOLUTIONARY END

1. Abbas Milani, *The Shah* (New York: Palgrave Macmillan, 2011), 203–4.

2. Homa Katouzian, *The Political Economy of Modern Iran, 1929–1979* (New York: New York University Press, 1981), 216–19.

3. T. Cuyler Young, "Iran in Continuing Crisis," *Foreign Affairs* 40, no. 2 (1962): 276–77.

4. Reza Arasteh, "The Role of Intellectuals in Administrative Development and Social Change in Modern Iran," *International Review of Education* 9, no. 3 (1963): 329–30.

5. G. Hossein Razi, "Genesis of Party in Iran: A Case Study of the Interaction between the Political System and Political Parties." *Iranian Studies* 3, no. 2 (1970): 81–82.

6. Roger Savory, "Social Development in Iran during the Pahlavi Era," in *Iran under the Pahlavis*, ed. George Lenczowski (Stanford: Hoover Institution Press, 1978), 104–25.

7. Gholam Afkhami, *The Life and Times of the Shah* (Berkeley: University of California Press, 2009), 220–26.

8. Jahangir Amuzegar and M. Ali Fekrat, *Iran: Economic Development under Dualistic Conditions* (Chicago: University of Chicago, 1971), 58–75.

9. Andrew Johns, "The Johnson Administration, the Shah of Iran, and the Changing Pattern of US-Iranian Relations, 1965–1967: 'Tired of Being Treated Like a Schoolboy,'" *Journal of Cold War Studies* 9, no. 2 (2007): 64–94.

10. Ferydoon Firoozi, "Income Distribution and Taxation Laws of Iran," *International Journal of Middle East Studies* 9, no. 1 (1978): 73–87.

11. Robert Looney, *Economic Origins of the Iranian Revolution* (New York: Pergamon, 1982), 140–67.

12. Irene Gendzier, *Notes from the Minefield: United States Intervention in Lebanon and the Middle East, 1945–1958*, 2nd ed. (New York: Columbia University Press, 2006), 303.

13. April Summitt, "For a White Revolution: John F. Kennedy and the Shah of Iran," *Middle East Journal* 58, no. 4 (2004): 563–65.

14. V. Webster Johnson, "Agriculture in the Economic Development of Iran," *Land Economics* 36, no. 4 (1960): 313–21; and United States Agency for International Development. *Technical Aid, An Investment in People: The Point Four Program in Iran* (Provo, UT: Brigham Young University Press, 1960).

15. James Goode, "Reforming Iran during the Kennedy Years," *Diplomatic History* 15, no. 1 (1991): 27–28.

16. James Bill, *The Eagle and the Lion: The Tragedy of American-Iranian Relations* (New Haven: Yale University Press, 1988), 157–59.

17. Julian Bharier, *Economic Development in Iran, 1900–1970* (London: Oxford University Press, 1971), 169.

18. Mohammad Majd, "Land Reform Policies in Iran," *American Journal of Agricultural Economics* 69, no. 4 (1987): 843–44.

19. Ahmad Ashraf, "State and Agrarian Relations before and after the Iranian Revolution, 1960–1990," in *Peasants and Politics in the Modern Middle East*, ed. Farhad Kazemi and John Waterbury (Miami: Florida International University Press, 1991), 281–84.

20. Kenneth Platt, "Land Reform in Iran," in *Land Reform in Iran, Iraq, Pakistan, Turkey, Indonesia* (Washington, D.C.: USAID, 1970), 48–51.

21. Jane Perry Clark Carey and Andrew Galbraith Care, "Iranian Agriculture and Its Development: 1952–1973," *International Journal of Middle East Studies* 7, no. 3 (1976): 364.

22. Reza Moghaddam, "Land Reform and Rural Development in Iran," *Land Economics* 48, no. 2 (1972): 165–67.

23. Seyed Farian Sabahi, "The Literacy Corps in Pahlavi Iran (1963–1979): Political, Social, and Literary Implications," *Cahiers d'études sur la Méditerranée orientale et le monde turco-iranien* 31 (2001).

24. Ali Ansari, *Modern Iran since 1921: The Pahlavis and After* (London: Longman, 2003), 168.

25. J. C. Hurewitz, *Middle East Politics: The Military Dimension* (Boulder, CO: Westview, 1982), 287.

26. Mohammad Majd, *Resistance to the Shah: Landowners and the Ulama in Iran* (Gainesville: University of Florida, 2000), 72–78.

27. Majd, "Land Reform Policies," 845–46.

28. James Bill, "Modernization and Reform From Above: The Case of Iran," *Journal of Politics* 32, no. 1 (1970): 36.

29. Nikki Keddie, ed., *Iran: Religion, Politics, and Society: Collected Essays* (London: Cass, 1980), 194–99.

30. Hossein Mahdavi, "The Coming Crisis in Iran," *Foreign Affairs* 44, no. 1 (1965): 139–40.

31. Mohammad Majd, "Small Landowners and Land Redistribution in Iran, 1962–1971," *International Journal of Middle East Studies* 32, no. 1 (2000): 128–35.

32. Helmut Richards, "Land Reform and Agribusiness in Iran," *Middle East Research and Information Project Reports* 43 (1975): 3–18, 24.

33. Fatemeh Moghadam, *From Land Reform to Revolution: The Political Economy of Agricultural Development in Iran, 1962–1979* (London: I. B. Tauris, 1996), 94–97.

34. Farhad Kazemi, *Poverty and Revolution in Iran: The Migrant Poor, Urban Marginality, and Politics* (New York: New York University Press, 1980), 28–63.

35. Fred Halliday, "The Economic Contradictions," *Middle East Research and Information Project Reports* 69 (1978): 10.

36. William Green Miller, "Political Organization in Iran: From Dowreh to Political Party," *Middle East Journal* 23, no. 2 (1969): 348–49.

37. Marvin Weinbaum, "Iran Finds a Party System: The Institutionalization of 'Iran Novin,'" *Middle East Journal* 27, no. 4 (1972): 445–48.

38. Hossein Bashiriyeh, *The State and Revolution in Iran, 1962–1982* (London: Croom Helm, 1984), 32.

39. Milani, *Shah*, 259.

40. Charles Issawi, "Iran's Economic Upsurge," *Middle East Journal* 21, no. 4 (1967): 451–54.

41. Kazemi, *Poverty and Revolution*, 105–6.

42. Katouzian, *The Political Economy*, 274–85.

43. Ferydoon Firoozi, "The Iranian Budgets: 1964–1970," *International Journal of Middle East Studies* 5, no. 3 (1974): 342–43.

44. James Scoville, "The Labor Market in Prerevolutionary Iran," *Economic Development and Cultural Change* 34, no. 1 (1985): 148–51.

45. Ervand Abrahamian, *Iran Between Two Revolutions* (Princeton: Princeton University Press, 1982), 433.

46. Arang Keshavarzian, *Bazaar and State in Iran: The Politics of the Tehran Marketplace* (New York: Cambridge Univeristy Press, 2007), 128–41.

47. Vali Nasr, "Politics within the Late Pahlavi State: The Ministry of Economy and Industrial Policy, 1963–1969," *International Journal of Middle East Studies* 32, no. 1 (2000): 109.

48. Bashiriyeh, *State and Revolution*, 67.

49. Reza Baraheni, *The Crowned Cannibals: Writings on Repression in Iran* (New York: Vintage, 1977), 5.

50. Ahmad Ashraf, "Bazaar-Mosque Alliance: The Social Basis of Revolts and Revolutions." *International Journal of Politics, Culture and Society* 1, no. 4 (1988): 577.

51. Asadollah Alam and Alinaghi Alikhani, *The Shah and I: The Confidential Diary of Iran's Royal Court, 1968–77* (London: I. B. Tauris, 1991), 321 and 506.

52. Nimah Mazaheri, "State Repression in the Iranian Bazaar, 1975–1977: The Anti-Profiteering Campaign and an Impending Revolution," *Iranian Studies* 39, no. 3 (2006): 404–10.

53. Norriss Hetherington, "Industrialization and Revolution in Iran: Forced Progress or Unmet Expectation?" *Middle East Journal* 36, no. 3 (1982): 364.

54. Misagh Parsa, *Social Origins of the Iranian Revolution* (New Brunswick, NJ: Rutgers University Press, 1989), 127–67.

55. P. Amini, "A Single Party State in Iran, 1975–78: The Rastakhiz Party: The Final Attempt by the Shah to Consolidate His Political Base," *Middle Eastern Studies* 38, no. 1 (2002): 161.

56. M. H. Pesaran, "Income Distribution in Iran," in *Iran: Past, Present, and Future*, ed. Jane Jacqz (Denver, CO: Aspen Institute for Humanistic Studies, 1976).

57. Mehdi Mozaffari, "Why the Bazar Rebels," *Journal of Peace Research* 28, no. 4 (1991): 384.

58. Ervand Abrahamian, "Structural Causes of the Iranian Revolution," *Middle East Research and Information Project Reports* 87 (1980): 23.

59. Weinbaum, "Iran Finds a Party," 450.

60. Said Amir Arjomand, *The Turban for the Crown: The Islamic Revolution in Iran* (New York: Oxford University Press, 1988), 216.

61. Majd, *Resistance to the Shah*, 194–216.

62. Mansoor Moaddel, "The Shi'i Ulama and the State in Iran," *Theory and Society* 15, no. 4 (1986): 543–45.

63. Moghadam, *From Land Reform to Revolution*, 199–202.

64. Willem Floor, "The Revolutionary Character of the Iranian Ulama: Wishful Thinking or Reality?" *International Journal of Middle East Studies* 12, no. 4 (1980): 509–12.

65. Nikki Keddie, *Modern Iran: Roots and Results of Revolution*, 3rd ed. (New Haven: Yale University Press, 2006), 146–47.

66. Arjomand, *Turban for the Crown*, 98.

67. Michael M. J. Fischer, *Iran: From Religious Dispute to Revolution* (Cambridge, MA: Harvard University Press, 1980), 124–29.

68. Mohsen Milani, *The Making of Iran's Islamic Revolution: From Monarchy to Islamic Republic*, 2nd ed. (Boulder, CO: Westview, 1994), 78–83.

69. Shahrough Akhavi, *Religion and Politics in Contemporary Iran Clergy-State Relations in the Pahlavi Period* (Albany: State University of New York Press, 1980), 105–10.

70. Ibid., 187; see also 129–43.

71. Alam and Alikhani, *The Shah and I*, 321.

72. Arjomand, *Turban for the Crown*, 92.

73. Behrooz Moazami, "The Islamization of the Social Movements and the Revolution, 1963–1979," *Comparative Studies of South Asia, Africa and the Middle East* 29, no. 1 (2009): 52–55.

74. Shahrough Akhavi, "The Ideology and Praxis of Shi'ism in the Iranian Revolution," *Comparative Studies in Society and History* 25, no. 2 (1983): 203–8.

75. Gholam Afkhami, *The Iranian Revolution: Thanatos on a National Scale* (Washington, D.C.: Middle East Institute, 1985), 71–75.

76. Robert Graham, *Iran: The Illusion of Power* (New York: St. Martin's Press, 1979), 134–36.

77. Benjamin Smith, *Hard Times in the Lands of Plenty: Oil Politics in Iran and Indonesia* (Ithaca, NY: Cornell University Press, 2007), 140–44.

78. Ervand Abrahamian, *A History of Modern Iran* (New York: Cambridge University Press, 2008), 151.

79. Milani, *Shah*, 380–81.

80. Khosrow Fatemi, "Leadership by Distrust: The Shah's Modus Operandi," *Middle East Journal* 36, no. 1 (1982): 48–54.

81. Hossein Razavi and Firouz Vakil, *The Political Environment of Economic Planning in Iran, 1971–1983: From Monarchy to Islamic Republic* (Boulder, CO: Westview, 1984), 79–84.

82. Amini, "A Single Party State," 139–40.

83. Graham, *Iran*, 152–69.

84. Abrahamian, *History of Modern Iran*, 127–28.

85. Ahmad Faroughy, "Repression in Iran," *Index on Censorship* 3, no. 4 (1974); and Baraheni, *The Crowned Cannibals*.

86. Abrahamian, *Iran Between Two Revolutions*, 480–95.

87. Lois Beck, "Tribe and State in Nineteeth- and Twentieth-Century Iran," in *Tribes and State Formation in the Middle East*, ed. Philip S. Khoury and Joseph Kostiner (Berkeley: University of California Press, 1990), 15–16.

88. Robert Looney, "The Role of Military Expenditures in Pre-revolutionary Iran's Economic Decline," *Iranian Studies* 21, no. 3 (1988): 52–83.

89. Theodore Moran, "Iranian Defense Expenditures and the Social Crisis," *International Security* 3, no. 3 (1978): 188–91.

90. Tore Petersen, *Richard Nixon, Great Britain and the Anglo-American Alignment in the Persian Gulf and Arabian Peninsula: Making Allies out of Clients* (Eastbourne, UK: Sussex Academic, 2009), 79–115.

91. Alvin Cottrell, "Iran's Armed Forces under the Pahlavi Dynasty," in *Iran under the Pahlavis*, ed. George Lenczowski (Stanford: Hoover Institution Press, 1978), 400–407.

92. See, for instance, United States Department of Commerce, *A Market for U.S. Products in Iran* (Washington, D.C.: Bureau of International Commerce, 1966).

93. Peter Mangold, *Superpower Intervention in the Middle East* (New York: St. Martin's, 1978), 22–24.

94. Petersen, *Richard Nixon*, 88.

95. Nayef Samhat, "Middle Powers and American Foreign Policy: Lessons from Irano-U.S. Relations, 1962–77," *Policy Studies Journal* 28, no. 1 (2000): 19.

96. Richard Cottam, *Iran and the United States: A Cold War Case Study* (Pittsburgh: University of Pittsburgh, 1988), 148.

97. Abrahamian, "Structural Causes;" Marvin Zonis, "Iran: A Theory of Revolution from Accounts of Revolution," *World Politics* 35, no. 4 (1983): 586–606; Nikki Keddie, "Iranian Revolutions in Comparative Perspective," *The American Historical Review* 88, no. 3 (1983): 579–98; Said Amir Arjomand, "Iran's Islamic Revolution in Comparative Perspective," *World Politics* 38, no. 3 (1986): 383–414; and Misagh Parsa, "Theories of Collective Action and the Iranian Revolution," *Sociological Forum* 3, no. 1 (1988): 44–71.

98. Charles Kurzman, *The Unthinkable Revolution in Iran* (Cambridge, MA: Harvard University Press, 2004), 136.

99. Desmond Harney, *The Priest and the King: An Eyewitness Account of the Iranian Revolution* (London: British Academic, 1998), 38–39.

100. Ahmad Ashraf and Alinaghi Banuazizi, "The State, Classes, and Modes of Mobilization in the Iranian Revolution," *State, Culture, and Society* 1, no. 3 (1985): 25.

101. Milani, *Making of Iran's Islamic Revolution*, 116.

102. Abrahamian, *Iran Between Two Revolutions*, 433.

103. Parsa, *Social Origins*, 144–56.
104. Fred Halliday, *Iran: Dictatorship and Development* (New York: Penguin, 1979), 62.
105. Parsa, *Social Origins*, 225–28.
106. By contrast, "[The opposition] marchers' discipline [demonstrated] considerable organizational and leadership capability. It meant the existence of a formidable number of trained cadres with the ability to produce, control, and lead the crowd at will against tactical and strategic targets. The crowd responded perfectly to cues, as for example in their slogans or the presentation of flowers to the military and police." Afkhami, *Iranian Revolution*, 97.
107. Smith, *Hard Times*, 159.
108. Arjomand, *Turban for the Crown*, 190.
109. Kurzman, *Unthinkable Revolution*, 105–24.
110. Consider this popular joke. The shah boasts about the growth under his reign: "When I came to the throne, Iran had only 16 million people, now there are 35 million," to which a citizen retorts, "But with the way things are going, there will be 16 million left when you leave it!" Desmond Harney, *Priest and the King*, 49.
111. Jeanne Kirkpatrick, *Dictatorships and Double Standards: Rationalism and Reason in Politics* (New York: Simon and Schuster, 1982).
112. Michael Arthur Ledeen and William Lewis, *Debacle, the American Failure in Iran* (New York: Knopf, 1981).
113. Gary Sick, *All Fall Down: America's Fateful Encounter with Iran* (London: I. B. Tauris, 1985), 132–34.
114. Afkhami, *Life and Times*, 488–89.
115. Sick, *All Fall Down*, 169.

7. A CONFLICT INTERRUPTED IN JORDAN

1. Sulayman Musa, *Ta'sis al-imarah al-urduniyyah, 1921–1925* (Amman: Maktabat al-muhtasib, 1989), 177–84.
2. Maan Abu Nowar, *The History of the Hashemite Kingdom of Jordan: The Creation and Development of Transjordan, 1920–1929* (Oxford, UK: Ithaca, 1989), 55–83.
3. Mary Wilson, *King Abdullah, Britain, and the Making of Jordan* (New York: Cambridge University Press, 1987); Sulayman Musa and Munib Al-Madi, *Ta'rikh al-urdunn fiil-qarn al-ʿishrin, 1900–1959* (Amman: Maktabat al-muhtasib, 1959); and Kamal Salibi, *The Modern History of Jordan* (London: I. B. Tauris, 1993).
4. Hassan Salih ʿUthman and Hamid Ahmad Al-Shubaki, *Rijalat maʿ al-malik ʿabdullah* (Amman: n.p., 1995).
5. Raphael Patai and Fahim Qubain, "The Town," in *The Hashemite Kingdom of Jordan*, ed. Raphael Patai (New Haven: Human Relations Area Files, 1956), 276–78.
6. Pete Moore, *Doing Business in the Middle East: Politics and Economic Crisis in Jordan and Kuwait* (New York: Cambridge University Press, 2004), 49–64.

7. Maan Abu Nowar, *The Development of Trans-Jordan 1929–1939: A History of the Hashemite Kingdom of Jordan* (Reading, UK: Ithaca, 2006), 117–18.

8. Haim Gerber, *The Social Origins of the Modern Middle East* (Boulder, CO: Lynne Rienner, 1987), 159.

9. Gabriel Baer, "Land Tenure in the Hashemite Kingdom of Jordan," *Land Economics* 33, no. 1 (1957): 193–95.

10. A useful English-language overview of the Transjordanian tribes remains F. G. Peake, *A History of Jordan and Its Tribes* (Coral Gables, FL: University of Miami Press, 1958), 143–221.

11. Others have rightly problematized the "cultural" origins of the tribal-state alliance. See Yoav Alon, *The Making of Jordan: Tribes, Colonialism, and the Modern State* (London: I. B. Tauris, 2007); and Tariq Moraiwed Tell, *The Social and Economic Origins of Monarchy in Jordan* (New York: Palgrave Macmillan, 2013).

12. Eugene Rogan, *Frontiers of the State in the Late Ottoman Empire: Transjordan, 1850–1921* (New York: Cambridge University Press, 2002), 9.

13. Alon, *Making of Jordan*, 92–95.

14. Tell, *Social and Economic Origins*, 84–86.

15. Alon, *Making of Jordan*, 110–49.

16. Michael Fischbach, *State, Society, and Land in Jordan* (Leiden, the Netherlands: Brill, 2000), 148–78.

17. Joseph Andoni Massad, *Colonial Effects: The Making of National Identity in Jordan* (New York: Columbia University Press, 2001), 60.

18. Riccardo Bocco and Tariq Tell, "Pax Britannica in the Steppe: British Policy and the Transjordan Bedouin," in *Village, Steppe and State: The Social Origins of Modern Jordan*, ed. Eugene L. Rogan and Tariq Tell (London: British Academic, 1994), 125–26.

19. Naseer Aruri, *Jordan: A Study in Political Development, 1921–1965* (The Hague, the Netherlands: Martinus Nijhoff, 1972), 39–42.

20. Ron Pundik, *The Struggle for Sovereignty: Relations between Great Britain and Jordan, 1946–1951* (Oxford: Oxford University Press, 1994), 89–102.

21. P. J. Vatikiotis, *Politics and the Military in Jordan: A Study of the Arab Legion, 1921–1957* (London: Cass, 1967), 10–11.

22. Massad, *Colonial Effects*, 100–65.

23. 'Abbas Murad, *Al-Dawr al-siyasi lil-jaysh al-urduni* (Beirut: PLO Research Center, 1973), 110–13.

24. William Roger Louis, "Britain and the Middle East after 1945," in *Diplomacy in the Middle East the International Relations of Regional and outside Powers*, ed. Carl Brown (London: I. B. Tauris, 2004), 23.

25. James Baster, "The Economic Problems of Jordan," *International Affairs* 31, no. 1 (1955): 29.

26. International Bank for Reconstruction and Development, *The Economic Development of Jordan* (Baltimore: Johns Hopkins Press, 1957), 10.

27. Ibrahim Ahmad Al-Shiyab, "Political Parties in Jordan, 1921–1956," *European Journal of Social Sciences* 21, no. 1 (2011): 32–36.
28. Marwan Hanania, "The Impact of Palestinian Refugee Crisis on the Development of Amman, 1947–1958," *British Journal of Middle East Studies* (2014): 3–6, doi: 10.1086/599247.
29. Ibid., 17–21.
30. Maan Abu Nowar, *The Struggle for Independence 1939–1947: A History of the Hashemite Kingdom of Jordan* (Reading, UK: Ithaca, 2001), 221–57.
31. Avi Plascov, *The Palestinian Refugees in Jordan, 1948–1957* (London: Cass, 1981), 44–50.
32. Kamel Abu Jaber, "The Legislature of the Hashemite Kingdom of Jordan: A Study in Political Development," *The Muslim World* 59, nos. 3–4 (1969): 220–50.
33. Ilan Pappé, "Jordan between Hashemite and Palestinian Identity," in *Jordan in the Middle East: The Making of a Pivotal State, 1948–1988*, ed. Joseph Nevo and Ilan Pappé (London: Cass, 1994), 64–65.
34. Peter Young, *The Arab Legion* (Reading, UK: Osprey Publishing, 1972), 35–36.
35. Shaul Mishal, *West Bank/East Bank: The Palestinians in Jordan, 1949–1967* (New Haven: Yale University Press, 1978), 28.
36. Amnon Cohen, *Political Parties in the West Bank under the Jordanian Regime, 1949–1967* (Ithaca, NY: Cornell University Press, 1982), 18–25.
37. Avi Plascov, *The Palestinian Refugees in Jordan, 1948–1957* (London: Frank Cass, 1981), 123–57.
38. Willard Beling, *Pan-Arabism and Labor* (Cambridge, MA: Harvard University Center for Middle Eastern Studies, 1961), 42–43.
39. Hani Al-Hourani, *Al-Haraka al-ʿamaliyyah al-urduniyyah, 1948–1988* (Nicosia, Cyprus: Majallat Al-Urdun Al-Jadid, 1989), 14–16.
40. Betty Anderson, *Nationalist Voices in Jordan: The Street and the State* (Austin: University of Texas, 2005), 117–46.
41. Muhammad Masalha, *Al-Tajriba al-hizbiyyah al-siyasiyyah fiil-urdun: dirasa tahliliyyah-muqaranah* (Amman: Dar waʾil lil-nashr, 1999), 39–67.
42. Vatikiotis, *Politics and the Military*, 117–19.
43. Sulayman Musa, *Tarʾikh al-urdun al-siyasi al-muʿasir: haziran 1967–1995* (Amman: Lajnat tarikh al-urdun, 1998), 48–52.
44. Michael Oren, "A Winter of Discontent: Britain's Crisis in Jordan, December 1955-March 1956," *International Journal of Middle East Studies* 22, no. 2 (1990): 171–84.
45. Murad, *Al-Dawr al-siyasi*, 90–96.
46. Benjamin Shwadran, *Jordan: A State of Tension* (New York: Council for Middle Eastern Affairs, 1959), 341.
47. Sahila Rimawi, "Ahzab al-tayar al-qawmi wa hukumat al-nabulsi," in *Hukumat sulayman al-nabulsi*, ed. Hani Al-Hourani (Amman: Dar sindbad lil-nashr, 1999), 101–12.

48. Dhiyab Mukhadimah, "Al-siyasiyyat al-kharijiyyah fii 'ahd hukumat al-nabulsi," in *Hukumat sulayman al-nabulsi*, 177–87.

49. Robert Satloff, *From Abdullah to Hussein: Jordan in Transition* (Oxford: Oxford University Press, 1994), 164–65.

50. Anderson, *Nationalist Voices*, 185.

51. Timothy Piro, *The Political Economy of Market Reform in Jordan* (Lanham, MD: Rowman and Littlefield, 1998), 25–30.

52. Shwadran, *State of Tension*, 343.

53. I am grateful to Falih Tawil for pointing this out. Falih Tawil, personal interview with author, Amman, Jordan, July 4, 2007.

54. Mishal, *West Bank/East Bank*, 94.

55. Hani Al-Hourani, *The Jordanian Labour Movement: History, Structure, and Challenges* (Bonn: Friedrich Ebert Stiftung, 2001), 13–15.

56. Hurewitz, *Military Dimension*, 323.

57. Satloff, *From Abdullah to Hussein*, 174.

58. Robert Stookey, *America and the Arab States: An Uneasy Encounter* (New York: Wiley, 1975), 151.

59. Stephen Kaplan, "United States Aid and Regime Maintenance in Jordan, 1957–1973," *Public Policy* 23, no. 2 (1975): 194–95. The Sixth Fleet was also tasked with a contingency plan to evacuate King Hussein. Gendzier, *Notes from the Minefield*, 301.

60. Mohammad Ibrahim Faddah, *The Middle East in Transition: A Study of Jordan's Foreign Policy* (New York: Asia Publishing House, 1974), 281–83.

61. Jan Morris, *The Hashemite Kings* (New York: Pantheon, 1959), 186.

62. United States Department of Defense, "Financial Crisis in Jordan," Memorandum prepared by the Office of Chief Naval Operations for the Secretary of the Navy, June 20, 1957.

63. Taysir 'Abdel Jaber, personal interview with author, Amman, Jordan, June 6, 2006.

64. Lawrence Tal, *Politics, the Military, and National Security in Jordan: 1955–1967* (New York: Palgrave Macmillan, 2002), 50–51.

65. Said Aburish, *A Brutal Friendship: The West and the Arab Elite* (New York: St. Martin's, 1997), 129–34.

66. Jack O'Connell, *King's Counsel: A Memoir of War, Espionage, and Diplomacy in the Middle East* (New York: Norton, 2011), 4–6.

67. Wilford, *America's Great Game*, 266–67.

68. Erica Schoenberger and Stephanie Reich, "Soviet Policy in the Middle East," *Middle East Research and Information Project Reports* 39 (1975): 10–14.

69. Salim Yaqub, *Containing Arab Nationalism: The Eisenhower Doctrine and the Middle East* (Chapel Hill: University of North Carolina Press, 2004), 57–117.

70. Walter Laqueur, *The Struggle for the Middle East: The Soviet Union in the Mediterranean, 1958–1968* (New York: Macmillan, 1969), 219.

71. Adeed Dawisha, "The Soviet Union in the Arab World: The Limits to Superpower Influence," in *The Soviet Union in the Middle East: Policies and Perspectives*, ed. Adeed Dawisha and Karen Dawisha (New York: Holmes and Meier, 1982), 8–23.

72. Taher Kanaan, personal interview with author, Amman, Jordan, August 2, 2006. See also Anne Mariel Peters, "Special Relationships, Dollars, and Development: U.S. Aid and Institutions in Egypt, Jordan, South Korea, and Taiwan" (PhD diss., University of Virginia, 2009).

73. United States Department of State, "Briefing Book for 5/30/61 US Visit of Prime Minister Ben-Gurion: Jordan as the Key to Stability in the Middle East," May 1961.

74. Faddah, *Middle East in Transition*, 285–88.

75. Nigel John Ashton, *King Hussein of Jordan: A Political Life* (New Haven: Yale University Press, 2008), 81.

76. Oles Smolansky, "Soviet-Jordanian Relations," in *The Hashemite Kingdom of Jordan and the West Bank*, ed. Anne Sinai and Allen Pollack (New York: American Academic Association for Peace in the Middle East, 1977), 175–87.

77. Malcolm Kerr, *The Arab Cold War: Gamal 'Abd Al-Nasir and His Rivals, 1958–1970* (Oxford: Oxford University Press, 1971).

78. Adnan Abu Odeh, *Jordanians, Palestinians, and the Hashemite Kingdom in the Middle East Peace Process* (Washington, D.C.: United States Institute of Peace, 1999), 110–12.

79. Sabri Rbeihat, personal interview with author, Amman, Jordan, June 14, 2006.

80. Philip Robins, *A History of Jordan* (New York: Cambridge University Press, 2004), 100.

81. John Bagot Glubb, *A Soldier with the Arabs* (New York: Harper and Brothers, 1957), 421.

82. Clinton Bailey, "Cabinet Formation in Jordan," in *The Hashemite Kingdom of Jordan and the West Bank*, 106–7.

83. Asher Susser, *On Both Banks of the Jordan: A Political Biography of Wasfi Al-Tall* (London: Frank Cass, 1994), 50–51.

84. Tal, *Politics, the Military, and National Security*, 60–62.

85. Douglas Little, "A Puppet in Search of a Puppeteer? The United States, King Hussein, and Jordan, 1953–1970," *The International History Review* 17, no. 3 (1995): 527–28.

86. Mishal, *West Bank/East Bank*, 49–50.

87. Zaki Shalom, *The Superpowers, Israel and the Future of Jordan, 1960–1963: The Perils of the Pro-Nasser Policy* (Brighton, UK: Sussex Academic, 1999), 38–74.

88. Uriel Dann, *King Hussein and the Challenge of Arab Radicalism: Jordan, 1955–1967* (Oxford: Oxford University Press, 1989), 129–33.

89. Khalil Hammad, "The Role of Foreign Aid in the Jordanian Economy, 1959–1983," in *The Economic Development of Jordan*, ed. Bichara Khader and Adnan Badran (London: Croom Helm, 1987).

90. Lester Mallory, personal interview with Hank Zivetz, November 18, 1988, in *Frontline Diplomacy: The Foreign Affairs Oral History Collection of the Association for Diplomatic Studies and Training* (Washington, D.C.: Library of Congress, 2007).

91. Kaplan, "Aid and Regime Maintenance," 204–5.

92. Avi Shlaim, *Lion of Jordan: The Life of King Hussein in War and Peace* (New York: Knopf, 2007), 212–13.

93. Tell, *Monarchy in Jordan*, 207–8.

94. Tal, *Politics, the Military, and National Security*, 10–19.

95. Imad Saliba Ma'ay'ah, personal interview with author, Amman, Jordan, June 16, 2012. This practice diminished in the early 2000s but still persists.

96. J. C. Hurewitz, *Middle East Politics: The Military Dimension* (Boulder, CO: Westview, 1982), 325.

97. Upon its termination in 1977, this program (Operation No-Beef) had funneled around $15 million to Hussein over two decades. Douglas Little, "Mission Impossible: The CIA and the Cult of Covert Action in the Middle East," *Diplomatic History* 28, no. 5 (2004): 684–85.

98. Nawaf Tell, "Jordanian Security Sector Governance: Between Theory and Practice" (Working Paper 145, Geneva Centre for the Democratic Control of Armed Forces, 2004), 16.

99. Wilbur Crane Eveland, *Ropes of Sand: America's Failure in the Middle East* (New York: Norton, 1980), 320–21.

100. Senior political official (confidential), personal interview with author, Amman, Jordan, June 22, 2011.

101. Raymond Cohen, *Saving the Holy Sepulchre: How Rival Christians Came Together to Rescue their Holiest Shrine* (New York: Oxford University Press, 2008), 156.

102. Dann, *King Hussein*, 16.

103. Susser, *On Both Banks*, 94–99.

104. I am thankful to Fayez Al-Tarawneh for pointing out the traditional mediating function of the Diwan. Fayez Al-Tarawneh, personal interview with author, Amman, Jordan, July 16, 2006.

105. Although the Muslim Brotherhood in Jordan today has a preponderance of Palestinians, until the 1970s it retained a mostly Transjordanian membership. Mansoor Moaddel, *Jordanian Exceptionalism: A Comparative Analysis of State-Religion Relationships in Egypt, Iran, Jordan, and Syria* (New York: Palgrave Macmillan, 2002), 100–105.

106. See, for instance, Hazim Zaki Nusseibeh, *Ta'rikh al-urdun al-siyasi al-mu'asir: ma baina 'ami 1952–1967* (Amman: Lajnat ta'rikh al-urdun, 1990), 99–102.

107. Michael P. Mazur, *Economic Growth and Development in Jordan* (London: Croom Helm, 1979), 112.

108. Eliyahu Kanovsky, *The Economic Development of Jordan* (New Brunswick, NJ: Transaction, 1976), 6–8.

109. Mazur, *Economic Growth*, 31.

110. Joel Migdal, *Palestinian Society and Politics* (Princeton: Princeton University Press, 1980), 39–43.

111. Abu Odeh, *Jordanians, Palestinians*, 83–84.

112. Jon Kimche, *The Second Arab Awakening: The Middle East, 1914–1970* (London: Holt, Rinehart, and Winston, 1970), 251.

113. Piro, *Political Economy*, 45–53.

114. Hamed El-Said and Kip Becker, *Management and International Business Issues in Jordan* (London: Routledge, 2002), 125–26.

115. Anne Mariel Peters and Peter Moore, "Beyond Boom and Bust: External Rents, Durable Authoritarianism, and Institutional Adaptation in the Hashemite Kingdom of Jordan," *Studies in Comparative International Development* 44, no. 3 (2009): 145–70.

116. Clinton Bailey, *Jordan's Palestinian Challenge, 1948–1983: A Political History* (Boulder, CO: Westview, 1984), 19–20.

117. Joseph Dees, "Jordan's East Ghor Canal Project," *Middle East Journal* 13, no. 4 (1959): 357–71.

118. Jared Hazleton, "Land Reform in Jordan: The East Ghor Canal Project," *Middle Eastern Studies* 15, no. 2 (1979): 565–67.

119. Peters and Moore, *Beyond Boom and Bust*, 271–72.

8. RECURRENT TENSIONS AND TENUOUS SURVIVAL UNDER HASHEMITE RULE

1. I am grateful to Mohammed Al-Momany for helping me visualize this neopatrimonial structure. For an analytical breakdown, see Saʿd Abu Diyah, ʿAmaliyat ittikhadh al-qirar fii siyasat al-urdun al-kharijiyyah: al-dhawabit wa al-muqawwimat (Amman: n.p., 1983), 159–211.

2. Samir Mutawi, *Jordan in the 1967 War* (New York: Cambridge University Press, 1987), 169–70.

3. Michael Mazur, *Economic Growth and Development in Jordan* (London: Croom Helm, 1979), 82.

4. Uriel Dann, "The Jordanian Entity in Changing Circumstances, 1967–1973," in *From June to October: The Middle East between 1967 and 1973*, ed. Itamar Rabinovich and Haim Shaked (New Brunswick, NJ: Transaction, 1978), 239.

5. Mutawi, *Jordan in the 1967 War*, 76–84.

6. Anne Sinai and Allen Pollock, "Jordan: Past and Present," in *The Hashemite Kingdom of Jordan and the West Bank*, ed. Anne Sinai and Allen Pollack (New York: American Academic Association for Peace in the Middle East, 1977), 55.

7. Adnan Abu Odeh, *Jordanians, Palestinians, and the Hashemite Kingdom in the Middle East Peace Process* (Washington, D.C.: United States Institute of Peace, 1999), 174–76.

8. Hume Horan, personal interview with Charles Kennedy, November 20, 2000, in *Frontline Diplomacy: The Foreign Affairs Oral History Collection* of the Association

for Diplomatic Studies and Training (Washington, D.C.: Library of Congress, 2007).

9. Yezid Sayigh, *Armed Struggle and the Search for State: The Palestinian National Movement, 1949–1993* (New York: Oxford University Press, 2000), 177.

10. Avi Shlaim, *Lion of Jordan: The Life of King Hussein in War and Peace* (New York: Knopf, 2007), 343.

11. Fakhry Abu Shakra, personal interview with author, Amman, Jordan, May 31, 2006.

12. Clinton Bailey, *Jordan's Palestinian Challenge, 1948–1983: A Political History* (Boulder, CO: Westview, 1984), 33–37.

13. Miriam Joyce, *Anglo-American Support for Jordan: The Career of King Hussein* (New York: Palgrave Macmillan, 2008), 52.

14. Syed Ali El-Edroos, *The Hashemite Arab Army, 1908–1979: An Appreciation and Analysis of Military Operations* (Amman: The Publishing Committee, 1980), 437–45.

15. Sulayman Musa, *A'lam min al-urdun: safahat min ta'rikh al-'arab al-hadith* (Amman: Dar al-sha'b, 1986), 144–48.

16. Palestinian Liberation Front, *Nawha Urdun Watani Dimuqrati* (Amman: n.p., 1980), 109–20.

17. Kamal Salibi, *The Modern History of Jordan* (London: I. B. Tauris, 1993), 229–30.

18. Asher Susser, *On Both Banks of the Jordan: A Political Biography of Wasfi Al-Tall* (London: Cass, 1994), 135.

19. Joyce, *Anglo-American Support*, 38.

20. Harrison Symmes, personal interview with Charles Kennedy, February 25, 1989, in *Frontline Diplomacy: The Foreign Affairs Oral History Collection*.

21. Joseph Nevo, "September 1970 in Jordan: A Civil War?" *Civil Wars* 10, no. 3 (2008): 223–24.

22. Nigel John Ashton, *King Hussein of Jordan: A Political Life* (New Haven: Yale University Press, 2008), 142–44.

23. Adnan Abu Odeh, personal interview with author, Amman, Jordan, July 2, 2006.

24. Sinai and Pollock, "Past and Present," 56.

25. For a personal (if stylized) account of such sieges, see Jihad Hattar, *Dhikriyat 'an ma'rika aylul: al-urdun 1970* (Beirut: Ittihad al-'am lil-kuttab wa al-suhufiyin al-filistiniyyin, 1977), 115–67.

26. Malcolm Kerr, *The Arab Cold War: Gamal 'Abd Al-Nasir and His Rivals, 1958–1970* (Oxford: Oxford University Press, 1971), 150.

27. Shlaim, *Lion of Jordan*, 339.

28. National Security Council, "Memorandum prepared by Alexander Haig for the White House Staff on Jordan," October 3, 1970.

29. Henry Brandon, "Were We Masterful . . . " *Foreign Policy* 10 (1973): 163.

30. William Quandt, *Decade of Decisions: American Policy toward the Arab-Israeli Conflict, 1967–1976* (Berkeley: University of California Press, 1977), 116–19.

31. Joyce, *Anglo-American Support*, 63–65.

32. Douglas Little, "A Puppet in Search of a Puppeteer? The United States, King Hussein, and Jordan, 1953–1970." *The International History Review* 17, no. 3 (1995): 543.

33. Alan Dowty, *Middle East Crisis: U.S. Decision-Making in 1958, 1970 and 1973* (Berkeley: University of California Press, 1984), 115–36.

34. Nigel John Ashton, " 'Special Relationship Sometimes in Spite of Ourselves:' Britain and Jordan, 1957–73," *Journal of Imperial and Commonwealth History* 33, no. 2 (2005): 236–37.

35. James Phillips, "As Israel and the Arabs Battle, Moscow Collects the Dividends," *Backgrounder* 291 (Washington, D.C.: Heritage Foundation, 1983), 6–7.

36. Zach Levey, "United States Arms Policy toward Jordan, 1963–68," *Journal of Contemporary History* 41, no. 3 (2006): 542.

37. Nawaf Tell, personal interview with author, Amman, Jordan, June 28, 2006.

38. Joyce, *Anglo-American Support*, 45.

39. Jack O'Connell, *King's Counsel: A Memoir of War, Espionage, and Diplomacy in the Middle East* (New York: Norton, 2011), 100.

40. El-Edroos, *Hashemite Arab Army*, 458–60.

41. Lawrence Axelrod, "Tribesmen in Uniform: The Demise of the Fida'iyyun in Jordan, 1970–71," *The Muslim World* 68, no. 1 (1978): 25–45.

42. Robert Satloff, *Troubles on the East Bank: Challenges to the Domestic Stability of Jordan* (Washington, D.C.: Center for Strategic and International Studies, 1986), 36–38.

43. Tariq Moraiwed Tell, *The Social and Economic Origins of Monarchy in Jordan* (New York: Palgrave Macmillan, 2013), 127.

44. Dann, "The Jordanian Entity," 237.

45. Iris Fruchter-Ronen, "Black September: The 1970–71 Events and Their Impact on the Formation of Jordanian National Identity," *Civil Wars* 10, no. 3 (2008): 254.

46. Sulayman Musa, *Tarʾikh al-urdun al-siyasi al-muʿasir: haziran 1967–1995* (Amman: Lajnat tarikh al-urdun, 1998), 118-20.

47. White House, "Memorandum of Conversation between King Hussein, Zeid Rifaʿi, Henry Kissinger, and State Department Officials," March 15, 1974.

48. Emile Sahliyeh, "Jordan and the Palestinians," in *The Middle East: Ten Years After Camp David*, ed. William B. Quandt (Washington, D.C.: Brookings Institution, 1988), 287–89.

49. Khalil Hammad, "The Role of Foreign Aid in the Jordanian Economy, 1959–1983," in *The Economic Development of Jordan*, ed. Bichara Khader and Adnan Badran (London: Croom Helm, 1987), 26–27.

50. Taher Masri, personal interview with author, Amman, Jordan, July 3, 2006.

51. Tariq Moraiwed Tell, "The Politics of Rural Policy in East Jordan," in *The Transformation of Nomadic Society in the Arab East*, ed. Martha Mundy and Basim Musallam (Cambridge: Cambridge University Press, 2000), 90–98.

52. Eliyahu Kanovsky, "Economic Development in Jordan since 1967," in *The Hashemite Kingdom of Jordan and the West Bank*, 77–82.

53. Mazur, *Economic Growth*, 113.

54. Eliyahu Kanovsky, *Jordan's Economy: From Prosperity to Crisis* (Tel Aviv: Moshe Dayan Center for Middle Eastern and African Studies, 1989), 46–49.

55. Satloff, *Troubles on the East Bank*, 16–19.

56. Pete Moore, *Doing Business in the Middle East: Politics and Economic Crisis in Jordan and Kuwait* (New York: Cambridge University Press, 2004), 110–13.

57. Michel Chatelus, "Rentier or Producer Economy in the Middle East? The Jordanian Response," in *The Economic Development of Jordan*, ed. Bichara Khader and Adnan Badran (London: Croom Helm, 1987), 215.

58. Moore, *Doing Business*, 117–18.

59. Ilan Pappé, "Jordan between Hashemite and Palestinian Identity," in *Jordan in the Middle East: The Making of a Pivotal State, 1948–1988*, ed. Joseph Nevo and Ilan Pappé (London: Cass, 1994), 86–87.

60. Walid Al-Turk, personal interview with author, Amman, Jordan, June 20, 2006.

61. Susser, *On Both Banks*, 156–57.

62. Yitzhak Reiter, "The Palestinian-Transjordanian Rift: Economic Might and Political Power in Jordan," *Middle East Journal* 58, no. 1 (2004): 72–92.

63. M. A. J. Share, "The Use of Jordanian Worker's Remittances," in *The Economic Development of Jordan*, ed. Bichara Khader and Adnan Badran (London: Croom Helm, 1987), 39–42.

64. Marwan Kardoosh and Taher Kanaan, *The Jordanian Economy into the Third Millennium* (Amman: Higher Council for Science and Technology, 2003), 10–12.

65. Arthur Day, *East Bank/West Bank: Jordan and the Prospects for Peace* (New York: Council on Foreign Relations, 1986), 79–82.

66. Jamil Jreisat, "Bureaucracy and Development in Jordan," *Journal of Asian and African Studies* 24, no. 1–2 (1989): 98–103.

67. Paul Jureidini and R. D. McLaurin, *Jordan: The Impact of Social Change on the Role of the Tribes* (Washington, D.C.: Center for Strategic and International Studies, 1984), 40 and 61–62.

68. Riad Al-Khouri, personal interview with author, June 16, 2011.

69. Joseph Nevo, "Professional Associations in Jordan: The Backbone of an Emerging Civil Society," *Asian Studies Review* 25, no. 2 (2001): 172–73.

70. Yitzhak Reiter, "Higher Education and Sociopolitical Transformation in Jordan," *British Journal of Middle Eastern Studies* 29, no. 2 (2002): 158–60.

71. Abu Odeh, *Hashemite Kingdom*, 190–236.

72. Abu Odeh, personal interview.

73. Jureidini and McLaurin, *Jordan: The Impact*, 39–40.

74. Moaddel, *Jordanian Exceptionalism*, 107.

75. Hani Al-Hourani et al., *Islamic Action Front Party* (Amman, Jordan: Al-Urdun Al-Jadid, 1993), 12–14.

76. Ibrahim Al-Shraah, "Al-Ittihad al-watani al-ʿarabi ʿal-urduni' baina ʿami 1971–1974: Dirasa taʾrikhiyyah tahliliyyah," *Al-Najah University Journal of Research in the Humane Sciences* 26, no. 3 (2012): 731–66.

77. Massad, *Colonial Effects*, 247–48.

78. Nabeel Khoury, "The National Consultative Council of Jordan: A Study in Legislative Development," *International Journal of Middle East Studies* 13, no. 4 (1981): 430–33.

79. Gil Feiler, "Jordan's Economy, 1970–90: The Primary of Exogenous Factors," in *Jordan in the Middle East: The Making of a Pivotal State, 1948–1988*, ed. Joseph Nevo and Ilan Pappé (London: Frank Cass, 1994), 52.

80. Fadel Ali Al-Sarhan, personal interview with author, Amman, Jordan, June 12, 2006.

81. Ibid.

82. Katherine Rath, "The Process of Democratization in Jordan," *Middle Eastern Studies* 30, no. 3 (1994): 530–57.

83. Hani Al-Hourani and Hussein Abu Rumman, *Al-Mujtamaʿ al-madani wa al-hukm fiil-urdun*, vol. 1 (Amman: Dar sindbad lil-nashr, 2004), 52–69.

84. Curtis Ryan, *Jordan in Transition: From Hussein to Abdullah* (Boulder, CO: Lynne Rienner, 2002), 15–45.

85. Glenn Robinson, "Defensive Democratization in Jordan," *International Journal of Middle East Studies* 30, no. 3 (1998): 387–410.

86. Hillel Frisch, "Fuzzy Nationalism: The Case of Jordan," *Nationalism and Ethnic Politics* 8, no. 4 (2002): 97–99.

87. Masri, personal interview.

88. Abu Odeh, *Jordanians, Palestinians*, 229.

89. Malik Mufti, "Elite Bargains and the Onset of Political Liberalization in Jordan," *Comparative Political Studies* 32, no. 1 (1999): 105–9.

90. Kamel Abu Jaber and Schirin H. Fathi, "The 1989 Jordanian Parliamentary Elections," *Orient* 31, no. 1 (1990): 72–73.

91. Tim Riedel, "The 1993 Parliamentary Elections in Jordan," *Orient* 35, no. 1 (1994): 53–6.

92. Khalid Samara Al-Zuʿbi, *Al-Nidham al-idari fiil-urdun* (Amman: Lajnat tarikh al-urdun, 1994), 50–52.

93. Ellen Lust-Okar, "Elections under Authoritarianism: Preliminary Lessons from Jordan," *Democratization* 13, no. 3 (2006): 456–71.

94. Yann Le Troquer and Rozenn Hommery Al-Oudat, "From Kuwait to Jordan: The Palestinians' Third Exodus," *Journal of Palestine Studies* 28, no. 3 (1999): 40–42.

95. Sean L. Yom and Mohammad H. Al-Momani, "The International Dimensions of Authoritarian Regime Stability: Jordan in the Post-Cold War Era," *Arab Studies Quarterly* 30, no. 1 (2008): 39–60.

96. Jane Harrigan, Hamed Al-Said, and Chengang Wang, "The IMF and the World Bank in Jordan: A Case of Over Optimism and Elusive Growth," *Review of International Organizations* 1, no. 3 (2006): 270.

97. ʿAbdel Jaber, personal interview.
98. Karim Nashashibi, "Fiscal Revenues in the South Mediterranean Arab Countries: Vulnerabilities and Growth Potential" (Working Paper, International Monetary Fund, 2002), 11–12.

9 THE GEOPOLITICAL ORIGINS OF DURABLE POLITICAL ORDER

1. Jennifer Gandhi and Adam Przeworski, "Cooperation, Cooptation, and Rebellion under Dictatorships," *Economics and Politics* 18, no. 1 (2006): 1–26; and Milan Svolik, *The Politics of Authoritarian Rule* (New York: Cambridge University Press, 2012).
2. Joel Migdal, *Strong Societies and Weak States: State-Society Relations and State Capabilities in the Third World* (Princeton: Princeton University Press, 1988).
3. Randall Wood and Carmine DeLuca, *Dictator's Handbook: A Practical Manual for the Aspiring Tyrant* (N.p.: Gull Pond Books, 2012); and Bruce Bueno de Mesquita and Alastair Smith, *The Dictator's Handbook: Why Bad Behavior Is Almost Always Good Politics* (New York: Public Affairs, 2012).

BIBLIOGRAPHY

SERIALS AND DATABASES

Central Bank of Iran. *Annual Review*. Tehran: Central Bank of Iran, serial.

Central Bank of Jordan. *Yearly Statistical Series*. Amman: Central Bank of Jordan, serial.

Kuwait Central Statistical Office. *Statistical Abstract in 25 Years*. Kuwait: Ministry of Planning, 1990.

United States Agency for International Development. *US Overseas Loans and Grants: Obligations and Loan Authorizations Database* ("Greenbook"). Washington, D.C.: US-AID, serial.

United States Arms Control and Disarmament Agency (ACDA). *World Military Expenditures and Arms Transfers*. Washington, D.C.: Department of State, serial.

World Bank. *World Development Indicators*. Washington, D.C.: The World Bank, serial.

GOVERNMENT DOCUMENTATION

Central Intelligence Agency. "The Tudeh Party: Vehicle of Communism in Iran," National Intelligence Estimate ORE 23–49. July 18, 1949. Reproduced in *Declassified Documents Reference System*. Farmington Hills, MI: Gale Group, 2006.

International Cooperation Administration. *Programs of the International Cooperation Administration under the Mutual Security Program*. Washington, D.C.: Department of State, 1959.

National Security Council. Memorandum prepared by Alexander Haig for the White House Staff on Jordan. October 3, 1970. Reproduced in *Declassified Documents Reference System*. Farmington Hills, MI: Gale Group, 2006.

———. "Report on Iran, NSC 5703/1." October 8, 1958. Reproduced in *Declassified Documents Reference System*. Farmington Hills, MI: Gale Group, 2006.

United States Agency for International Development. *Technical Aid, An Investment in People: The Point Four Program in Iran*. Provo, UT: Brigham Young University Press, 1960.

———. *US Economic Assistance to Iran, 1950–1965*. Washington, D.C.: USAID, 1965.

United States Department of Commerce. *A Market for U.S. Products in Iran*. Washington, D.C.: Bureau of International Commerce, 1966.

United States Department of Defense. "Financial Crisis in Jordan." Memorandum prepared by the Office of Chief Naval Operations for the Secretary of the Navy. June 20, 1957. Reproduced in *Declassified Documents Reference System*. Farmington Hills, MI: Gale Group, 2006.

United States Department of State. "Briefing Book for 5/30/61 US Visit of Prime Minister Ben-Gurion: Jordan as the Key to Stability in the Middle East." May 1961. Reproduced in *Declassified Documents Reference System*. Farmington Hills, MI: Gale Group, 2006.

White House. Memorandum of conversation between King Hussein, Zeid Rifai, Henry Kissinger, and state department officials. March 15, 1974. Reproduced in *Declassified Documents Reference System*. Farmington Hills, MI: Gale Group, 2006.

BOOKS AND BOOK CHAPTERS

Abrahamian, Ervand. *A History of Modern Iran*. New York: Cambridge University Press, 2008.

———. *Iran between Two Revolutions*. Princeton: Princeton University Press, 1982.

Abu Diyah, Sa'd. *'Amaliyat ittikhadh al-qirar fii siyasat al-urdun al-kharijiya: al-dhawabit wa al-muqawwimat*. Amman: n.p., 1983.

Abu Hakima, Ahmad M. *The Modern History of Kuwait, 1750–1965*. London: Luzac, 1983.

Abu Nowar, Maan. *The Development of Trans-Jordan 1929–1939: A History of the Hashemite Kingdom of Jordan*. Reading, UK: Ithaca, 2006.

———. *The History of the Hashemite Kingdom of Jordan: The Creation and Development of Transjordan, 1920–1929*. Oxford: Ithaca, 1989.

———. *The Struggle for Independence, 1939–1947: A History of the Hashemite Kingdom of Jordan*. Reading, UK: Ithaca, 2001.

Abu Odeh, Adnan. *Jordanians, Palestinians, and the Hashemite Kingdom in the Middle East Peace Process*. Washington, D.C.: United States Institute of Peace, 1999.

Aburish, Said. *A Brutal Friendship: The West and the Arab Elite*. New York: St. Martin's, 1997.

Acemoglu, Daron, and James Robinson. *Economic Origins of Dictatorship and Democracy*. New York: Cambridge University Press, 2006.

Adelman, Jonathan, ed. *Superpowers and Revolution*. New York: Praeger, 1986.

Afkhami, Gholam. *The Iranian Revolution: Thanatos on a National Scale.* Washington, D.C.: Middle East Institute, 1985.

———. *The Life and Times of the Shah.* Berkeley: University of California Press, 2009.

Akhavi, Shahrough. *Religion and Politics in Contemporary Iran Clergy-State Relations in the Pahlavi Period.* Albany: State University of New York Press, 1980.

Al-ʿAdsani, Khalid Sulayman. *Muthakirrat khalid sulayman al-ʿadsani, sikritir majlis al-umma al-tashriʿ al-awwal wa al-thani.* Kuwait: n.p., 1939.

Al-ʿAjami, Dhafir Muhammad Nasir. *Jaysh al-kuwayt fii ʿasr mubarak al-sabah.* Kuwait: n.p., 2000.

Al-ʿAnazi, Muhammad Nayif. *Dirasat fii taʾrikh al-kuwayt al-hadith wa al-muʿasir.* Kuwait: Matbaʿ al-fajr al-kuwaytiyyah, 2004.

Al-Ebraheem, Hassan Ali. *ʿAjz al-mizaniyyah—awdhaʿ al-maliyyah al-ʿama fiil-kuwayt: al-waqiʿ, al-ihtimal, wa subul al-muwajahah.* Kuwait: Maktabat dar al-qirtas, 1995.

———. *Kuwait and the Gulf: Small States and the International System.* London: Croom Helm, 1984.

Al-Ghabra, Shafeeq. *Al-Kuwayt: dirasa fiil-aliyat al-dawla al-qutriyyah wa al-sulta wa al-mujtamaʿ.* Cairo: Ibn Khaldun Center for Development Studies, 1995.

Al-Hatim, Musa Ghadban. *Taʾrikh al-shurta fiil-kuwayt.* Kuwait: Dar al-qirtas lil-nashr, 1999.

Al-Humeidi, Sabri Falih. *Al-Kuwayt: nushuʾha wa tatawwurha, 1760–1871.* London: Dar al-hikma, 2005.

Al-Hourani, Hani. *Al-Haraka al-ʿamaliyyah al-urduniyyah, 1948–1988.* Nicosia, Cyprus: Majallat Al-Urdun Al-Jadid, 1989.

———. *The Jordanian Labour Movement: History, Structure, and Challenges.* Bonn: Friedrich Ebert Stiftung, 2001.

Al-Hourani, Hani, Taleb Awad, Hammed Dabbas, and Saʿeda Kilani. *Islamic Action Front Party.* Amman: Al-Urdun Al-Jadid, 1993.

Al-Hourani, Hani, and Hussein Abu Rumman. *Al-Mujtamaʿ al-madani wa al-hukm fiil-urdun,* vol. 1 (Amman: Dar sindbad lil-nashr, 2004).

Al-Jasim, Najat ʿAbd Al-Qadir. *Al-Tatawwur al-siyasi wa al-iqtisadi lil-kuwayt baina al-harbayni.* Kuwait: n.p., 1997.

Al-Mudayris, Falah ʿAbdullah. *Al-Haraka al-dusturiyyah fiil-kuwayt.* Kuwait: Dar al-qirtas lil-nashr, 2002.

Al-Najjar, Ghanim. *Madkhal lil-tatawwar al-siyasi fiil-kuwayt.* Kuwait: Dar al- qirtas lil-nashr, 1996.

Al-Naqib, Khaldun. *Siraʿ baina al-qabaliyyah wa al-dimuqratiyyah: halat al-kuwayt.* London: Dar Al-Saqi, 1996.

Al-Qinaʿi, Yusuf Bin ʿIsa. *Safahat min taʾrikh al-kuwayt.* Kuwait: n.p., 1968.

Al-Rushayd, ʿAbd Al-ʿAziz. *Taʾrikh al-kuwayt.* Beirut: Maktabat al-hayat, 1971.

Al-Sabah, Y. S. F. *The Oil Economy of Kuwait.* London: Kegan Paul, 1980.

Al-Sharqawi, Ibrahim. *Al-Kuwayt wa al-luʾluʾ,* 2nd ed. Kuwait: n.p., 1998.

Al-Sultan, Fawzi. *Averting Financial Crisis—Kuwait.* Washington, D.C.: World Bank, 1989.

Al-Taher, Isam. *Kuwait: The Reality.* Pittsburgh: Dorrance, 1995.

Al-Yahya, Mohammad Abdul Rahman. *Kuwait: Fall and Rebirth.* London: Kegan Paul, 1993.

Al-Zuʿbi, Khalid Samara. *Al-Nidham al-idari fiil-urdun.* Amman: Lajnat tarikh al-urdun, 1994.

Alam, Asadollah, and Alinaghi Alikhani. *The Shah and I: The Confidential Diary of Iran's Royal Court, 1968–77.* London: I. B. Tauris, 1991.

Albrecht, Holger, ed. *Contentious Politics in the Middle East: Political Opposition under Authoritarianism.* Gainesville: University Press of Florida, 2010.

Alessa, Shamlan. *The Manpower Problem in Kuwait.* London: Kegan Paul, 1981.

Alghanim, Salwa. *The Reign of Mubarak al-Sabah: Shaikh of Kuwait, 1896–1915.* London: I. B. Tauris, 1998.

Alon, Yoav. *The Making of Jordan: Tribes, Colonialism and the Modern State.* London: I. B. Tauris, 2007.

Ames, Barry. *Political Survival: Politicians and Public Policy in Latin America.* Berkeley: University of California Press, 1987.

Amuzegar, Jahangir, and M. Ali Fekrat. *Iran: Economic Development under Dualistic Conditions.* Chicago: University of Chicago, 1971.

Anderson, Betty. *Nationalist Voices in Jordan: the Street and the State.* Austin: University of Texas, 2005.

Anderson, Lisa. *The State and Social Transformation in Tunisia and Libya, 1830–1980.* Princeton: Princeton University Press, 1986.

Ansari, Ali. *Modern Iran since 1921: The Pahlavis and After.* London: Longman, 2003.

Anscombe, Frederick. *The Ottoman Gulf: The Creation of Kuwait, Saudi Arabia, and Qatar.* New York: Columbia University Press, 1997.

Arjomand, Said Amir. *The Turban for the Crown: The Islamic Revolution in Iran.* New York: Oxford University Press, 1988.

Aruri, Naseer. *Jordan: A Study in Political Development, 1921–1965.* The Hague, the Netherlands: Martinus Nijhoff, 1972.

Ashraf, Ahmad. "State and Agrarian Relations Before and After the Iranian Revolution, 1960–1990." In *Peasants and Politics in the Modern Middle East,* edited by Farhad Kazemi and John Waterbury, 277–311. Miami: Florida International University Press, 1991.

Ashton, Nigel John. *King Hussein of Jordan: A Political Life.* New Haven: Yale University Press, 2008.

Assiri, Abdul-Reda. *Kuwait's Foreign Policy: City-State in World Politics.* Boulder, CO: Westview, 1990.

Ayoob, Mohammed. "The Muslim World's Poor Record of Modernization and Democratization: The Interplay of External and Internal Factors." In *Modernization, Democ-*

racy, and Islam, edited by Shireen Hunter and Huma Malik, 186–202. Norwalk, CT: Greenwood Press, 2005.

——. *The Third World Security Predicament: State Making, Regional Conflict, and the International System*. Boulder, CO: Lynne Rienner, 1995.

Ayubi, Nazih. *Over-stating the Arab State: Politics and Society in the Middle East*. London: I. B. Tauris, 1995.

Azoulay, Rivka. "The Politics of Shi'i Merchants in Kuwait." In *Business Politics in the Middle East*, edited by Steffen Hertog, Giacomo Luciani, and Mark Valeri, 67–100. London: Hurst, 2012.

Bailey, Clinton. "Cabinet Formation in Jordan." In *The Hashemite Kingdom of Jordan and the West Bank: A Handbook*, edited by Anne Sinai and Allen Pollack, 102–13. New York: American Academic Association for Peace in the Middle East, 1977.

——. *Jordan's Palestinian Challenge, 1948–1983: A Political History*. Boulder, CO: Westview, 1984.

Baraheni, Reza. *The Crowned Cannibals: Writings on Repression in Iran*. New York: Vintage, 1977.

Bashiriyeh, Hossein. *The State and Revolution in Iran, 1962–1982*. London: Croom Helm, 1984.

Beblawi, Hazem. "The Rentier State in the Arab World." In *The Arab State*, edited by Giacomo Luciani, 85–98. London: Routledge, 1990.

Beck, Lois. "Tribe and State in Nineteenth- and Twentieth-Century Iran." In *Tribes and State Formation in the Middle East*, edited by Philip S. Khoury and Joseph Kostiner, 185–225. Berkeley: University of California Press, 1990.

Beling, Willard. *Pan-Arabism and Labor*. Cambridge, MA: Harvard University Center for Middle Eastern Studies, 1961.

Bell, Gawain. *Shadows on the Sand: The Memoirs of Sir Gawain Bell*. London: Hurst, 1983.

Bharier, Julian. *Economic Development in Iran, 1900–1970*. London: Oxford University Press, 1971.

Bill, James. *The Eagle and the Lion: The Tragedy of American-Iranian Relations*. New Haven: Yale University Press, 1988.

Binder, Leonard. *Iran: Political Development in a Changing Society*. Berkeley: University of California Press, 1962.

Bocco, Riccardo, and Tariq Tell. "Pax Britannica in the Steppe: British Policy and the Transjordan Bedouin." In *Village, Steppe and State: The Social Origins of Modern Jordan*, edited by Eugene L. Rogan and Tariq Tell, 108–27. London: British Academic, 1994.

Boghardt, Lori Plotkin. *Kuwait amid War, Peace and Revolution: 1979–1991 and New Challenges*. New York: Palgrave Macmillan, 2006.

Brand, Laurie. *Jordan's Inter-Arab Relations: The Political Economy of Alliance Making*. New York: Columbia University Press, 1995.

Brautigam, Deborah. *Taxation and State-Building in Developing Countries: Capacity and Consent*. New York: Cambridge University Press, 2008.

Brown, L. Carl. *International Politics and the Middle East: Old Rules, Dangerous Game*. Princeton: Princeton University Press, 1984.

Brownlee, Jason. *Authoritarianism in an Age of Democratization*. New York: Cambridge University Press, 2007.

Brownlee, Jason, Tarek Masoud, and Andrew Reynolds. *The Arab Spring: Pathways of Repression and Reform*. New York: Oxford University Press, 2015.

Brynen, Rex, Bahgat Korany, and Paul Noble, eds. *Political Liberalization and Democratization in the Arab World*, vols. 1 and 2. Boulder, CO: Lynne Rienner, 1995, 1998.

Bueno de Mesquita, Bruce, and Alastair Smith. *The Dictator's Handbook: Why Bad Behavior is Almost Always Good Politics*. New York: Public Affairs, 2012.

Bueno de Mesquita, Bruce, Alastair Smith, Randolph Siverson, and James Morrow. *The Logic of Political Survival*. Cambridge, MA: MIT Press, 2005.

Bunce, Valerie, and Sharon Wolchik. *Defeating Authoritarian Leaders in Postcommunist Countries*. New York: Cambridge University Press, 2011.

Campbell, John. *Defense of the Middle East: Problems of American Policy*. New York: Harper, 1958.

Carter, J. R. L. *Merchant Families of Kuwait*. London: Scorpion, 1984.

Centeno, Miguel Angel. *Blood and Debt: War and the Nation-State in Latin America*. University Park: Pennsylvania State University Press, 2002.

Chatelus, Michel. "Rentier or Producer Economy in the Middle East? The Jordanian Response." In *The Economic Development of Jordan*, edited by Bichara Khader and Adnan Badran, 204–20. London: Croom Helm, 1987.

Chaudhry, Kiren Aziz. *The Price of Wealth: Economies and Institutions in the Middle East*. Ithaca, NY: Cornell University Press, 1997.

Chong, Ja Ian. *External Intervention and the Politics of State Formation: China, Indonesia, and Thailand, 1893–1952*. New York: Cambridge University Press, 2012.

Cohen, Amnon. *Political Parties in the West Bank under the Jordanian Regime, 1949–1967*. Ithaca, NY: Cornell University Press, 1982.

Cohen, Raymond. *Saving the Holy Sepulchre: How Rival Christians Came Together to Rescue their Holiest Shrine*. New York: Oxford University Press, 2008.

Cottam, Richard. *Iran and the United States: A Cold War Case Study*. Pittsburgh: University of Pittsburgh, 1988.

Cottrell, Alvin. "Iran's Armed Forces under the Pahlavi Dynasty." In *Iran Under the Pahlavis*, edited by George Lenczowski, 389–432. Stanford: Hoover Institution Press, 1978.

Cronin, Stephanie. *Tribal Politics in Iran Rural Conflict and the New State, 1921–1941*. London: Routledge, 2007.

Crystal, Jill. *Oil and Politics in the Gulf: Rulers and Merchants in Kuwait and Qatar*. New York: Cambridge University Press, 1990.

——. "Public Order and Authority: Policing Kuwait." In *Monarchies and Nations: Globalisation and Identity in the Arab States of the Gulf*, edited by Paul Dresch and James Piscatori, 158–81. London: I. B. Tauris, 2005.

Crystal, Jill, and Abdallah Al-Shayeji. "The Pro-Democratic Agenda in Kuwait: Structures and Context." In *Political Liberalization and Democratization in the Arab World*, vol. 2, edited by Rex Brynen, Bahgat Korany, and Paul Noble, 101–25. Boulder, CO: Lynne Rienner, 1998.

Dann, Uriel. *King Hussein and the Challenge of Arab Radicalism: Jordan, 1955–1967*. Oxford: Oxford University Press, 1989.

——. "The Jordanian Entity in Changing Circumstances, 1967–1973." In *From June to October: The Middle East between 1967 and 1973*, edited by Itamar Rabinovich and Haim Shaked, 231–244. New Brunswick, NJ: Transaction, 1978.

Dawisha, Adeed. "The Soviet Union in the Arab World: The Limits to Superpower Influence." In *The Soviet Union in the Middle East: Policies and Perspectives*, edited by Adeed Dawisha and Karen Dawisha, 8–23. New York: Holmes and Meier, 1982.

Day, Arthur. *East Bank/West Bank: Jordan and the Prospects for Peace*. New York: Council on Foreign Relations, 1986.

Dekhayel, Abdulkarim. *Kuwait: Oil, State and Political Legitimation*. Reading, UK: Ithaca, 2000.

Dickson, Harold R. P. *Kuwait and Her Neighbors*. London: Allen and Unwin, 1956.

Dimuqratiyyah al-shuyukh: Asrar al-hayat al-siyasiyyah fiil-kuwayt. Kuwait: Dar al-qirtas lil-nashr, 1986.

Downing, Brian. *The Military Revolution and Political Change: Origins of Democracy and Autocracy in Early Modern Europe*. Princeton: Princeton University Press, 1992.

Dowty, Alan. *Middle East Crisis: U.S. Decision-Making in 1958, 1970 and 1973*. Berkeley: University of California Press, 1984.

Dunning, Thad. *Crude Democracy*. New York: Cambridge University Press, 2008.

El-Edroos, Syed Ali. *The Hashemite Arab Army, 1908–1979: An Appreciation and Analysis of Military Operations*. Amman: The Publishing Committee, 1980.

El-Mallakh, Ragaei. *Economic Development and Regional Cooperation: Kuwait*. Chicago: University of Chicago, 1968.

El-Said, Hamed, and Kip Becker. *Management and International Business Issues in Jordan*. London: Routledge, 2002.

Ertman, Thomas. *Birth of the Leviathan: Building States and Regimes in Medieval and Early Modern Europe*. New York: Cambridge University Press, 1997.

Eveland, Wilbur Crane. *Ropes of Sand: America's Failure in the Middle East*. New York: Norton, 1980.

Evron, Yair. "Great Power Military Intervention in the Middle East." In *Great Power Intervention in the Middle East*, edited by Milton Leitenberg and Gabriel Sheffer, 17–45. New York: Pergamon, 1979.

Faddah, Mohammad Ibrahim. *The Middle East in Transition: A Study of Jordan's Foreign Policy*. New York: Asia Publishing House, 1974.

Feiler, Gil. "Jordan's Economy, 1970–90: The Primary of Exogenous Factors." In *Jordan in the Middle East: The Making of a Pivotal State, 1948–1988*, edited by Joseph Nevo and Ilan Pappé, 45–60. London: Cass, 1994.

Ferrier, Ronald. "The Anglo-Iranian Oil Dispute: A Triangular Relationship." In *Musaddiq, Iranian Nationalism, and Oil*, edited by James A. Bill and William Roger Louis, 164–99. London: I. B. Tauris, 1988.

Fischbach, Michael. *State, Society, and Land in Jordan*. Leiden: Brill, 2000.

Fischer, Michael M. J. *Iran: From Religious Dispute to Revolution*. Cambridge, MA: Harvard University Press, 1980.

Foran, John. *Taking Power: On the Origins of Third World Revolutions*. New York: Cambridge University Press, 2005.

Gandhi, Jennifer. *Political Institutions Under Dictatorships*. New York: Cambridge University Press, 2008.

Gasiorowski, Mark. *U.S. Foreign Policy and the Shah: Building a Client State in Iran*. Ithaca, NY: Cornell University Press, 1991.

Gavrielides, Nicolas. "Tribal Democracy: The Anatomy of Parliamentary Elections in Kuwait." In *Elections in the Middle East: Implications of Recent Trends*, edited by Linda L. Layne, 187–213. Boulder, CO: Westview, 1987.

Geddes, Barbara. *Politician's Dilemma: Building State Capacity in Latin America*. Berkeley: University of California Press, 1994.

Gendzier, Irene. *Notes from the Minefield United States Intervention in Lebanon and the Middle East, 1945–1958*, 2nd ed. New York: Columbia University Press, 2006.

Gerber, Haim. *The Social Origins of the Modern Middle East*. Boulder, CO: Lynne Rienner, 1987.

Gerges, Fawaz. *The Superpowers and the Middle East: Regional and International Politics, 1955–1967*. Boulder, CO: Westview, 1994.

Giustozzi, Antonio. *The Art of Coercion: The Primitive Accumulation and Management of Coercive Power*. New York: Columbia University Press, 2011.

Glubb, John Bagot. *A Soldier with the Arabs*. New York: Harper and Brothers, 1957.

Goodwin, Jeff. *No Other Way Out: States and Revolutionary Movements, 1945–1991*. New York: Cambridge University Press, 2001.

Graham, Robert. *Iran: The Illusion of Power*. New York: St. Martin's Press, 1979.

Grzymala-Busse, Anna. 2007. *Rebuilding Leviathan: Party Competition and State Exploitation in Post-Communist Democracies*. New York: Cambridge University Press.

Haggard, Stephan, and Robert R. Kaufman. *The Political Economy of Democratic Transitions*. Princeton: Princeton University Press, 1995.

Halliday, Fred. *Arabia without Sultans*. London: Penguin, 1974.

——. *Iran: Dictatorship and Development*. New York: Penguin, 1979.

——. *The Middle East in International Relations: Power, Politics and Ideology*. Cambridge: Cambridge University Press, 2005.

Halpern, Manfred. *The Politics of Social Change in the Middle East and North Africa*. Princeton: Princeton University Press, 1963.

Hammad, Khalil. "The Role of Foreign Aid in the Jordanian Economy, 1959–1983." In *The Economic Development of Jordan*, edited by Bichara Khader and Adnan Badran, 11–31. London: Croom Helm, 1987.

Harney, Desmond. *The Priest and the King: An Eyewitness Account of the Iranian Revolution*. London: British Academic, 1998.

Hay, Rupert. *The Persian Gulf States*. Washington, D.C.: Middle East Institute, 1959.

Heiss, Mary Ann. *Empire and Nationhood: The United States, Great Britain, and Iranian Oil, 1950–1954*. New York: Columbia University Press, 1997.

Henry, Clement Moore, and Robert Springborg. *Globalization and the Politics of Development in the Middle East*. New York: Cambridge University Press, 2010.

Herb, Michael. *All in the Family: Absolutism, Revolution, and Democracy in the Middle Eastern Monarchies*. Albany: State University of New York Press, 1999.

Herbst, Jeffrey Ira. *States and Power in Africa: Comparative Lessons in Authority and Control*. Princeton: Princeton University Press, 2000.

Herrmann, Richard. "The Role of Iran in Soviet Perceptions and Policy, 1946–1988." In *Neither East nor West: Iran, the Soviet Union, and the United States*, edited by Nikki Keddie and Mark J. Gasiorowski, 63–99. New Haven: Yale University Press, 1990.

Hertog, Steffen. *Princes, Brokers, and Bureaucrats: Oil and the State in Saudi Arabia*. Ithaca, NY: Cornell University Press, 2011.

Heydemann, Steven. *Authoritarianism in Syria: Institutions and Social Conflict, 1946–1970*. Ithaca, NY: Cornell University Press, 1999.

——. "War, Institutions, and Social Change in the Middle East." In *War, Institutions, and Social Change in the Middle East*, edited by Steven Heydemann, 1–32. Berkeley: University of California Press, 2000.

Hicks, Neil, and Ghanim Al-Najjar. "The Utility of Tradition: Civil Society in Kuwait." In *Civil Society in the Middle East*, vol. 1, edited by Augustus Richard Norton, 186–213. Leiden, the Netherlands: Brill, 1995.

Hiro, Dilip. *Iran under the Ayatollahs*. New York: Routledge, 1985.

Hollis, Rosemary. "Great Britain." In *The Powers in the Middle East: The Ultimate Strategic Arena*, edited by Bernard Reich, 179–225. New York: Praeger, 1987.

Hudson, Michael. *Arab Politics: The Search for Legitimacy*. New Haven: Yale University Press, 1977.

——, ed. *The Middle East Dilemma: The Politics and Economics of Arab Integration*. New York: Columbia University Press, 1998.

Hui, Victoria Tin-Bor. *War and State Formation in Ancient China and Early Modern Europe*. New York: Cambridge University Press, 2005.

Huntington, Samuel. *Political Order in Changing Societies*. New Haven: Yale University Press, 1968.

Huntington, Samuel, and Clement H. Moore, eds. *Authoritarian Politics in Modern Society: The Dynamics of Established One-Party Systems*. New York: Basic, 1970.

Hurewitz, J. C. *Middle East Politics: The Military Dimension*. Boulder, CO: Westview, 1982.

Ikegami, Eiko. *The Taming of the Samurai: Honorific Individualism and the Making of Modern Japan.* Cambridge, MA: Harvard University Press, 1995.

International Bank for Reconstruction and Development. *The Economic Development of Jordan.* Baltimore: Johns Hopkins Press, 1957.

——. *The Economic Development of Kuwait.* Baltimore: Johns Hopkins Press, 1965.

Ismael, Jacqueline. *Kuwait: Dependency and Class in a Rentier State.* 2nd ed. Gainesville: University of Florida, 1993.

Ismael, Tareq, and Glenn Perry, eds. *The International Relations of the Contemporary Middle East: Subordination and Beyond.* New York: Routledge, 2014.

Jamal, ʿAbdullah Yusif. *Al-Muʿaradha al-siyasiyyah fiil-kuwayt.* Kuwait: Dar al-qirtas lil-nashr, 2004.

Jarmon, Robert. *Sabah Al-Salim Al-Sabah, Amir of Kuwait, 1965–1977: A Political Biography.* London: London Center for Arab Studies, 2002.

Joyce, Miriam. *Kuwait, 1945–1996: An Anglo-American Perspective.* London: Cass, 1998.

——. *Anglo-American Support for Jordan: The Career of King Hussein.* New York: Palgrave Macmillan, 2008.

Jureidini, Paul, and R. D. McLaurin. *Jordan: The Impact of Social Change on the Role of the Tribes.* Washington D.C.: Center for Strategic and International Studies, 1984.

Kanovsky, Eliyahu. "Economic Development in Jordan Since 1967." In *The Hashemite Kingdom of Jordan and the West Bank: A Handbook,* edited by Anne Sinai and Allen Pollack, 73–88. New York: American Academic Association for Peace in the Middle East, 1977.

——. *The Economic Development of Jordan.* New Brunswick, NJ: Transaction Publishers, 1976.

——. *Jordan's Economy: From Prosperity to Crisis.* Tel Aviv: Moshe Dayan Center for Middle Eastern and African Studies, 1989.

Kardoosh, Marwan, and Taher Kanaan. *The Jordanian Economy into the Third Millennium,* Amman: Higher Council for Science and Technology, 2003.

Katouzian, Homa. *Mussaddiq and the Struggle for Power in Iran.* London: I. B. Tauris, 1990.

——. *The Political Economy of Modern Iran, 1929–1979.* New York: New York University Press, 1981.

——. *State and Society in Iran: The Eclipse of the Qajars and the Emergence of the Pahlavis.* London: I. B. Tauris, 2000.

Kazemi, Farhad. *Poverty and Revolution in Iran: The Migrant Poor, Urban Marginality, and Politics.* New York: New York University Press, 1980.

Keddie, Nikki. *Modern Iran: Roots and Results of Revolution,* 3rd ed. New Haven: Yale University Press, 2006.

——. "The Roots of Ulama Power in Modern Iran." In *Scholars, Saints, and Sufis: Muslim Religious Institutions in the Middle East Since 1500,* edited by Nikki Keddie, 211–29. Los Angeles: University of California Press, 1972.

Keddie, Nikki, ed. *Iran: Religion, Politics, and Society: Collected Essays.* London: Cass, 1980.

Kelly, J. B. *Arabia, the Gulf, and the West.* New York: Basic, 1980.

Kerr, Malcolm. *The Arab Cold War: Gamal 'Abd Al-Nasir and His Rivals, 1958–1970.* Oxford: Oxford University Press, 1971.

Keshavarzian, Arang. *Bazaar and State in Iran: The Politics of the Tehran Marketplace.* New York: Cambridge University Press, 2007.

Khadduri, Majid, and Edmund Ghareeb. *War in the Gulf, 1990–91: The Iraq-Kuwait Conflict and Its Implications.* New York: Oxford University Press, 1997.

Khouja, M. W., and P. G. Sadler. *The Economy of Kuwait: Development and Role in International Finance.* London: Macmillan, 1979.

Kimche, Jon. *The Second Arab Awakening: The Middle East, 1914–1970.* London: Holt, Rinehart, and Winston, 1970.

Kinzer, Stephen. *All the Shah's Men: An American Coup and the Roots of Middle East Terror,* 2nd ed. New York: Wiley, 2008.

Kirkpatrick, Jeane. *Dictatorships and Double Standards: Rationalism and Reason in Politics.* New York: Simon and Schuster, 1982.

Kohli, Atül. *State-Directed Development: Political Power and Industrialization in the Global Periphery.* New York: Cambridge University Press, 2004.

Korany, Bahgat, and Ali E. Hillal Dessouki. "The Global System and Arab Foreign Policies: The Primacy of Constraints." In *The Foreign Policies of Arab States: The Challenge of Change,* edited by Bahgat Korany and Ali E. Hillal Dessouki, 18–39. Cairo: American University in Cairo Press, 1984.

Krasner, Stephen. *Sovereignty: Organized Hypocrisy.* Princeton: Princeton University Press, 1999.

Kurzman, Charles. *The Unthinkable Revolution in Iran.* Cambridge, MA: Harvard University Press, 2004.

Kuwait Economic Society. *Kuwaiti Public Opinion Survey Report.* Kuwait: KES, 2005.

Lake, David. *Hierarchy in International Relations.* Ithaca, NY: Cornell University Press, 2009.

Laqueur, Walter. *The Struggle for the Middle East: The Soviet Union in the Mediterranean, 1958–1968.* New York: Macmillan, 1969.

Lavy, Victor, and Eliezer Sheffer. *Foreign Aid and Economic Development in the Middle East: Egypt, Syria, and Jordan.* Westport, CT: Praeger, 1991.

Ledeen, Michael Arthur, and William Lewis. *Debacle, the American Failure in Iran.* New York: Knopf, 1981.

Lenczowski, George. *Oil and State in the Middle East.* Ithaca, NY: Cornell University Press, 1960.

Levitsky, Steven, and Lucan Way. *Competitive Authoritarianism: Hybrid Regimes after the Cold War.* New York: Cambridge University Press, 2010.

Lichbach, Mark Irving. *The Rebel's Dilemma.* Ann Arbor: University of Michigan, 1995.

Lorimer, J. G. *Gazeteer of the Persian Gulf, Oman, and Central Asia*, vol. 1. Kolkata, India: Superintendent Government Printing, 1915.

Looney, Robert. *Economic Origins of the Iranian Revolution*. New York: Pergamon, 1982.

Louër, Laurence. *Transnational Shia Politics: Religious and Political Networks in the Gulf*. New York: Columbia University Press, 2008.

Louis, William Roger. "Britain and the Middle East after 1945." In *Diplomacy in the Middle East the International Relations of Regional and Outside Powers*, edited by L. Carl Brown, 21–58. London: I. B. Tauris, 2004.

Luciani, Giacomo. "The Oil Rent, the Fiscal Crisis of the State, and Democratization." In *Democracy without Democrats: The Renewal of Politics in the Muslim World*, edited by Ghassan Salamé, 130–55. London: I. B. Tauris, 1994.

Luong, Pauline Jones, and Erika Weinthal. *Oil Is Not a Curse: Ownership Structure and Institutions in Soviet Successor States*. New York: Cambridge University Press, 2010.

Lust-Okar, Ellen. *Structuring Conflict in the Arab World: Incumbents, Opponents, and Institutions*. New York: Cambridge University Press, 2005.

Magaloni, Beatriz. *Voting for Autocracy: Hegemonic Party Survival and Its Demise in Mexico*. New York: Cambridge University Press, 2006.

Mahdavy, Hossein. "The Patterns and Problems of Economic Development in Rentier States: The Case of Iran." In *Studies in the Economic History of the Middle East: From the Rise of Islam to the Present Day*, edited by Michael Cook, 428–67. London: Oxford University Press, 1970.

Mahoney, James. *Colonialism and Postcolonial Development: Spanish America in Comparative Perspective*. New York: Cambridge University Press, 2010.

Mahoney, James, and Dietrich Rueschemeyer. "Comparative-Historical Analysis: Achievements and Agendas." In *Comparative Historical Analysis in the Social Sciences*, edited by James Mahoney and Dietrich Rueschemeyer, 3–40. New York: Cambridge University Press, 2003.

Majd, Mohammad. *Resistance to the Shah Landowners and the Ulama in Iran*. Gainesville: University of Florida, 2000.

Mangold, Peter. *Superpower Intervention in the Middle East*. New York: St. Martin's, 1978.

Masalha, Muhammad. *Al-Tajriba al-hizbiyyah al-siyasiyyah fiil-urdun: dirasa tahliliyyah-muqaranah*. Amman: Dar wa'il lil-nashr, 1999.

Massad, Joseph Andoni. *Colonial Effects: The Making of National Identity in Jordan*. New York: Columbia University Press, 2001.

Mazur, Michael. *Economic Growth and Development in Jordan*. London: Croom Helm, 1979.

McLachlan, Keith. "Oil in the Persian Gulf Area." In *The Persian Gulf States: A General Survey*, edited by Alvin Cottrell, C. Edmund Bosworth, R. Michael Burrell, Keith McLachlan, and Roger Savory, 195–224. Baltimore: Johns Hopkins University Press, 1980.

268

Migdal, Joel. *Palestinian Society and Politics*. Princeton: Princeton University Press, 1980.

——. *Strong Societies and Weak States: State-Society Relations and State Capabilities in the Third World*. Princeton: Princeton University Press, 1988.

Milani, Abbas. *The Shah*. New York: Palgrave Macmillan, 2011.

Milani, Mohsen. *The Making of Iran's Islamic Revolution: From Monarchy to Islamic Republic*, 2nd ed. Boulder, CO: Westview, 1994.

Mishal, Shaul. *West Bank/East Bank: The Palestinians in Jordan, 1949–1967*. New Haven: Yale University Press, 1978.

Moaddel, Mansoor. *Jordanian Exceptionalism: A Comparative Analysis of State-Religion Relationships in Egypt, Iran, Jordan, and Syria*. New York: Palgrave Macmillan, 2002.

Moghadam, Fatemeh. *From Land Reform to Revolution: The Political Economy of Agricultural Development in Iran, 1962–1979*. London: I. B. Tauris, 1996.

Moore, Barrington. *Social Origins of Dictatorship and Democracy: Lord and Peasant in the Making of the Modern World*. Boston: Beacon, 1966.

Moore, Pete. *Doing Business in the Middle East: Politics and Economic Crisis in Jordan and Kuwait*. New York: Cambridge University Press, 2004.

Morris, Jan. *The Hashemite Kings*. New York: Pantheon, 1959.

Mukhadimah, Dhiyab. "Al-siyasiyyat al-kharijiyyah fii ʿahd hukumat al-nabulsi," In *Hukumat sulayman al-nabulsi*, edited by Hani Hourani. 177–87. Amman: Dar sindbad lil-nashr, 1999.

Murad, ʿAbbas. *Al-Dawr al-siyasi lil-jaysh al-urduni*. Beirut: PLO Research Center, 1973.

Musa, Sulayman. *Aʿlam min al-urdun: safahat min taʾrikh al-ʿarab al-hadith*. Amman: Dar al-shaʾb, 1986.

——. *Taʾsis al-imarah al-urduniyyah, 1921–1925*. Amman: Maktabat al-muhtasib, 1989.

——. *Tarʾikh al-urdun al-siyasi al-muʿasir: haziran 1967–1995*. Amman: Lajnat tarikh al-urdun, 1998.

Musa, Sulayman, and Munib Al-Madi. *Taʾrikh al-urdunn fiil-qarn al-ʿishrin, 1900–1959*. Amman: Maktabat al-muhtasib, 1959.

Mutawi, Samir. *Jordan in the 1967 War*. New York: Cambridge University Press, 1987.

Norton, Augustus Richard, ed. *Civil Society in the Middle East*, vols. 1 and 2. Leiden, the Netherlands: Brill, 1995, 1996.

Nusseibeh, Hazim Zaki. *Taʾrikh al-urdun al-siyasi al-muʿasir: ma baina ʿami 1952–1967*. Amman: Lajnat taʾrikh al-urdun, 1990.

O'Connell, Jack. *King's Counsel: A Memoir of War, Espionage, and Diplomacy in the Middle East*. New York: Norton, 2011.

Onley, James. *The Arabian Frontier of the British Raj: Merchants, Rulers, and the British in the Nineteenth Century Gulf*. Oxford: Oxford University Press, 2007.

Owen, Roger, and Sevket Pamuk. *A History of Middle East Economies in the Twentieth Century*. Cambridge, MA: Harvard University Press, 1999.

Palestinian Liberation Front. *Nawha Urdun Watani Dimuqrati*. Amman: n.p., 1980.

Pappé, Ilan. "Jordan Between Hashemite and Palestinian Identity." In *Jordan in the Middle East: The Making of a Pivotal State, 1948–1988*, edited by Joseph Nevo and Ilan Pappé, 61–91. London: Cass, 1994.

Parsa, Misagh. *Social Origins of the Iranian Revolution*. New Brunswick, NJ: Rutgers University Press, 1989.

Patai, Raphael and Fahim Qubain. "The Town." In *The Hashemite Kingdom of Jordan*, edited by Raphael Patai, 250–91. New Haven: Human Relations Area Files, 1956.

Peake, F. G. *A History of Jordan and Its Tribes*. Coral Gables, FL: University of Miami Press, 1958.

Pepinsky, Thomas. *Economic Crises and the Breakdown of Authoritarian Regimes: Indonesia and Malaysia in Comparative Perspective*. New York: Cambridge University Press, 2009.

Perlmutter, Amos. *Modern Authoritarianism: A Comparative Institutional Analysis*. New Haven: Yale University Press, 1981.

Pesaran, M. H. "Income Distribution in Iran." In *Iran: Past, Present, and Future*, edited by Jane Jacqz, 267–86. Denver, CO: Aspen Institute for Humanistic Studies, 1976.

Petersen, Tore. *Richard Nixon, Great Britain and the Anglo-American Alignment in the Persian Gulf and Arabian Peninsula: Making Allies out of Clients*. Eastbourne, UK: Sussex Academic, 2009.

Peterson, J. E. "Britain and the Gulf: At the Periphery of Empire." In *The Persian Gulf in History*, edited by Lawrence G. Potter, 277–93. New York: Palgrave Macmillan, 2009.

Pevehouse, Jon. *Democracy from Above: Regional Organizations and Democratization*. New York: Cambridge University Press, 2005.

Pierson, Paul. *Politics in Time: History, Institutions, and Social Analysis*. Princeton: Princeton University Press, 2004.

Piro, Timothy. *The Political Economy of Market Reform in Jordan*. Lanham, MD: Rowman and Littlefield, 1998.

Plascov, Avi. *The Palestinian Refugees in Jordan, 1948–1957*. London: Cass, 1981.

Platt, Kenneth. "Land Reform in Iran." In *Land Reform in Iran, Iraq, Pakistan, Turkey, Indonesia*, 1–101. Washington, D.C.: USAID, 1970.

Posusney, Marsha Pripstein, and Michele Penner Angrist, eds. *Authoritarianism in the Middle East: Regimes and Resistance*. Boulder, CO: Lynne Rienner, 2005.

Pundik, Ron. *The Struggle for Sovereignty: Relations Between Great Britain and Jordan, 1946–1951*. Oxford: Oxford University Press, 1994.

Quandt, William. *Decade of Decisions: American Policy Toward the Arab-Israeli Conflict, 1967–1976*. Berkeley: University of California Press, 1977.

Ravenhill, John. *Collective Clientelism: The Lomé Conventions and North-South Relations*. New York: Columbia University Press, 1985.

Razavi, Hossein, and Firouz Vakil. *The Political Environment of Economic Planning in Iran, 1971–1983: From Monarchy to Islamic Republic*. Boulder, CO: Westview, 1984.

Rich, Paul. *Creating the Arabian Gulf: The British Raj and the Invasions of the Gulf.* Lanham, MD: Lexington, 2009.

Richards, Alan, and John Waterbury. *A Political Economy of the Middle East: State, Class, and Economic Development,* 3rd ed. Boulder, CO: Westview, 2008.

Riker, William. *The Theory of Political Coalitions.* New Haven: Yale University Press, 1962.

Rimawi, Sahila. "Ahzab al-tayar al-qawmi wa hukumat al-nabulsi." In *Hukumat sulayman al-nabulsi,* edited by Hani Hourani, 101–12. Amman: Dar sindbad lil-nashr, 1999.

Robins, Philip. *A History of Jordan.* New York: Cambridge University Press, 2004.

Rogan, Eugene. *Frontiers of the State in the Late Ottoman Empire: Transjordan, 1850–1921.* New York: Cambridge University Press, 2002.

Rumaihi, Muhammed Al-Ghanim. "The Mode of Production in the Arab Gulf before the Discovery of Oil." In *Social and Economic Development in the Arab Gulf,* edited by Tim Niblock, 49–60. London: Croom Helm, 1980.

Rush, Alan. *Al-Sabah: History and Genealogy of Kuwait's Ruling Family, 1752–1987.* London: Ithaca, 1987.

Ryan, Curtis. *Jordan in Transition: From Hussein to Abdullah.* Boulder, CO: Lynne Rienner, 2002.

Sadowski, Yahya. *Scuds or Butter? The Political Economy of Arms Control in the Middle East.* Washington, D.C.: Brookings Institution Press, 1993.

Sahliyeh, Emile. "Jordan and the Palestinians." In *The Middle East: Ten Years After Camp David,* edited by William B. Quandt, 269–318. Washington, D.C.: Brookings Institution Press, 1988.

Saikal, Amin. *The Rise and Fall of the Shah.* Princeton: Princeton University Press, 1980.

Salem, Paul. "Kuwait: Politics in a Participatory Emirate." In *Beyond the Facade: Political Reform in the Arab World,* edited by Marina Ottaway and Julia Choucair-Vizoso, 211–30. Washington, D.C.: Carnegie Endowment for International Peace, 2008.

Salibi, Kamal. *The Modern History of Jordan.* London: I. B. Tauris, 1993.

Salloukh, Bassel, and Rex Brynen, eds. *Persistent Permeability? Regionalism, Localism, and Globalization in the Middle East.* Aldershot, UK: Ashgate, 2004.

Satloff, Robert. *From Abdullah to Hussein: Jordan in Transition.* Oxford: Oxford University Press, 1994.

——. *Troubles on the East Bank: Challenges to the Domestic Stability of Jordan.* Washington, D.C.: Center for Strategic and International Studies, 1986.

Savory, Roger. "Social Development in Iran during the Pahlavi Era." In *Iran Under the Pahlavis,* edited by George Lenczowski, 85–107. Stanford: Hoover Institution Press, 1978.

Sayigh, Yezid. *Armed Struggle and the Search for State: The Palestinian National Movement, 1949–1993.* New York: Oxford University Press, 2000.

Schedler, Andreas, ed. *Electoral Authoritarianism: The Dynamics of Unfree Competition.* Boulder, CO: Lynne Rienner, 2006.

Schlumberger, Oliver, ed. *Debating Arab Authoritarianism: Dynamics and Durability in Nondemocratic Regimes*. Stanford: Stanford University Press, 2007.

Schofield, Richard. *Kuwait and Iraq: Historical Claims and Territorial Disputes*, 2nd ed. London: Royal Institute for International Affairs, 1993.

Schwarz, Rolf. *War and State Building in the Middle East*. Gainesville: University Press of Florida, 2012.

Shaji'i, Zahra. *Namayandagan-i majlis-i shura-yi milli dar bist-o-yak dowrah-yi qanun-guzari*. Tehran: Institute for Social Studies and Research, 1965.

Shalom, Zaki. *The Superpowers, Israel and the Future of Jordan, 1960–1963: The Perils of the Pro-Nasser Policy*. Brighton, UK: Sussex Academic, 1999.

Shamlan, Sayf Marzuq. *Min ta'rikh al-kuwayt*. Kuwait: n.p., 1986.

Sharabi, Hisham, *Neopatriarchy: A Theory of Distorted Change in Arab Society*. New York: Oxford University Press, 1988.

Share, M. A. J. "The Use of Jordanian Worker's Remittances." In *The Economic Development of Jordan*, edited by Bichara Khader and Adnan Badran, 32–44. London: Croom Helm, 1987.

Shefter, Martin. *Political Parties and the State: The American Historical Experience*. Princeton: Princeton University Press, 1994.

Shiber, Saba George. *The Kuwait Urbanization: Documentation, Analysis, Critique*. Kuwait: Kuwait Government Printing, 1964.

Shlaim, Avi. *Lion of Jordan: The Life of King Hussein in War and Peace*. New York: Knopf, 2007.

Shuhaiber, Suhail. "Social and Political Developments in Kuwait Prior to 1961." In *Kuwait: The Growth of a Historic Identity*, edited by Ben Slot, 95–110. London: Gulf Museum Consultancy, 2003.

Shwadran, Benjamin. *Jordan: A State of Tension*. New York: Council for Middle Eastern Affairs, 1959.

Siavoshi, Sussan. "The Oil Nationalization Movement, 1949–1953." In *A Century of Revolution Social Movements in Iran*, edited by John Foran, 106–34. Minneapolis: University of Minnesota, 1994.

Sick, Gary. *All Fall Down: America's Fateful Encounter with Iran*. London: I. B. Tauris, 1985.

Sinai, Anne, and Allen Pollack. "Jordan: Past and Present." In *The Hashemite Kingdom of Jordan and the West Bank: A Handbook*, edited by Anne Sinai and Allen Pollack, 17–61. New York: American Academic Association for Peace in the Middle East, 1977

Skocpol, Theda. *States and Social Revolutions: A Comparative Analysis of France, Russia, and China*. New York: Cambridge University Press, 1979.

——. "Reflections on Recent Scholarship about Social Revolutions, and How to Study Them." In *Social Revolutions in the Modern World*, edited by Theda Skocpol, 301–44. New York: Cambridge University Press, 1994.

Slater, Dan. *Ordering Power: Contentious Politics and Authoritarian Leviathans in Southeast Asia*. New York: Cambridge University Press, 2010.

Slot, Ben. *Mubarak Al-Sabah: Founder of Modern Kuwait, 1896–1915.* London: Arabian Publishing, 2005.

Smith, Benjamin. *Hard Times in the Lands of Plenty: Oil Politics in Iran and Indonesia.* Ithaca, NY: Cornell University Press, 2007.

Smith, Simon. *Kuwait, 1950–1965: Britain, the Al-Sabah, and Oil.* Oxford: Oxford University Press, 1999.

Smolansky, Oles. "Soviet-Jordanian Relations." In *The Hashemite Kingdom of Jordan and the West Bank*, edited by Anne Sinai and Allen Pollack, 175–87. New York: American Academic Association for Peace in the Middle East, 1997.

Spector, Ivar. "Soviet Cultural Propaganda in the Near and Middle East." In *The Middle East in Transition: Studies in Contemporary History*, edited by Walter Laqueur, 378–87. New York: Praeger, 1958.

Stepan, Alfred. *Rethinking Military Politics: Brazil and the Southern Cone.* Princeton: Princeton University Press, 1988.

Stookey, Robert. *America and the Arab States: An Uneasy Encounter.* New York: Wiley, 1975.

Svolik, Milan. *The Politics of Authoritarian Rule.* New York: Cambridge University Press, 2012.

Susser, Asher. *On Both Banks of the Jordan: A Political Biography of Wasfi Al-Tall.* London: Cass, 1994.

Sylvan, David, and Stephen Majeski. *US Foreign Policy in Perspective: Clients, Enemies and Empire.* London: Routledge, 2009.

Tal, Lawrence. *Politics, the Military and National Security in Jordan: 1955–1967.* New York: Palgrave Macmillan, 2002.

Tell, Tariq Moraiwed. "The Politics of Rural Policy in East Jordan." In *The Transformation of Nomadic Society in the Arab East*, edited by Martha Mundy and Basim Musallam, 90–98. Cambridge: Cambridge University Press, 2000.

——. *The Social and Economic Origins of Monarchy in Jordon.* New York: Palgrave Macmillan, 2013.

Tétreault, Mary Ann. *Stories of Democracy: Politics and Society in Contemporary Kuwait.* New York: Columbia University Press, 2000.

Thelen, Kathleen, and Sven Steinmo. "Historical Institutionalism in Comparative Analysis." In *Structuring Politics: Historical Institutionalism in Comparative Analysis*, edited by Sven Steinmo, Kathleen Thelen, and Frank Longstreth, 1–29. New York: Cambridge University Press, 1992.

Tilly, Charles. *Big Structures, Large Processes, Huge Comparisons.* New York: Russell Sage Foundation, 1984.

——. *Coercion, Capital, and European States, AD 990–1992.* Cambridge, MA: Blackwell, 1990.

Triska, Jan F., ed. *Dominant Powers and Subordinate States: The United States in Latin America and the Soviet Union in Eastern Europe.* Durham, NC: Duke University Press, 1986.

Vatikiotis, P. J. *Politics and the Military in Jordan: A Study of the Arab Legion, 1921–1957.* London: Cass, 1967.

ʿUthman, Hassan Salih, and Hamid Ahmad Al-Shubaki. *Rijalat maʿ al-malik ʿabdullah.* Amman: n.p., 1995.

Vu, Tuong. *Paths to Development in Asia: South Korea, Vietnam, China, and Indonesia.* New York: Cambridge University Press, 2010.

Waldner, David. *State Building and Late Development.* Ithaca, NY: Cornell University Press, 1999.

Waterbury, John. "Democracy without Democrats? The Potential for Political Liberalization in the Middle East." In *Democracy without Democrats? The Renewal of Politics in the Muslim World,* edited by Ghassan Salamé, 23–47. London: I. B. Tauris, 1994.

Whitehead, Laurence, ed. *The International Dimensions of Democratization: Europe and the Americas.* New York: Oxford University Press, 1996.

Wickham-Crowley, Timothy P. *Guerrillas and Revolution in Latin America: A Comparative Study of Insurgents and Regimes since 1956.* Princeton: Princeton University Press, 1992.

Wilber, Donald N. *Clandestine Service History: Overthrow of Premier Mossadegh of Iran, November 1952–August 1953.* Langley, VA: Central Intelligence Agency, 1969.

Wilford, Hugh. *America's Great Game: The CIA's Secret Arabists and the Shaping of the Modern Middle East.* New York: Basic, 2013.

Wilson, Mary. *King Abdullah, Britain, and the Making of Jordan.* New York: Cambridge University Press, 1987.

Winstone, H. V. F., and Zahra Dickson Freeth. *Kuwait: Prospect and Reality.* New York: Crane and Russak, 1972.

Wood, Randall, and Carmine DeLuca. *The Dictator's Handbook: A Practical Manual for the Aspiring Tyrant.* N.p.: Gull Pond Books, 2012.

Wriggins, W. Howard. *The Ruler's Imperative: Strategies for Political Survival in Asia and Africa.* New York: Columbia University Press, 1969.

Yapp, Malcolm. "British Policy in the Persian Gulf." In *The Persian Gulf States: A General Survey,* edited by Alvin Cottrell, C. Edmund Bosworth, R. Michael Burrell, Keith McLachlan, and Roger Savory, 70–100. Baltimore: Johns Hopkins University Press, 1980.

Yaqub, Salim. *Containing Arab Nationalism: The Eisenhower Doctrine and the Middle East.* Chapel Hill: University of North Carolina Press, 2004.

Yergin, Daniel. *The Prize: The Epic Quest for Oil, Money, and Power.* New York: Simon and Schuster, 1991.

Young, Peter. *The Arab Legion.* Reading, UK: Osprey, 1972.

Zabih, Sepehr. *The Communist Movement in Iran.* Berkeley: University of California Press, 1966.

Zahlan, Rosemarie Said. *The Making of the Modern Gulf States: Kuwait, Bahrain, Qatar, the United Arab Emirates, and Oman.* London: Ithaca, 1998.

JOURNAL ARTICLES AND REPORTS

Abrahamian, Ervand. "The Crowd in Iranian Politics 1905–1953." *Past and Present* 41 (1968): 184–210.

——. "Structural Causes of the Iranian Revolution." *Middle East Research and Information Project Reports* 87 (1980): 21–26.

Abu Jaber, Kamel. "The Legislature of the Hashemite Kingdom of Jordan: A Study in Political Development." *The Muslim World* 59, nos. 3–4 (1969): 220–50.

Abu Jaber, Kamel, and Schirin H. Fathi. "The 1989 Jordanian Parliamentary Elections." *Orient* 31, no. 1 (1990): 67–86.

Akhavi, Shahrough. "The Ideology and Praxis of Shi'ism in the Iranian Revolution." *Comparative Studies in Society and History* 25, no. 2 (1983): 195–221.

Albertus, Michael, and Victor Menaldo. "Coercive Capacity and the Prospects for Democratization." *Comparative Politics* 44, no. 2 (2012): 151–69.

Al-Ebraheem, Hassan Ali. "Kuwait's Economic Travails." *Middle East Quarterly* 3, no. 3 (1996): 17–23.

Al-Najjar, Ghanim. "Challenges of Security Sector Governance in Kuwait." Working Paper 142, Geneva Centre for the Democratic Control of Armed Forces, 2004.

Al-Nakib, Farah. "Public Space and Public Protest in Kuwait, 1938–2012." *City: Analysis of Urban Trends, Culture, Theory, Policy, Action* 18, no. 6 (2014): 726–27.

——. "Revisiting Hadar and Badu in Kuwait: Citizenship, Housing, and the Construction of a Dichotomy." *International Journal of Middle East Studies* 46, no. 1 (2014): 5–30.

——. "The Lost 'Two-Thirds:' Kuwait's Territorial Decline between 1913 and 1922." *Journal of Arabian Studies: Arabia, the Gulf, and the Red Sea* 2, no. 1 (2012): 19–37.

Al-Remaidhi, Abdullah, and Bob Watt. "Electoral Constituencies and Political Parties in Kuwait: An Assessment." *Election Law Journal: Rules, Politics, and Policy* 11, no. 4 (2012): 518–28.

Al-Shiyab, Ibrahim Ahmad. "Political Parties in Jordan, 1921–1956." *European Journal of Social Sciences* 21, no. 1 (2011): 28–46.

Al-Shraah, Ibrahim. "Al-Ittihad al-watani al-'arabi 'al-urduni' baina 'ami 1971–1974: Dirasa ta'rikhiyyah tahliliyyah." *Al-Najah University Journal of Research in the Humane Sciences* 26, no. 3 (2012): 731–66.

Amini, P. "A Single Party State in Iran, 1975–78: The Rastakhiz Party, the Final Attempt by the Shah to Consolidate His Political Base." *Middle Eastern Studies* 38, no. 1 (2002): 131–68.

Anderson, Lisa. "Absolutism and the Resilience of Monarchy in the Middle East." *Political Science Quarterly* 106, no. 2 (1991): 1–15.

——. "Searching Where the Light Shines: Studying Democratization in the Middle East." *Annual Review of Political Science* 9 (2006): 189–214.

Arasteh, Reza. "The Role of Intellectuals in Administrative Development and Social Change in Modern Iran." *International Review of Education* 9, no. 3 (1963): 326–34.

Arjomand, Said Amir. "Iran's Islamic Revolution in Comparative Perspective." *World Politics* 38, no. 3 (1986): 383–414.

Art, David. "What Do We Know About Authoritarianism After Ten Years?" *Comparative Politics* 44, no. 3 (2012): 351–73.

Aruri, Naseer. "Kuwait: A Political Study." *The Muslim World* 60, no. 4 (1970): 321–43.

Ashraf, Ahmad. "Bazaar-Mosque Alliance: The Social Basis of Revolts and Revolutions." *International Journal of Politics, Culture and Society* 1, no. 4 (1988): 538–67.

——. "Historical Obstacles to the Development of a Bourgeoisie in Iran." *Iranian Studies* 2, no. 2 (1969): 54–79.

Ashraf, Ahmad, and Alinaghi Banuazizi. "The State, Classes, and Modes of Mobilization in the Iranian Revolution." *State, Culture, and Society* 1, no. 3 (1985): 3–40.

Ashton, Nigel John. "A Microcosm of Decline: British Loss of Nerve and Military Intervention in Jordan and Kuwait, 1958 and 1961." *The Historical Journal* 40, no. 4 (1997): 1069–83.

——. "'A Special Relationship Sometimes in Spite of Ourselves:' Britain and Jordan, 1957–73." *Journal of Imperial and Commonwealth History* 33, no. 2 (2005): 221–44.

Assiri, Abdul-Reda, and Kamal Al-Manoufi. "Kuwait's Political Elite: The Cabinet." *Middle East Journal* 42, no. 1 (1988): 48–58.

Axelrod, Lawrence. "Tribesmen in Uniform: The Demise of the Fida'iyyun in Jordan, 1970–71." *The Muslim World* 68, no. 1 (1978): 25–45.

Baaklini, Abdo. "Legislatures in the Gulf Area: The Experience of Kuwait, 1961–1976." *International Journal of Middle East Studies* 14, no. 3 (1982): 359–79.

Baer, Gabriel. "Land Tenure in the Hashemite Kingdom of Jordan." *Land Economics* 33, no. 1 (1957): 187–97.

Barany, Zoltan. "Unrest and State Response in Arab Monarchies." *Mediterranean Quarterly* 24, no. 2 (2013): 5–38.

Baster, James. "The Economic Problems of Jordan." *International Affairs* 31, no. 1 (1955): 26–35.

Behrooz, Maziar. "Tudeh Factionalism and the 1953 Coup In Iran." *International Journal of Middle East Studies* 33, no. 3 (2001): 363–82.

Bellin, Eva. "The Robustness of Authoritarianism in the Middle East: Exceptionalism in Comparative Perspective." *Comparative Politics* 36, no. 2 (2004): 139–57.

Bill, James A. "Modernization and Reform From Above: The Case of Iran." *Journal of Politics* 32, no. 1 (1970): 19–40.

Boix, Carles, and Milan Svolik. "The Foundations of Limited Authoritarian Government: Institutions, Commitment, and Power-Sharing in Dictatorships." *Journal of Politics* 75, no. 2 (2013): 300–16.

Brandon, Henry. "Were We Masterful . . . " *Foreign Policy* 10 (1973): 158–70.

Brumberg, Daniel. "The Trap of Liberalized Autocracy." *Journal of Democracy* 13, no. 4 (2002): 56–68.

Capoccia, Giovanni, and R. Daniel Kelemen. "The Study of Critical Junctures: Theory, Narrative, and Counterfactuals in Historical Institutionalism." *World Politics* 59, no. 3 (2007): 341–69.

Carey, Jane Perry Clark, and Andrew Galbraith Carey. "Iranian Agriculture and Its De-velopment: 1952–1973." *International Journal of Middle East Studies* 7, no. 3 (1976): 359–82.

Carney, Christopher. "International Patron-Client Relationships: A Conceptual Frame-work." *Studies in Comparative International Development* 24, no. 2 (1989): 42–55.

Celine, K. "Kuwait Living on Its Nerves." *Middle East Research and Information Project Reports* 130 (1985): 10–12.

Cottam, Richard. "The United States, Iran, and the Cold War." *Iranian Studies* 2, no. 1 (1970): 2–22.

Daftary, Farhad. "The Balance of Payment Deficit and the Problem of Inflation in Iran, 1955–1962." *Iranian Studies* 5, no. 1 (1972): 2–24.

Davenport, Christian. "State Repression and Political Order." *Annual Review of Political Science* 10 (2007): 1–23.

David, Steven. "Explaining Third World Alignment." *World Politics* 43, no. 2 (1991): 233–56.

Dees, Joseph. "Jordan's East Ghor Canal Project." *Middle East Journal* 13, no. 4 (1959): 357–71.

Diamond, Larry. "Thinking About Hybrid Regimes." *Journal of Democracy* 13, no. 2 (2002): 21–35.

Efimenco, N. Marbury. "An Experiment with Civilian Dictatorship in Iran: The Case of Mohammed Mossadegh." *Journal of Politics* 17, no. 3 (1955): 390–406.

Ehlers, Eckart, and Willem Floor. "Urban Change in Iran, 1920–1941." *Iranian Studies* 26, no. 3 (1993): 251–75.

Elwell-Sutton, L. P. "Political Parties in Iran, 1941–1948." *Middle East Journal* 3, no. 1 (1949): 45–62.

Escribà-Folch, Abel. "Repression, Political Threats, and Survival under Autocracy." *International Political Science Review* 34, no. 5 (2013): 543–60.

Eshraghi, F. "The Immediate Aftermath of Anglo-Soviet Occupation of Iran in August 1941." *Middle Eastern Studies* 20, no. 3 (1984): 324–51.

Faghfoory, Mohammad. "The Impact of Modernization on the Ulama in Iran, 1925–1941." *Iranian Studies* 26, no. 3 (1993): 277–312.

Faroughy, Ahmad. "Repression in Iran." *Index on Censorship* 3, no. 4 (1974): 9–18.

Fatemi, Khosrow. "Leadership by Distrust: The Shah's Modus Operandi." *Middle East Journal* 36, no. 1 (1982): 48–61.

Firoozi, Ferydoon. "Income Distribution and Taxation Laws of Iran." *International Journal of Middle East Studies* 9, no. 1 (1978): 73–87.

——. "The Iranian Budgets: 1964–1970." *International Journal of Middle East Studies* 5, no. 3 (1974): 328–43.

Floor, Willem. "The Revolutionary Character of the Iranian Ulama: Wishful Think-ing or Reality?" *International Journal of Middle East Studies* 12, no. 4 (1980): 501–24.

Frisch, Hillel. "Fuzzy Nationalism: The Case of Jordan." *Nationalism and Ethnic Politics* 8, no. 4 (2002): 86–103.

Fruchter-Ronen, Iris. "Black September: The 1970–71 Events and Their Impact on the Formation of Jordanian National Identity." *Civil Wars* 10, no. 3 (2008): 244–60.

Gandhi, Jennifer, and Adam Przeworski. "Cooperation, Cooptation, and Rebellion under Dictatorships." *Economics and Politics* 18, no. 1 (2006): 1–26.

Gasiorowski, Mark. "The 1953 Coup D'état in Iran." *International Journal of Middle East Studies* 19, no. 3 (1987): 261–86.

Gause, F. Gregory, III. "Systemic Approaches to Middle East International Relations." *International Studies Review* 1, no. 1 (1999): 11–31.

Gavin, Francis. "Politics, Power, and US Policy in Iran, 1950–1953." *Journal of Cold War Studies* 1, no. 1 (1999): 56–89.

Geddes, Barbara. "What Do We Know about Democratization after Twenty Years?" *Annual Review of Political Science* 2 (1999): 115–44.

Gerges, Fawaz. "The Study of Middle East International Relations: A Critique." *British Journal for Middle Eastern Studies.* Bulletin 18, no. 2 (1991): 208–20.

Ghabra, Shafeeq. "Kuwait and the Dynamics of Socio-Economic Change." *Middle East Journal* 51, no. 3 (1997): 358–72.

——. "Voluntary Associations in Kuwait: The Foundation of a New System?" *Middle East Journal* 45, no. 2 (1991): 199–215.

Ghods, M. Reza. "Iranian Nationalism and Reza Shah." *Middle Eastern Studies* 27, no. 1 (1991): 35–45.

Goldstone, Jack. "Toward a Fourth Generation of Revolutionary Theory." *Annual Review of Political Science* 4 (2001): 139–87.

Goode, James. "Reforming Iran during the Kennedy Years." *Diplomatic History* 15, no. 1 (1991): 13–29.

Goodwin, Jeff, and Theda Skocpol. "Explaining Revolutions in the Contemporary Third World." *Politics and Society* 17, no. 4 (1989): 489–509.

Gourevitch, Peter. "The Second Image Reversed: The International Sources of Domestic Politics." *International Organization* 32, no. 4 (1978): 881–912.

Grzymala-Busse, Anna. "Time Will Tell? Temporality and the Analysis of Causal Mechanisms and Processes." *Comparative Political Studies* 44, no. 9 (2011): 1267–97.

Hadenius, Axel, and Jan Teorell. "Pathways from Authoritarianism." *Journal of Democracy* 18, no. 1 (2007): 143–57.

Hall, Peter, and Rosemary C. R. Taylor. "Political Science and the Three New Institutionalisms." *Political Studies* 44, no. 5 (1996): 936–57.

Halliday, Fred. "The Economic Contradictions." *Middle East Research and Information Project Reports* 69 (1978): 9–18, 23.

Hanania, Marwan. "The Impact of Palestinian Refugee Crisis on the Development of Amman, 1947–1958," *British Journal of Middle East Studies* (2014): 1–22, doi: 10.1086/599247.

Harrigan, Jane, Hamed Al-Said, and Chengang Wang. "The IMF and the World Bank in Jordan: A Case of Over Optimism and Elusive Growth." *Review of International Organizations* 1, no. 3 (2006): 263–92.

278

Hattar, Jihad. *Dhikriyat ʿan maʿrika aylul: al-urdun 1970*. Beirut: Ittihad al-ʿam lil-kuttab wa al-suhufiyin al-filistiniyyin, 1977.

Hazleton, Jared. "Land Reform in Jordan: The East Ghor Canal Project." *Middle Eastern Studies* 15, no. 2 (1979): 258–69.

Hetherington, Norriss. "Industrialization and Revolution in Iran: Forced Progress or Unmet Expectation?" *Middle East Journal* 36, no. 3 (1982): 362–73.

Hijazi, Ahmad. "Kuwait: Development from a Semitribal, Semicolonial Society to Democracy and Sovereignty." *American Journal of Comparative Law* 13, no. 3 (1964): 428–38.

Howard, Marc Morjé, and Philip Roessler. "Liberalizing Electoral Outcomes in Competitive Authoritarian Regimes." *American Journal of Political Science* 50, no. 2 (2006): 365–81.

Issawi, Charles. "Iran's Economic Upsurge." *Middle East Journal* 21, no. 4 (1967): 447–61.

Jacoby, Wade. "Inspiration, Coalition, and Substitution: External Influences on Postcommunist Transformations." *World Politics* 58, no. 4 (2006): 623–51.

Jamal, Amaney, and Mark Tessler. "Attitudes in the Arab World." *Journal of Democracy* 19, no. 1 (2008): 97–110.

Johns, Andrew. "The Johnson Administration, the Shah of Iran, and the Changing Pattern of US-Iranian Relations, 1965–1967: 'Tired of Being Treated like a Schoolboy.' " *Journal of Cold War Studies* 9, no. 2 (2007): 64–94.

Johnson, V. Webster. "Agriculture in the Economic Development of Iran." *Land Economics* 36, no. 4 (1960): 313–21.

Jowitt, Kenneth. "Inclusion and Mobilization in European Leninist Regimes." *World Politics* 28, no. 1 (1975): 69–96.

Jreisat, Jamil. "Bureaucracy and Development in Jordan." *Journal of Asian and African Studies* 24, nos. 1 and 2 (1989): 94–105.

Kaplan, Stephen. "United States Aid and Regime Maintenance in Jordan, 1957–1973." *Public Policy* 23, no. 2 (1975): 189–217.

Karam, Jasem. "Kuwait National Assembly—1992: A Study in Electoral Geography." *GeoJournal* 31, no. 4 (1993): 383–92.

Kazemi, Farhad, and Ervand Abrahamian. "The Nonrevolutionary Peasantry of Modern Iran." *Iranian Studies* 11, no. 1 (1978): 259–304.

Keddie, Nikki. "Iranian Revolutions in Comparative Perspective." *The American Historical Review* 88, no. 3 (1983): 579–98.

Khoury, Nabeel. "The National Consultative Council of Jordan: A Study in Legislative Development." *International Journal of Middle East Studies* 13, no. 4 (1981): 427–39.

Krasner, Stephen. "Sharing Sovereignty: New Institutions for Collapsed and Failing States." *International Security* 29, no. 2 (2004): 85–120.

Ladjevardi, Habib. "The Origins of US Support for an Autocratic Iran." *International Journal of Middle East Studies* 15, no. 2 (1983): 225–39.

Le Troquer, Yann, and Rozenn Hommery Al-Oudat. "From Kuwait to Jordan: The Palestinians' Third Exodus." *Journal of Palestine Studies* 28, no. 3 (1999): 37–51.

Lenczowski, George. "United States' Support for Iran's Independence and Integrity, 1945–1959." *Annals of the American Academy of Political and Social Science* 401 (1972): 45–55.

Levey, Zach. "United States Arms Policy toward Jordan, 1963–68." *Journal of Contemporary History* 41, no. 3 (2006): 527–43.

Little, Douglas. "A Puppet in Search of a Puppeteer? The United States, King Hussein, and Jordan, 1953–1970." *International History Review* 17, no. 3 (1995): 512–44.

——. "Mission Impossible: The CIA and the Cult of Covert Action in the Middle East." *Diplomatic History* 28, no. 5 (2004): 663–701.

Loewenstein, Andrew. " 'The Veiled Protectorate of Kowait:' Liberalized Imperialism and British Efforts to Influence Kuwaiti Domestic Policy during the Reign of Sheikh Ahmad Al-Jaber, 1938–50." *Middle Eastern Studies* 36, no. 2 (2000): 103–23.

Longva, Anh Nga. "Nationalism in Pre-Modern Guise: The Discourse on Hadhar and Badu in Kuwait." *International Journal of Middle East Studies* 38, no. 2 (2006): 171–87.

Looney, Robert. "The Role of Military Expenditures in Pre-Revolutionary Iran's Economic Decline." *Iranian Studies* 21, no. 3 (1988): 52–83.

Lust-Okar, Ellen. "Elections under Authoritarianism: Preliminary Lessons from Jordan." *Democratization* 13, no. 3 (2006): 456–71.

Lustick, Ian. "The Absence of Middle Eastern Great Powers: Political 'Backwardness' in Historical Perspective." *International Organization* 51, no. 4 (1997): 653–83.

Magaloni, Beatriz. "Credible Power-Sharing and the Longevity of Authoritarian Rule." *Comparative Political Studies* 41, nos. 4–5 (2008): 715–41.

Mahdavi, Hossein. "The Coming Crisis in Iran." *Foreign Affairs* 44, no. 1 (1965): 134–46.

Majd, Mohammad. "The 1951–53 Oil Nationalization Dispute and the Iranian Economy: A Rejoinder." *Middle Eastern Studies* 31, no. 3 (1995): 449–59.

——. "Land Reform Policies in Iran." *American Journal of Agricultural Economics* 69, no. 4 (1987): 843–48.

——. "Small Landowners and Land Redistribution in Iran, 1962–1971." *International Journal of Middle East Studies* 32, no. 1 (2000): 123–53.

Marsh, Steve. "Continuity and Change: Reinterpreting the Policies of the Truman and Eisenhower Administrations toward Iran, 1950–1954." *Journal of Cold War Studies* 7, no. 3 (2005): 79–123.

Mazaheri, Nimah. "State Repression in the Iranian Bazaar, 1975–1977: The Anti-Profiteering Campaign and an Impending Revolution." *Iranian Studies* 39, no. 3 (2006): 401–14.

Mclean, David. "Finance and 'Informal Empire' before the First World War." *Economic History Review* 29, no. 2 (1976): 291–305.

Menaldo, Victor. "The Middle East and North Africa's Resilient Monarchs." *Journal of Politics* 74, no. 3 (2012): 707–22.

Miller, William Green. "Political Organization in Iran: From Dowreh to Political Party." *Middle East Journal* 23, no. 2 (1969): 159–67.

Miyata, Osamu. "The Tudeh Military Network during the Oil Nationalization Period." *Middle Eastern Studies* 23, no. 3 (1987): 313–28.

Moaddel, Mansoor. "The Shi'i Ulama and the State in Iran." *Theory and Society* 15, no. 4 (1986): 519–56.

Moazami, Behrooz. "The Islamization of the Social Movements and the Revolution, 1963–1979." *Comparative Studies of South Asia, Africa and the Middle East* 29, no. 1 (2009): 47–62.

Moghaddam, Reza. "Land Reform and Rural Development in Iran." *Land Economics* 48, no. 2 (1972): 160–68.

Mokhtari, Fariborz. "Iran's 1953 Coup Revisited: Internal Dynamics versus External Intrigue." *Middle East Journal* 62, no. 3 (2008): 457–88.

Moran, Theodore. "Iranian Defense Expenditures and the Social Crisis." *International Security* 3, no. 3 (1978): 178–92.

Mozaffari, Mehdi. "Why the Bazar Rebels." *Journal of Peace Research* 28, no. 4 (1991): 377–91.

Mufti, Malik. "Elite Bargains and the Onset of Political Liberalization in Jordan." *Comparative Political Studies* 32, no. 1 (1999): 100–29.

Nashashibi, Karim. "Fiscal Revenues in the South Mediterranean Arab Countries: Vulnerabilities and Growth Potential." Working Paper, International Monetary Fund, 2002.

Nasr, Vali. "Politics within the Late Pahlavi State: The Ministry of Economy and Industrial Policy, 1963–1969." *International Journal of Middle East Studies* 32, no. 1 (2000): 97–122.

Nevo, Joseph. "Professional Associations in Jordan: The Backbone of an Emerging Civil Society." *Asian Studies Review* 25, no. 2 (2001): 169–84.

——. "September 1970 in Jordan: A Civil War?" *Civil Wars* 10, no. 3 (2008): 217–30.

Onley, James, and Sulayman Khalaf. "Shaikhly Authority in the Pre-oil Gulf: An Historical-Anthropological Study." *History and Anthropology* 17, no. 3 (2006): 189–208.

Oren, Michael. "A Winter of Discontent: Britain's Crisis in Jordan, December 1955–March 1956." *International Journal of Middle East Studies* 22, no. 2 (1990): 171–84.

Parsa, Misagh. "Theories of Collective Action and the Iranian Revolution." *Sociological Forum* 3, no. 1 (1988): 44–71.

Pepinsky, Thomas. "The Institutional Turn in Comparative Authoritarianism." *British Journal of Political Science* 44, no. 3 (2014): 631–53.

Peters, Anne Mariel, and Pete Moore. "Beyond Boom and Bust: External Rents, Durable Authoritarianism, and Institutional Adaptation in the Hashemite Kingdom of Jordan." *Studies in Comparative International Development* 44, no. 3 (2009): 256–85.

Phillips, James. "As Israel and the Arabs Battle, Moscow Collects the Dividends." Backgrounder 291. Washington, D.C.: Heritage Foundation. 1983.

Potrafke, Niklas. "Islam and Democracy." *Public Choice* 151, no. 1 (2012): 185–92.

Qayed, Hasan. "Press and Authorities in the Arab World: The Case of Kuwait." *Arab Affairs* 1, no. 9 (1989): 94–108.

Rath, Kathrine. "The Process of Democratization in Jordan." *Middle Eastern Studies* 30, no. 3 (1994): 530–57.

Razi, G. Hossein. "Genesis of Party in Iran: A Case Study of the Interaction between the Political System and Political Parties." *Iranian Studies* 3, no. 2 (1970): 58–90.

Reiter, Yitzhak. "Higher Education and Sociopolitical Transformation in Jordan." *British Journal of Middle Eastern Studies* 29, no. 2 (2002): 137–64.

——. "The Palestinian-Transjordanian Rift: Economic Might and Political Power in Jordan." *Middle East Journal* 58, no. 1 (2004): 72–92.

Richards, Gordon. "Stabilization Crises and the Breakdown of Military Authoritarianism in Latin America." *Comparative Political Studies* 18, no. 4 (1986): 449–85.

Richards, Helmut. "Land Reform and Agribusiness in Iran." *Middle East Research and Information Project Reports* 43 (1975): 3–18, 24.

Ricks, Thomas. "US Military Missions to Iran, 1943–1978: The Political Economy of Military Assistance." *Iranian Studies* 12, no. 3 (1979): 163–93.

Riedel, Tim. "The 1993 Parliamentary Elections in Jordan." *Orient* 35, no. 1 (1994): 51–63.

Robinson, Glenn. "Defensive Democratization In Jordan." *International Journal of Middle East Studies* 30, no. 3 (1998): 387–410.

Rose, Richard. "Dynamic Tendencies in the Authority of Regimes." *World Politics* 21, no. 4 (1969): 602–28.

Ross, Michael. "Does Oil Hinder Democracy?" *World Politics* 53, no. 3 (2001): 325–61.

Rudolph, Lloyd, and Susanne Hoeber Rudolph. "Authority and Power in Bureaucratic and Patrimonial Administration: A Revisionist Interpretation of Weber on Bureaucracy." *World Politics* 31, no. 2 (1979): 195–227.

Ruehsen, Moyara De Moraes. "Operation 'Ajax' Revisited: Iran, 1953." *Middle Eastern Studies* 29, no. 3 (1993): 467–86.

Sabahi, Seyed Farian. "The Literacy Corps in Pahlavi Iran (1963–1979): Political, Social, and Literary Implications." *Cahiers d'études sur la Méditerranée orientale et le monde turco-iranien* 31 (2001): 191–220.

Salih, Kamal Osman. "The 1938 Kuwait Legislative Council." *Middle Eastern Studies* 28, no. 1 (1992): 66–100.

——. "Kuwait Primary (Tribal) Elections, 1975–2008: An Evaluative Study." *British Journal of Middle Eastern Studies* 38, no. 2 (2011): 141–67.

——. "Parliamentary Control of the Executive: Evaluation of the Interpellation Mechanism, Case Study Kuwait National Assembly, 1992–2004." *South Asian and Middle Eastern Studies* 29, no. 3 (2006): 36–69.

Samhat, Nayef. "Middle Powers and American Foreign Policy: Lessons from Irano-U.S. Relations, 1962–77." *Policy Studies Journal* 28, no. 1 (2000): 11–26.

Schoenberger, Erica, and Stephanie Reich. "Soviet Policy in the Middle East." *Middle East Research and Information Project Reports* 39 (1975): 3–28.

Scoville, James. "The Labor Market in Prerevolutionary Iran." *Economic Development and Cultural Change* 34, no. 1 (1985): 143–55.

Segal, Eran. "Formal and Informal Political Participation in Kuwait: Diwaniya, Majlis, and Parliament." *Journal of Arabian Studies: Arabia, the Gulf, and the Red Sea* 2, no. 2 (2012): 127–41.

——. "Merchants' Networks in Kuwait: The Story of Yusuf Al-Marzuk." *Middle Eastern Studies* 45, no. 5 (2009): 709–19.

Selvik, Kjetil. "Elite Rivalry in a Semi-Democracy: The Kuwaiti Press Scene." *Middle Eastern Studies* 47, no. 3 (2011): 477–96.

Shafq, S. Rezazadeh, and J. D. Lotz. "The Iranian Seven Year Development Plan." *Middle East Journal* 4, no. 1 (1950): 100–105.

Shehab, Fakhri. "Kuwait: A Super-Affluent Society." *Foreign Affairs* 42, no. 3 (1964): 461–74.

Slater, Dan, and Daniel Ziblatt. "The Enduring Indispensability of Controlled Comparison." *Comparative Political Studies* 46, no. 10 (2013): 1301–27.

Smith, Benjamin. "Life of the Party: The Origins of Regime Breakdown and Persistence under Single-Party Rule." *World Politics* 57, no. 3 (2005): 421–51.

——. "Rethinking the Economic Origins of Dictatorship and Democracy: The Continuing Value of Cases and Comparisons." *American Political Science Association—Comparative Politics Newsletter* 19, no. 1 (2008): 16–20.

Summitt, April. "For a White Revolution: John F. Kennedy and the Shah of Iran." *Middle East Journal* 58, no. 4 (2004): 560–75.

Tell, Nawaf. "Jordanian Security Sector Governance: Between Theory and Practice." Working Paper 145, Geneva Centre for the Democratic Control of Armed Forces, 2004.

Tétreault, Mary Ann. "Autonomy, Necessity, and the Small State: Ruling Kuwait in the Twentieth Century." *International Organization* 45, no. 4 (1991): 565–91.

Tétreault, Mary Ann, and Mohammad Al-Ghanim. "The Day After 'Victory:' Kuwait's 2009 Election and the Contentious Present." *Middle East Report Online* (2009). http://www.merip.org/mero/mero070809.

Toth, Anthony. "Tribes and Tribulations: Bedouin Losses in the Saudi and Iraqi Struggles over Kuwait's Frontiers, 1921–1943." *British Journal of Middle Eastern Studies* 32, no. 2 (2005): 145–67.

Vu, Tuong. "Studying the State through State Formation." *World Politics* 62, no. 1 (2010): 148–75.

Way, Lucan. "Authoritarian State Building and the Sources of Regime Competitiveness in the Fourth Wave: The Cases of Belarus, Moldova, Russia, and Ukraine." *World Politics* 57, no. 2 (2005): 231–61.

Weinbaum, Marvin. "Iran Finds a Party System: The Institutionalization of 'Iran Novin.'" *Middle East Journal* 27, no. 4 (1972): 439–55.

Yazdi, Majid. "Patterns of Clerical Political Behavior in Postwar Iran, 1941–53." *Middle Eastern Studies* 26, no. 3 (1990): 281–307.

Yetiv, Steve. "Kuwait's Democratic Experiment in Its Broader International Context." *Middle East Journal* 56, no. 2 (2002): 257–71.

Yom, Sean L. "Oil, Coalitions, and Regime Durability: The Origins and Persistence of Popular Rentierism in Kuwait." *Studies in Comparative International Development* 46, no. 2 (2011): 217–41.

Yom, Sean L., and F. Gregory Gause III. "Resilient Royals: How Arab Monarchies Hang On." *Journal of Democracy* 23, no. 4 (2012): 74–88.

Yom, Sean L., and Mohammad H. Al-Momani. "The International Dimensions of Authoritarian Regime Stability: Jordan in the Post-Cold War Era." *Arab Studies Quarterly* 30, no. 1 (2008): 39–60.

Young, T. Cuyler. "Iran in Continuing Crisis." *Foreign Affairs* 40, no. 2 (1962): 275–92.

Zonis, Marvin. "Iran: A Theory of Revolution from Accounts of the Revolution." *World Politics* 35, no. 4 (1983): 586–606.

DISSERTATIONS AND THESES

Alhabib, Mohammad. "The Shia Migration from Southwestern Iran to Kuwait: Push-Pull Factors during the Late Nineteenth and Early Twentieth Centuries." MA thesis, Georgia State University, 2010.

Al-Najjar, Ghanim. "Decision-Making Process in Kuwait: The Land Acquisition Policy as a Case Study." PhD diss., University of Exeter, 1984.

Al-Naqeeb, Sula. "The Question of Citizenship and Integration in Kuwait: Looking at the Bidoun as a Case Study." MA thesis, School of Oriental and African Studies, University of London, 2006.

Al-Shayeji, Abdullah Khalifah. "Democratization in Kuwait: The National Assembly as a Strategy for Political Survival." PhD diss., University of Texas at Austin, 1988.

Falah Al-Mdairis. "The Arab Nationalist Movement in Kuwait from its Origins to 1970." PhD diss., University of Oxford, 1987.

Khalaf, Jassim Muhammad. "The Kuwait National Assembly: A Study of Its Structure and Function." PhD diss., State University of New York at Albany, 1984.

Peters, Anne Mariel. "Special Relationships, Dollars, and Development: U.S. Aid and Institutions in Egypt, Jordan, South Korea, and Taiwan." PhD diss., University of Virginia, 2009.

Rossiter, Ash. "Britain and the Development of Professional Security Forces in the Gulf Arab States, 1921–71: Local Forces and Informal Empire." PhD diss., University of Exeter, 2014.

INDEX